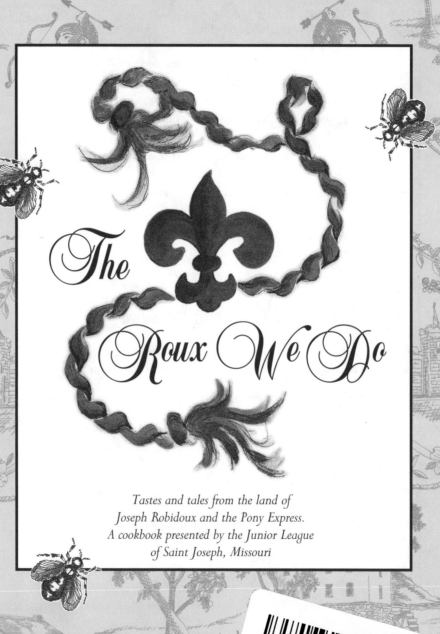

The Roux We Do

Tastes and tales from the land of
Joseph Robidoux and the Pony Express.
A cookbook presented by the Junior League
of Saint Joseph, Missouri

Junior League Prayer

We pray that we shall never be so blind that
our small world is all we ever see,
Or so supremely satisfied
That what we are is all we ever want to be.
Give us the joy of feeling someone's need;
Make us gracious followers -
Make gracious those who lead.
And more than all, we pray that through
the years
We will remember there are always
new frontiers.

Mission Statement

The Junior League of St. Joseph is an organization of women committed to promoting voluntarism and to improving the community through the effective action and leadership of trained volunteers. Its purpose is exclusively educational and charitable.

Vision Statement

Through the power of association the Junior League of St. Joseph will affect change to better the lives of women and children by embracing diverse perspectives, building community partnerships, and inspiring shared solutions.

ISBN 0-9709814-0-6

Printed in the USA by
WIMMER
The Wimmer Companies
Memphis
1-800-548-2537

Table of Contents

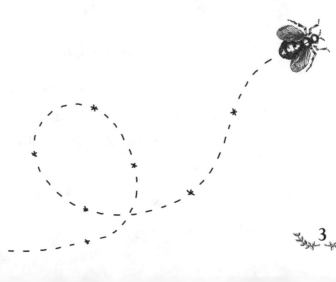

Editorial Team

Co-Chairs:
Laura Nelson and Jeanne Schanze

Assistant Chairs:
Ramona Steele and Jackie Grimwood

Recipe Editor: Sheryl Gossett
Sustainer Advisor: Carol Burns

Copy Editor: Nancy Reese-Dillon
Sustainer Advisors:
Mary Jo Hornaday and Christy Barber

Design Editor: Lou Wyeth
Sustainer Advisor: Janet Taylor

Artist:
Tina Cox and Lou Wyeth

Internal Marketing Chair:
Michelle Turner
Sustainer Advisor:
Laura Baade

External Marketing Chair: Jackie Grimwood
Sustainer Advisor: Margaret O'Malley

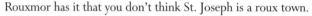

Introduction

Rouxmor has it that you don't think St. Joseph is a roux town.

"It just can't be!" one might say.

"Only the French do a great roux," another might add.

"Don't forget New Orleans and their roux," yet another might chime in.

We don't mean to be rouxd or rouxthless, but St. Joseph is the original roux town. Our roux is Joseph Robidoux, (pronounced roo-be-do), founding father of St. Joseph, and French through and through.

Maybe not exactly the type of roux you may have been thinking of, but saucy, nonetheless. A lot like our city's history, in fact.

Robidoux was of French and French Canadian descent starting with Manuel Robidoux, who lived in Paris in the 1500's. His son, Andre Robidoux, went to Canada in 1667. The first in the line of Joseph Robidoux's was a shoe dealer in Montreal. His son, Joseph Robidoux II, migrated to St. Louis. It was there that Joseph Robidoux III was born and the rest, they say, is St. Joseph history.

Before finally settling here, Joseph Robidoux conducted business as baker and a confectioner; he surely must have mastered some sort of a sweet roux. (At least that's the story we're sticking to!) While his culinary skills were not well documented, his business savvy was.

Robidoux opened a trading post at Blacksnake Hills, the precursor to St. Joseph. As a fur trader, he had a reputation as a shrewd business man and spoke with a strong French accent. He quickly made friends with the Indians. To make a long story short, he settled in an area eventually to be named after his patron saint, St. Joseph, and then watched as the city took central stage to the Westward migration. St. Joseph became a boom town and Robidoux was its man of the hour.

Robidoux's spirit is alive in many of St. Joseph's business ventures past and present. He lived long enough to see the start (and finish) of the Pony Express mail service, which can probably lay claim to being the most romantic chapter in the history of transcontinental communication, complete with orphans, outlaws, and other outlandish characters.

Since then, St. Joseph's history has been a wonderful mixture of entrepreneurial spirit and the Wild West; complete with the notorious bank robber Jesse James, hat maker John Stetson, John Patee and his World Hotel, and a one-time world class stockyards and meat processing center; as well as Quaker Oats, Goetz Brewery, and Mead Paper, to mention a few. Native sons include world renowned journalist Walter Cronkite, poet Eugene Field, actress Jayne Wyman, the fictional Aunt Jemima, and jazz saxophonist great, Coleman Hawkins.

Just as St. Joseph truly played a pivotal role in the development of the west with several historically noteworthy accomplishments, the Junior League of St. Joseph, beginning in 1921, has also laid claim to many great accomplishments and advancements in St. Joseph. The Junior League of St. Joseph was responsible for starting many St. Joseph services and agencies including: Family Guidance, the Allied Arts Council, the Volunteer Action Center, Legal Aide, Leadership St. Joseph. Through the years the Junior League of St. Joseph has devoted itself to projects which enable women and children and that promote safety, wellness, and literacy.

The city's history is filled with colorful, intriguing, and sometimes bizarre characters and stories. In this book we've tried to capture part of the allure and charm of a bygone era and combine it with the modern day intrigue often found in St. Joseph.

Dare we say that you'll "roux the day" that you neglected to think of St. Joseph as a roux town?

Yep. Right down to the Blacksnake in our hills; down to the stock in our yards. Right down to the Pony in our Express right down to the Wild in our West. In fact, right down to the roux in our Robidoux.

And So It Began

True, it was a far cry from the shouts and commotion of a chaotic Wall Street trading floor. Joseph Robidoux practiced an entirely different sort of trading. The somewhat nomadic Robidoux spent years as the only white man in the territory as a registered fur trader, establishing a trading post in the soon-to-be St. Joseph area.

Frequently Robidoux looked to the north and watched as a group of Indians approached carrying bundles of buffalo, otter, beaver and other skins. Robidoux himself was so tanned and weather beaten that it was hard to tell whether he was a white or Indian. Robidoux spoke fluent French and a number of Indian dialects, and greeted the Indian traders.

Eventually settlers swarmed to the fertile country surrounding Robidoux's trading post. When the fur trade declined because beaver hats were no longer in style, Robidoux realized that he had resources even more cherished than the animal skins. He had rich soil and timberland. No one, especially Joseph Robidoux, imagined that his trading post would become the cradle of St. Joseph civilization.

Today Robidoux's cabin no longer exists, but the apartment house he built to accommodate newcomers to St. Joseph has been restored by the St. Joseph Historical Society.

Robidoux Row provides visitors with a view of life in the early 1800's. It includes the room Robidoux lived in after his wife died until his own death in 1868. The quarters are furnished with some of his belongings and throughout the city, Robidoux's adventuresome spirit permeates not only the museum but the streets and hills of St. Joseph.

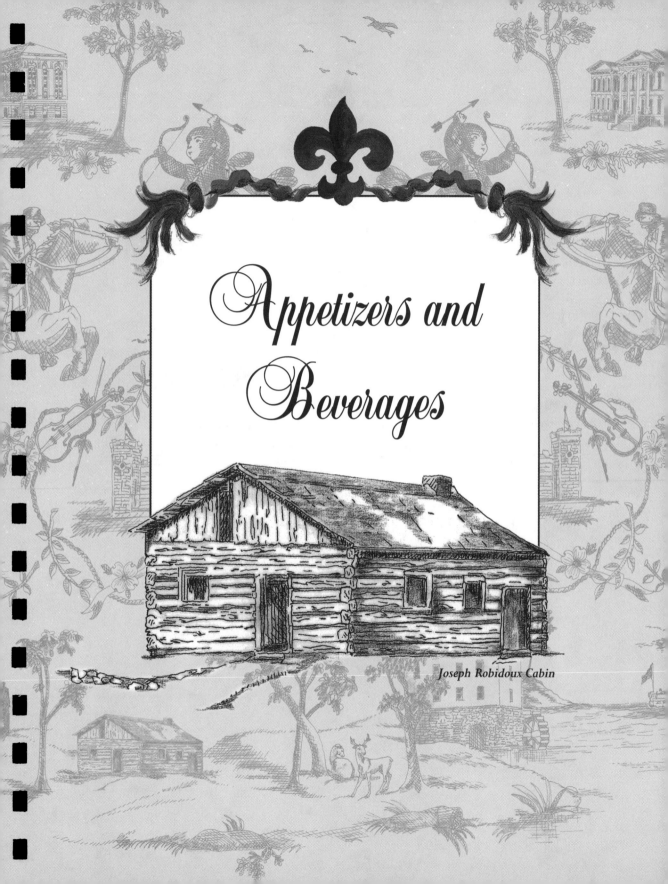

Appetizers and Beverages

Joseph Robidoux Cabin

Appetizers and Beverages

Black Bean Bundles

1	(15 ounce) can black beans, drained and rinsed	¾	cup shredded jalapeño Monterey Jack cheese
6	green onions, chopped	1	teaspoon cumin
1	clove garlic, minced	6	tablespoons butter
¾	cup chopped cilantro	1	box phyllo dough

Preheat oven to 400 degrees. Coat a cookie sheet with nonstick spray. In medium bowl, combine beans, green onions, garlic, cilantro, cheese, and cumin. Mix until well blended and set aside.

Melt butter in a small bowl in microwave. Unfold phyllo dough onto clean counter. Place 1 sheet on work surface and keep the remaining sheets covered with a moistened towel. Lightly brush the phyllo with melted butter. Place a second sheet on top of the first and brush lightly with butter. Repeat with a third sheet. Using a sharp knife cut phyllo into 3-inch squares. Place 1 rounded teaspoon of black bean filling in center of each square. Bring the 4 corners and the edges of each square together in the center. Pinch around the filling and flare the tops. Place the bundle on prepared cookie sheet. Repeat procedure with remaining ingredients. Bake for 8 to 10 minutes, until phyllo dough is crisp and golden. Transfer to serving platter and serve with salsa. May be prepared 2 days in advance and may be frozen for up to a month.

Hint: Young and old alike clamor for more. Keep a supply in your freezer for unexpected company.

Yield: 12 servings

Rouxminations

Street Smart

Less than 20 years after Joseph Robidoux, St. Joseph founding father, built his first home, more than 3400 people lived on the streets named after his family: Angelique, Messanie, Charles, Felix, Faraon, Francis, Edmond, Sylvanie and Jule(s). These streets remain major thoroughfares today. The surveyor who suggested "St. Joseph," Frederick Smith, also staked his claim to fame by naming a street Frederick Avenue.

Red and Yellow Roasted Pepper Artichoke Puffs

2	tablespoons butter	¾	cup grated Parmesan cheese
1	bunch green onions, chopped	1	tablespoon fresh lemon juice
2	cloves garlic, minced		Pepper to taste
1	(14 ounce) can artichokes, drained and diced	½	cup mayonnaise
3	ounces thinly sliced prosciutto, minced	3	red bell peppers
3	tablespoons finely shredded fresh basil or 1 teaspoon dried	3	yellow bell peppers
		¼	cup olive oil
		2	tablespoons balsamic vinegar
			Salt and pepper

Melt butter in skillet. Add green onions and garlic and cook, stirring frequently, just until softened, 2 to 3 minutes. Transfer to a medium mixing bowl. Add artichokes, prosciutto, basil and Parmesan, and stir to combine. Sprinkle with lemon juice and pepper. Stir in mayonnaise, cover, and refrigerate for 1 hour.

Preheat oven to 400 degrees. Stem and seed peppers and cut into 2 x 1½-inch pieces. Place peppers in a single layer on baking sheet and drizzle with olive oil and vinegar. Sprinkle with salt and pepper. Bake for 15 minutes, stirring once halfway through. Remove from oven and let cool.

Preheat broiler and mound 2 tablespoons of artichoke mixture on each pepper piece. Arrange in rows on baking sheet and broil 3 to 4 inches from heat until puffed and bubbly, 2 to 3 minutes. Let cool a few minutes, then transfer to serving tray.

Hint: Simply put, these are awesome.

Yield: 4 dozen

Rouxminations

80 Years and Counting

The Junior League of St. Joseph was founded in 1921, making it one of the oldest Junior Leagues in the nation. In 2001, the Junior League celebrated its 80th birthday.

Artichoke Puffs

1 box Pepperidge Farm pastry
   sheets, thawed
1 egg, lightly beaten
2 teaspoons water
1 cup grated Provolone cheese
1 cup grated Parmesan cheese
¼ cup mayonnaise
1 (12 ounce) can artichoke
   hearts, drained and chopped,
   juice reserved
1 teaspoon garlic powder
2-3 teaspoons Tabasco sauce,
   or to taste
½ teaspoon reserved artichoke
   juice
½ teaspoon paprika
2 teaspoons minced garlic
   Salt and pepper

Preheat oven to 350 degrees. Brush pastry with an egg wash made from the egg and water. Mix remaining ingredients and spread on pastry. Cut into 2-inch squares and transfer to a lightly greased baking sheet. Bake until puffed and lightly browned, about 20 minutes.

Yield: 10 servings

Broccoli Bites with Horseradish Sauce

Bites

2 (10 ounce) packages frozen
   chopped broccoli
2 cups herb stuffing
1 cup grated Parmesan cheese
6 eggs, beaten
¾ cup butter, softened
   Salt and pepper

Horseradish Sauce

4 tablespoons butter, melted
¾ cup mayonnaise
2 tablespoons horseradish, or
   more to taste
1 tablespoon grated onion
¼ teaspoon salt
¼ teaspoon dry mustard
   Dash of red pepper

For Broccoli Bites: Preheat oven 350 degrees. Cook broccoli and drain well. Place in a large bowl and add stuffing, cheese, eggs, butter, and salt and pepper to taste. Mix well. Roll into small balls and place on a baking sheet which has been coated with nonstick spray. Bake for 20 minutes.

For Sauce: Mix all ingredients until well blended. Serve bites with sauce for dipping.

Hint: These bites are always a surprising hit.

Yield: 10 to 12 servings

Rouxminations

Apartment C-5

Robidoux Row, built by Joseph Robidoux in about 1850, is said to be the first apartment house west of the Mississippi River. The apartments were free to transients whom Robidoux thought would be good citizens. Joseph Robidoux retired to one of the apartments and died there in 1868 and the ripe old age of 85. According to one report, he died from choking on a cove oyster.

Cocktail Corn Cakes with Spicy Mango Salsa

Corn Cakes

3	tablespoons medium cornmeal	1	tablespoon melted butter
½	cup all-purpose flour	⅔	cup small shoepeg corn kernels
¼	teaspoon salt		Cayenne pepper
¼	teaspoon baking powder	1	tablespoon sunflower or other
1	egg, beaten		vegetable oil
5	tablespoons milk		

Salsa

½	mango, finely diced		Juice of 1 lime
½	medium red onion, finely chopped		Salt and pepper
1	fresh green chili, seeded and finely diced	20	cilantro leaves to garnish

For Corn Cakes: Mix cornmeal, flour, salt, baking powder, egg, milk, and butter to make a smooth batter. Stir in corn kernels. Add cayenne pepper to taste. Brush a frying pan or griddle with oil and heat over medium heat. Working in batches, drop heaped teaspoonfuls of batter onto hot surface. Cook until crisp and golden, about 2 minutes and 30 seconds per side. Brush pan with oil between each batch of pancakes. Cool pancakes to room temperature.

For Salsa: Combine mango, onion, chili, and lime juice. Add salt and pepper to taste. Top each cake with 1 heaping teaspoon of salsa. Garnish with cilantro leaves. Serve at room temperature.

Hint: Make cakes up to 1 day in advance. Store in airtight container in the refrigerator. Crisp in preheated 400 degree oven for 3 minutes. Make salsa up to 5 hours in advance. For best flavor, use fresh corn. May also top salsa with a ½ teaspoon of sour cream before garnishing.

Yield: 8 servings

Blue Cheese Bacon Stuffed Mushrooms

24 medium mushrooms	4 ounces blue cheese
3 tablespoons butter, divided	1 (3 ounce) package cream cheese, softened
1 shallot, minced	1 teaspoon lemon juice
2 tablespoons crumbled cooked bacon	½ teaspoon dried thyme

Preheat oven to 375 degrees. Remove stems from mushrooms. Set caps aside and finely chop stems. In a medium skillet, melt 1 tablespoon butter. Add shallot and mushroom stems and sauté for about 3 minutes. Transfer to a bowl and stir in bacon, blue cheese, cream cheese, lemon juice, and thyme. Blend well. In same skillet, melt remaining butter and immediately remove from heat. Add mushroom caps and toss until well-coated. Arrange caps with stem side up on a baking sheet. Mound about 2 tablespoons filling in each. (May prepare to this step up to 8 hours in advance; cover with plastic wrap and refrigerate.) Bake until bubbly and mushrooms are tender but still hold their shape, about 10 minutes.

Hint: These are an outstanding variation of the stuffed mushroom.

Yield: 12 servings

Zucchini Rounds with Gorgonzola

10 small zucchini	Baby basil leaves
½ pound Gorgonzola, cut in small pieces	⅓ pound Parmesan cheese, grated
2 pints cherry tomatoes, thinly sliced	Freshly ground pepper

Preheat oven to 400 degrees. Line a baking sheet with parchment paper. Wash zucchini and slice into ½-inch rounds. Scoop out an indentation with a melon baller, leaving bottom intact. Place ½ teaspoon Gorgonzola on each zucchini round. Put a tomato slice over cheese and top with a tiny basil leaf. Sprinkle with Parmesan cheese and pepper. Place rounds on baking sheet and bake 5 to 7 minutes. Cheese should be melted but not browned. Garnish with fresh basil leaves. Serve immediately.

Hint: Can be prepared several hours ahead. Refrigerate and bake at the last minute.

Yield: 10 servings

Rouxminations

Doobie, Doobie, Don't

When the city of St. Joseph was originally laid out, part of the area was a hemp field.

Who Let The Dogs Out? (Or, 101 ways to wok your dog!)

Two of the chief items in Joseph Robidoux Senior's diet were prime roast of dog and dog stew. Sorry, we didn't include the recipes in this cookbook!

Rouxminations

Fit For A King

The Missouri Theater was an example of a "Palace" theater and has been considered one of the four finest theaters in the United States. The theater is now a renovated movie palace which serves as a regional center for the arts. It is decorated in a pre-Persian motif, and the canopy-like ceiling appears to be held in place by ropes attached to the side walls.

Coconut Curried Chicken Balls

⅔ cup raisins
2 tablespoons dark rum
1⅓ cups pineapple cream cheese
3 tablespoons Major Grey's mango chutney
3 tablespoons mayonnaise
1 tablespoon teriyaki sauce
2 teaspoons curry powder
½ teaspoon ground ginger
½ teaspoon salt
¼ teaspoon red pepper
4 chicken breasts, cooked and coarsely chopped
1 cup sliced almonds, toasted
1½ cups flaked coconut

Combine raisins and rum and set aside. Combine cream cheese, chutney, mayonnaise, teriyaki sauce, curry powder, ginger, salt, and red pepper. Drain raisins. Add raisins, chicken, and almonds to cream cheese mixture and stir until well blended. Shape into 1-inch balls and roll in coconut. Chill before serving.

Hint: May be made in advance and frozen up to a week ahead of time.

Yield: 12 servings

Sticky Chicken Drummers

¾ cup soy sauce
½ cup teriyaki sauce
½ cup butter, melted
1 cup firmly packed brown sugar
1 tablespoon Creole seasoning
1 teaspoon dry mustard
3 pounds chicken drummies

Combine soy sauce, teriyaki sauce, butter, brown sugar, Creole seasoning, and dry mustard. Mix well. Add chicken, turning to coat. Chill at least 1 hour, or up to 24, in marinade, turning chicken occasionally.

Preheat oven to 375 degrees. Drain chicken and discard marinade. Arrange chicken on a cookie sheet with high sides. Bake for about 1 hour. Turn oven up to broil and broil about 5 inches from the heat for about 5 minutes with the oven door open. Remove and turn each piece over; return to broil for 5 more minutes. Serve on a platter with blue cheese dressing and celery stalks.

Hint: The best oven for this job is actually a convection oven. If doing it this way, preheat to 375 degrees and cook 25 minutes, remove from oven and flip chicken pieces, return to oven for 25 minutes.

Yield: 12 servings

King of the Hill Dip

1½ cups grated Monterey Jack cheese
1½ cups grated Parmesan cheese
1 cup mayonnaise
2 (4 ounce) cans chopped green chiles, undrained
¼ teaspoon cumin
1 cup finely chopped cooked chicken

Preheat oven to 350 degrees. Combine all ingredients and turn into a greased casserole dish. Bake for 20 minutes. Serve warm with tortilla chips.

Yield: 10 to 12 servings

Tequila Marinated Shrimp

3 tablespoons finely chopped onion
5 cloves garlic, minced
¼ cup olive oil
2 pounds medium fresh raw shrimp, peeled and deveined with tails left intact
¼ cup tequila
½ cup lime juice
⅛ teaspoon salt
3 tablespoons snipped fresh cilantro
Cilantro sprigs, garnish
Cocktail sauce

Cook onion and garlic in olive oil in large skillet over medium heat about 3 minutes, until tender. Add shrimp and tequila and bring to a boil. Boil gently, uncovered, for 3 to 5 minutes, until shrimp turn pink, stirring occasionally. Transfer shrimp mixture to a bowl. Add lime juice, salt, and cilantro and toss to mix. Cover and refrigerate 2 to 24 hours, stirring occasionally. Drain before serving. Garnish with cilantro sprigs and serve with cocktail sauce.

Yield: 8 servings

Rouxminations

King Of The Hill

A Missouri River observation point and historic Indian site is King Hill. The hill takes its name from John King, a trader and trapper for Joseph Robidoux. The hill boasts an American flag which is a beacon to Kansas travelers entering St. Joseph. The flag is battleship-sized and flies from a 100 foot tall pole.

Bacon Wrapped Scallops

¾ cup orange marmalade
½ cup soy sauce
2 dozen sea scallops

1 bunch green onions, julienned
12 slices bacon, halved

Mix marmalade and soy sauce. Wrap a scallop and a piece of green onion with a half slice of bacon, securing with a toothpick. Place in a dish and repeat with remaining scallops. Cover with marmalade mixture and marinate several hours.

Preheat oven to broil. Broil for 4 to 5 minutes per side and serve immediately.

Hint: These always disappear quickly! May need to halve scallops if too large. This is also great with jumbo shrimp.

Yield: 10 servings

Stuffed Baked Brie

1 (4 ounce) Brie round
¼ cup prepared pesto or ¼ cup Cranberry Chutney on page 187

1 package puff pastry, thawed
1 egg, beaten

Cut Brie in half horizontally and spread pesto or chutney on 1 half and top with the other half.

Roll pastry to ⅛-inch thickness. Place Brie in center and wrap carefully, removing any air pockets. Seal pastry edges with beaten egg. Place on a plate overlapped-edges-down. Brush with egg and decorate with pastry shapes, such as grape clusters or leaves, if desired. Freeze, uncovered, for 1 hour. Preheat oven to 375 degrees. Place Brie on a cookie sheet which has been coated with nonstick spray. Bake until golden brown, about 25 minutes. Cool 5 minutes before serving.

Hint: To make ahead, wrap Brie in foil after freezing it uncovered for an hour. It will keep for up to 2 weeks in the freezer.

Yield: 10 servings

Shrimp and Avocado Salsa on Pita Toasts with Chipotle Dip

Chipotle Dip

6   green onions, finely chopped
1   cup good mayonnaise
⅓   cup lite sour cream
1   teaspoon fresh lime juice
3   small chipotle chiles, chopped

¼   teaspoon adobo sauce (from chipotle can), or more, to taste
   Kosher salt

Shrimp Avocado Salsa

½   pound salad shrimp, rinsed
¼   cup finely chopped red onion
1½   cups chopped ripe red tomatoes
1   ripe avocado, peeled and cut into ¼-inch dice
1   fresh jalapeño, seeded and minced

1   tablespoon fresh lime juice
2   tablespoons seafood cocktail sauce
½   cup coarsely chopped cilantro
   Kosher salt

Pita Toasts

4   pita rounds, split in half and each half quartered

   Cilantro sprigs, garnish

For Chipotle Dip: Whisk together green onions, mayonnaise, sour cream, and lime juice. Add chipotles and sauce and mix well. Season to taste with kosher salt. (May be made up to 3 days ahead. Tightly cover and refrigerate.)

For Shrimp and Avocado Salsa: Combine shrimp, onion, tomatoes, avocado, jalapeño, lime juice, cocktail sauce, and cilantro in a medium, non-reactive bowl. Mix thoroughly but gently. Refrigerate, covered, for 2 to 3 hours. Season to taste with kosher salt.

For Pita Toasts: Preheat oven to 350 degrees. Arrange pita wedges on cookie sheet and bake until crispy, about 10 minutes.

To Assemble: Brush each toast lightly with the Chipotle Dip. Top with Shrimp Salsa. Arrange on platter with remaining dip in center. Garnish with cilantro sprigs.

Hint: The Chipotle Dip can be served alone with chips, crackers, etc. BUT it really makes this appetizer great. The chipotles can be found in the ethnic food section of most grocery stores. This is very colorful and pretty unique.

Yield: 12 servings

Rouxminations

Was It or Wasn't It?

While it's never been decided definitively, there was a cabin at Krug Park thought to have been the first St. Joseph house built for Joseph Robidoux by Indians and visited by thousands of people. Sometime in the 1930's, city officials decided the cabin was a hoax and had it removed. Some historians believe the cabin was indeed Robidoux's. Questions about the cabin's authenticity still linger today.

Rouxminations

Just Like Mom's

The Jerre Anne Cafeteria opened for business in 1930. The grand opening specials included a five pound bag of sugar for 29 cents and coffee for 35 cents a pound. The family got out of the grocery business and concentrated on the delicatessen and cafeteria featuring home cooking and homemade pastries. The Cafeteria is still opened today.

Coconut Chutney Ball

2	(8 ounce) packages of ⅓ less fat cream cheese, softened	3	large green onions, white parts only, chopped
1½	teaspoons curry powder	1½	cups chutney, divided
⅔	cup currants or raisins	½-¾	cup coconut, divided
1	cup salted peanuts, chopped		

Mix cream cheese and curry in a medium bowl. Add currants, nuts, green onions, and 1½ tablespoons chutney. Mix well and form into a mound. Chill, if possible for several hours. Remove from refrigerator and spread with 3 tablespoons chutney. Sprinkle with coconut. Top with remaining chutney and once again sprinkle with coconut. Refrigerate until ready to serve. Serve with an assortment of crackers.

Hint: We tested many different versions of this recipe and decided this was THE ONE!

Yield: 8 to 10 servings

Roasted Red Pepper Dip Crostini

1	(12 ounce) jar roasted red bell peppers, drained and chopped	¼	teaspoon salt
			Dash of black pepper
2	large cloves garlic, chopped	½	cup coarsely grated Parmesan cheese
¼	cup olive oil	1	loaf baguette bread
1½	tablespoons balsamic vinegar	¼-½	cup butter, melted
1½	teaspoons sugar		

Combine peppers, garlic, olive oil, vinegar, sugar, salt, and pepper. Stir until mixture has a cloudy appearance and is blended. Let sit at room temperature for at least 4 hours, stirring occasionally. Add Parmesan.

Preheat oven to 400 degrees. Slice bread and brush both sides with butter. Arrange on a baking sheet and bake for about 10 minutes. Turn bread slices over and bake an additional 10 minutes.

Before serving, microwave dip for 1 minute and stir. Serve bowl of dip on a dish surrounded by crostini.

Hint: Leftover dip makes a great condiment for sandwiches.

Yield: 12 servings

Sun-Dried Tomato Basil Torte

Filling

¼ cup chopped fresh basil
4 ounces oil-packed sun-dried tomatoes, drained and oil reserved

1 clove garlic, peeled
⅛ teaspoon freshly ground pepper
½ teaspoon fresh lemon juice

Torte

2 (8 ounce) packages cream cheese, softened
2 tablespoons olive oil
6 tablespoons blue cheese, divided

⅓ cup finely chopped walnuts
1 (7 ounce) container basil pesto
3-4 fresh large basil leaves

For Filling: Combine basil, sun-dried tomatoes, garlic, pepper, and lemon juice in a food processor. Process until a spreadable, but not too thin, paste forms. Add a small amount of reserved oil from sun-dried tomatoes if texture is too dry. Set aside.

For Torte: Line the bottom only of a 6-inch springform pan with plastic wrap or wax paper. Using an electric mixer, beat together cream cheese, olive oil, and 4 tablespoons blue cheese. Beat until smooth. Spread half evenly on bottom of prepared pan. Sprinkle remaining blue cheese on top. Spread Tomato Basil Filling on top of blue cheese. Sprinkle evenly with walnuts. Remove oily top layer from pesto. Spread pesto over walnuts. Top pesto with remaining cream cheese mixture. Cover and refrigerate for several hours. To serve, remove from springform pan and garnish with basil leaves arranged on top of torte in a clover leaf pattern.

Hint: Always a sure fire hit!

Yield: 10 to 12 servings

Rouxminations

Too Much H2O

In 1881, the Missouri River crested at 27.2 feet. It was a record that stood for more than 100 years Another flood occurred in 1952 and ultimately changed the course of the river. After the '52 flood, travelers had to go across the river and enter Kansas before arriving at Rosecrans airfield in Missouri. There are still several St. Joseph residences and business that are located on the other side of the river.

Rouxminations

It's All In The Name

According to some sources, the original name of St. Joseph was Blacksnake Hills. Blacksnake Hills was once a frontier trading post and settlement so named because its crooked, treacherous path among the winding hills resembled the blacksnake. It was also so-named because of the numerous blacksnakes found in the timbered area. Joseph Robidoux's trading post was also known as Le Post Du Serpent Noir (The Post of the Black Snake) by Canadian traders.

Missouri Basil Bruschetta

¾	cup extra virgin olive oil, divided	10-12	kalamata olives, pitted and chopped (do not substitute other olives)
2	cloves garlic, minced	12	large fresh basil leaves, finely chopped
1	tablespoon red wine vinegar Salt and pepper		
½	pound roma tomatoes, diced (about 3 large)	1	sour dough baguette, sliced in ½-inch thick slices
¼	cup finely chopped red onion	5	cloves garlic, peeled

Combine ½ cup of olive oil and minced garlic in a medium bowl and let stand for at least 1 hour. (To tone down the recipe a bit, you may strain the garlic out of the oil before proceeding.) Add vinegar and salt and pepper to olive oil and whisk until emulsified. Add tomatoes, red onion, olives, and basil and gently toss. If time allows, cover and set aside at room temperature for a couple of hours to combine flavors.

Preheat oven to broil. Arrange bread slices on a baking sheet and toast on both sides until lightly browned. Remove from oven. Rub 1 side with peeled garlic clove and then lightly brush with remaining olive oil.

To serve, top toasts with about 2 tablespoons of tomato mixture, or place tomato mixture in decorative bowl surrounded by toasts on a platter.

Hint: Basil and tomatoes grow profusely in our Saint Joseph gardens!

Yield: 12 servings

Pecan Cheese Squares

12	strips bacon	1	teaspoon grated onion
½	cup chopped pecans	½	cup mayonnaise
1	cup shredded sharp Cheddar cheese		Dash of salt
			Party rye bread slices

Preheat oven to 350 degrees. Cook bacon until crisp; drain and crumble. Blend bacon with pecans, cheese, onion, mayonnaise, and salt. Spread mixture on bread slices. Place on cookie sheet and toast in oven until lightly browned.

Hint: May be prepared ahead.

Yield: 10 to 12 servings

Polenta Crostini with Two Toppings

3	cups water	½	teaspoon black pepper
1	cup instant polenta	2	cloves garlic, crushed, optional
1	teaspoon salt	1	tablespoon finely chopped fresh herbs, optional
4	tablespoons grated Parmesan cheese	2	tablespoons olive oil

Blue Cheese and Balsamic Red Onion Topping

2	tablespoons olive oil	1	tablespoon balsamic vinegar
2	medium red onions, sliced		Black pepper
½	teaspoon salt	1	cup crumbled blue cheese

Tomato and Black Olive Salsa

2	ripe tomatoes, peeled, seeded and diced	¼	cup pitted black olives, finely chopped
1	medium red onion, finely chopped	2	teaspoons olive oil
		1	teaspoon red wine vinegar Salt and pepper to taste

For Crostini: Coat a jelly-roll pan with nonstick spray and set aside. Bring water to a boil in a large pan. Stir in the polenta and salt. Cook, stirring constantly, until thick, 5 to 10 minutes. Add Parmesan and pepper. Add optional ingredients, if desired. Stir well to combine and pour into prepared pan. Cover and refrigerate. (May do up to this step 3 days in advance.) After cooling completely, preheat oven to broil and unmold polenta from pan. Slice into 10 slices; then cut each slice diagonally into 2 triangles. Place triangles on greased cookie sheets. Brush with olive oil. Toast under the broiler until lightly golden and crisp, about 5 minutes. Cool to room temperature before topping.

For Blue Cheese and Balsamic Red Onion Topping: Heat oil in a pan over medium heat. Add onions and salt. Cook, stirring occasionally, until soft and tender, about 10 minutes. Add vinegar and cook until evaporated, about 3 minutes. Add pepper to taste. Cool to room temperature. Divide onions evenly among crostini; then top each with 1 teaspoon crumbled cheese. Serve at room temperature.

For Tomato and Black Olive Salsa: Combine all ingredients. Cover and let stand at room temperature 30 minutes.

Hint: Make toppings up to a day in advance, but do not add salt and pepper to salsa until ready to use. Top crostini an hour in advance.

Yield: 12 servings

Rouxminations

Early Explorations

Even before Joseph Robidoux settled in St. Joseph, the area was visited by two important historical figures: Lewis and Clark. The famous explorers and their Corps of Discovery reached Buchanan County, Missouri on July 4, 1804. They spent four days traveling through the area known as St. Michael's Prairie. They also camped there on a return trip in 1806. St. Joseph was part of the national celebration of the Lewis and Clark Bicentennial in July of 2004.

**Now That's
A Jigsaw Puzzle!**

*The house at 2809 Frederick
Avenue was the home of a
local physician, James
Heddens. The home was built
in 1902. It has been
speculated that the two story,
Classical-Revival style home
with a monumental front
portico on the main
facade was actually the
top-end Magnolia style of the
Sears and Roebucks model
homes, sent with numbered
pieces to be assembled on site,
and sold for $3500. Those
speculations proved false,
but it makes for a
great story!*

Italian Pinwheels

2	cups Italian cheese blend, divided
1	tablespoon dried Italian seasoning
1½	cups chopped roma tomatoes
1½	cups chopped yellow bell pepper
½	cup chopped shallots, green onion, and yellow onion, in whatever combination you have on hand
¼	pound prosciutto, minced
	Garlic or olive oil-flavored cooking spray
48	refrigerated won ton wrappers
½	cup water, in small bowl

Preheat oven to 375 degrees. Mix 1½ cups cheese, dried Italian seasoning, tomatoes, yellow pepper, onions, and prosciutto in a medium bowl. Set aside. (This may be prepared a day in advance.)

Spray a large cookie sheet with garlic or olive oil cooking spray. Hold a won ton wrapper in outstretched hand and dab the center with water. At an offset angle, top with another wrapper (you should be able to see all 8 corners). Pinch in center and twist center to form a pinwheel. Place on prepared cookie sheet. Repeat process until you have 24 pinwheels on the cookie sheet and spray evenly with flavored cooking spray. Place about 1½ tablespoons cheese mixture on top of center of each pinwheel, leaving the points bare. Bake until edges are golden brown, about 10 to 12 minutes. Remove from oven and immediately sprinkle with remaining cheese. Transfer to serving platter. Serve warm or at room temperature.

Yield: 12 servings

Parmesan Twists

1	package frozen puff pastry, thawed in refrigerator
	All-purpose flour for dusting
4	tablespoons unsalted butter, melted

2½ cups finely grated Parmesan cheese, divided
4 teaspoons kosher salt, divided
1 large egg, lightly beaten

Preheat oven to 425 degrees. Place 1 sheet of puff pastry on a lightly floured surface, keeping the remaining sheet in refrigerator until ready to use. Roll out dough until it is about ⅛-inch thick, making a 24 x 26-inch rectangle. Use a sharp knife to trim edges into a uniform rectangle; this will help make the twists uniform as they cook. Brush the dough lightly with the melted butter and sprinkle with ¾ cup Parmesan and 1 teaspoon salt.

With the short side of the dough facing you, fold it in half, bringing the top edge down toward you. Brush with the egg. Sprinkle with 1 teaspoon salt and ½ cup Parmesan. Using a very sharp knife cut the dough vertically into ½-inch wide strips. Transfer 6 of the strips to a baking sheet, spacing them evenly apart. Grab each end of a dough strip with your fingers, and carefully stretch and twist the strip in opposite directions. Continue with the remaining strips of dough. Follow this same procedure for the other sheet of dough.

Bake until golden brown, 10 to 12 minutes. Remove from oven and cool on baking sheet for at least 5 minutes to firm up before transferring to wire rack or serving platter.

Variations: Parmesan-Chive Twists: Add 3 tablespoons minced fresh chives to Parmesan.

Parmesan Rosemary Twists: Add 3 tablespoons minced fresh rosemary to Parmesan.

Parmesan Pepper Twists: Add 1 tablespoon plus 2 teaspoons red pepper flakes to Parmesan.

Parmesan Poppy Twists: Add 1 tablespoon plus 1 teaspoon poppy seeds to Parmesan.

Yield: 10 servings

Rouxminations

Every Day's A Party

Curious residents and travelers have the opportunity almost year round to step back and time and relive the days of a bygone with the city's 13 museums and eight annual parades, festivals and events. The festivals and events represent the historic, the ethnic, the artistic, and culinary achievements of St. Joseph residents, past and present.

Savory Cheese Pastries

Pastry

3½ cups all-purpose flour
1¼ cups butter, chilled and cut in small pieces

2½ cups shredded sharp Cheddar cheese
Pinch of salt
2   large eggs

Filling

4   tablespoons butter
2   leeks, rinsed well and minced, white and light green parts only
⅓   pound portobello mushrooms, chopped

2   cloves garlic, minced
12   ounces prosciutto, thinly sliced and minced
¾   cup grated Parmesan cheese

For Pastry: Place flour, butter, cheese, and salt in food processor. Process until mixture resembles coarse meal. Add the eggs and process just until the dough comes together. Wrap in plastic wrap and refrigerate several hours or overnight.

For Filling: Melt butter in large skillet over medium heat. Stir in leeks and mushrooms and sauté until softened, about 5 minutes. Add garlic and cook 2 more minutes. Stir in prosciutto and Parmesan cheese and mix until well blended. Remove from heat.

Preheat oven to 375 degrees. On a lightly floured surface, roll pastry out ⅛-inch thick. With a 2-inch cookie cutter, cut out as many circles as you can from the dough. Save scraps to roll out for additional circles. Put a teaspoon of filling in the center of the circle and cover it with another circle. Seal circles by pressing them together with the tines of a fork. Repeat until as many pastries as you can make are formed, then transfer to a baking sheet. (May be frozen at this point.) Bake until a light brown, about 20 minutes. Serve warm.

Yield: 10 to 12 servings

Salsa Stars

24 won ton squares
1   pound ground turkey meat
1   cup salsa
1   package dry ranch dressing mix

1   small can of sliced black olives, drained
½   cup shredded Cheddar cheese
½   cup shredded mozzarella cheese

Preheat oven to 450 degrees. Coat muffin tins with nonstick cooking spray. Place a won ton square in each muffin cup and bake for 8 minutes. Cool.

Cook turkey and drain. Add salsa, dressing mix, olives, and cheeses. Divide turkey mixture among won ton cups and bake until cheeses melt.

Hint: Pork sausage can be substituted for turkey.

Yield: 12 servings

Portobello Mushroom Nachos

4   (6 inch) flour tortillas, quartered
2   small portobello mushrooms, sliced (about ½ pound)
¼   cup low-salt chicken broth
1   tablespoon fresh lemon juice
1   tablespoon low-sodium soy sauce
1   teaspoon olive oil
2   tablespoons chopped fresh basil or 2 teaspoons dried

1   tablespoon chopped fresh thyme or 1 teaspoon dried
1   cup Refried White Beans (see page 192)
⅓   cup roasted tomato sauce
⅓   cup crumbled feta cheese, about 1½ ounces
    Lime slices, optional

Preheat oven to 350 degrees. Place tortilla quarters on a baking sheet which has been coated with nonstick spray. Bake until crisp, about 8 minutes.

Place mushrooms in a shallow 2-quart baking dish. Drizzle with broth, lemon juice, soy sauce, and olive oil; sprinkle with basil and thyme. Toss well. Cover and bake until tender, about 15 minutes. Drain mushrooms and discard liquid.

Spread 1 tablespoon refried white beans over each tortilla quarter and top with mushrooms. Top each serving with 1 teaspoon roasted tomato sauce and 1 teaspoon feta cheese. Return tortilla quarters to baking sheet and bake 5 minutes, until tortillas are thoroughly heated. Garnish with lime, if desired. Serve immediately.

Yield: 8 servings

Rouxminations

Madison Square Gardens in St. Joseph

Newton S. Hillyard arrived in St. Joseph with "only $5 in his pocket but rich with determination." Hillyard built a new plant and office building in St. Joseph that had the largest wood gymnasium west of the Mississippi River. He used it as a test site to perfect new wood gym seals and finishes. To simulate tournament conditions, he organized a company basketball team that twice won the AAU championship. The company is still family-owned.

Rouxminations

Cable Network

Wire Rope Corporation of American relocated in St. Joseph in 1948 in response to a need for a central location to serve the growing markets for wire rope. Wire Rope Corporation is the largest producer of wire rope in North America. The company is still family-owned.

Wild Mushroom and Brie Toasts

1	narrow French bread baguette, thinly sliced	2	pounds assorted wild mushrooms, sliced
¼	cup olive oil	2	tablespoons white wine or brandy
3	tablespoons butter		Salt and pepper
1½	cups chopped onion	1	pound Brie, sliced
1	teaspoon minced garlic	¼	cup chopped fresh parsley

Preheat oven to 350 degrees. Lightly brush each slice of bread with olive oil and arrange on a large cookie sheet. Bake in oven for about 6 minutes, until toasted a golden color. Remove from oven and set aside.

In a large skillet or sauté pan, melt butter and add onions, garlic, and mushrooms. Sauté 5 to 7 minutes. Add wine or brandy and bring to a boil. Boil just until liquid evaporates. Season to taste with salt and pepper.

Mound a heaping tablespoon of mushroom mixture onto each toast and top with a slice of Brie. Bake 5 minutes. Remove from oven and immediately sprinkle with fresh parsley.

Yield: 12 servings

Artichoke-Roasted Pepper Tapenade

1	(7 ounce) jar roasted red bell peppers, drained and coarsely chopped	½	cup freshly grated Parmesan cheese
1	(6 ounce) jar marinated artichokes, drained and coarsely chopped	¼	cup olive oil
		¼	cup drained capers
½	cup minced fresh parsley	2	cloves garlic, chopped
		1	tablespoon fresh lemon juice

Combine all ingredients in food processor. Process using on/off turns until mixture is well blended and finely chopped. Transfer to a medium bowl and season to taste with salt and pepper. Serve as a dip for vegetables or crackers, or as a spread for crostini.

Hint: Keeps well in the refrigerator for several days. It is also good on sandwiches.

Yield: 3½ cups

Artichoke and Sun-Dried Tomato Dip

¼	cup grated Parmesan cheese	8	ounces (2 cups) shredded Swiss cheese
½	cup sour cream (light can be used)	1	(14 ounce) can artichoke hearts, rinsed, drained, and chopped
½	cup mayonnaise (light can be used)	1	clove garlic, chopped
⅓	cup sun-dried tomatoes, softened and coarsely chopped	¼	teaspoon hot pepper sauce Fresh rosemary, optional

Preheat oven to 350 degrees. Combine Parmesan, sour cream, mayonnaise, sun-dried tomatoes, Swiss cheese, artichoke heart, garlic, and hot pepper sauce in a large bowl. Place in a greased 9-inch ovenproof shallow dish and bake for 22 to 26 minutes, until brown around edges. Garnish with rosemary, if desired, and serve with crackers or breadsticks.

Hint: Works best with purchased oil-packed sun-dried tomatoes.

Yield: 8 to 10 servings

Black Bean Hummus

⅓	cup fresh lime juice	2	jalapeño peppers, stemmed, seeded, and minced
3	cloves garlic, minced	½	cup chopped cilantro
½	cup smooth peanut butter	2	tablespoons olive oil
2	cups canned black beans, drained and rinsed		Salt to taste
½-¾	cup water		Lime wedges and black olives for garnish

Place lime juice, garlic, and peanut butter in a food processor fitted with a steel blade, and process to a smooth paste. Add black beans and process until mixture is very smooth, thinning it to spreading consistency with the water while processing. Add jalapeño peppers and cilantro and pulse just to incorporate. Season to taste with salt. Transfer to a serving bowl and drizzle with olive oil. Garnish with lime wedges and black olives. Serve at room temperature with crackers or pita bread.

Hint: May be prepared 2 days in advance.

Yield: 3½ cups

Rouxminations

Santa Claus Is Coming To Town

A St. Joseph holiday landmark since 1958, the Santa and his reindeer Christmas display sits atop the Mead building at 11th and Mitchell during most of December. The display is 100 feet long. It is a beacon to many young Santa admirers.

Fabulous Chicken Jalapeño Dip

4	boneless, skinless chicken breasts	½	cup milk
3	teaspoons garlic powder, or to taste	½	cup mayonnaise
		½	cup minced red bell pepper
1	teaspoon salt	4	tablespoons minced jalapeño pepper
1	teaspoon pepper	2	tablespoons lemon juice
2	tablespoons olive oil	1½	teaspoons salt
16	ounces cream cheese, softened	1½	teaspoons Tabasco sauce

Preheat oven to 350 degrees. Season chicken breasts with garlic powder, salt, and pepper. Sauté chicken in olive oil in a 12-inch skillet over medium heat for 5 minutes. Chop breasts into thirds and continue cooking until chicken is cooked through, but not overcooked. Transfer to cutting board and finely chop.

Combine remaining ingredients in a medium bowl. Mix well and add chicken, stirring until completely blended. Transfer to a greased 8-inch square ovenproof dish. (May prepare to this point a day ahead.) Bake until mixture is hot and bubbly, about 20 minutes. Serve with crackers or pita triangles.

Hint: Well-seasoned chicken makes this a hit. Once you dip into this, it cannot be left alone.

Yield: 10 servings

Our Favorite Guacamole Dip

2	large ripe avocados, peeled and chopped, pits reserved	1	tablespoon lime juice
		3	tablespoons olive oil
1	large tomato, peeled, seeded, and chopped		Salt and pepper
		1	can chopped chiles, drained
1	large onion, chopped		

Combine avocado, tomato, and onion in a medium bowl. Add lime juice and olive oil. Season with salt and pepper to taste. Mix well and add chiles. Stick the avocado pits on top to prevent browning. Cover tightly with plastic wrap and refrigerate until ready to serve. Remove pits and serve with tortilla chips.

Yield: 3½ cups

Hot Onion Fromage

1 cup chopped sweet onion
   (such as Vidalia)
1 cup mayonnaise

1 cup shredded Swiss cheese
   Ground cayenne pepper

Preheat oven to 350 degrees. Combine onion, mayonnaise and Swiss cheese in a medium bowl. Mix well and transfer to a greased 1-quart baking dish. Sprinkle with cayenne pepper. Bake, uncovered, until hot and bubbly, about 30 minutes. Serve hot with large dipping Fritos or other sturdy chips.

Yield: 6 servings

Pan-Fried Onion Dip

3 large yellow onions
4 tablespoons unsalted butter
¼ cup vegetable oil
¼ teaspoon ground cayenne
   pepper
1 teaspoon kosher salt

½ teaspoon freshly ground black
   pepper
4 ounces cream cheese, room
   temperature
½ cup sour cream
½ cup Hellmann's mayonnaise

Cut onions in half, and then slice into ⅛-inch thick, half rounds, or slice in food processor with the slicing blade attached. Heat butter and oil in a large sauté or frying pan over medium heat. Add onions, cayenne, salt, and pepper and sauté for 10 minutes Reduce heat to medium-low and cook, stirring occasionally, for about 20 more minutes, until onions are browned and caramelized. Remove from pan to a plate with a slotted spoon, leaving much of the butter and oil in the pan so the dip doesn't get greasy. Allow onions to cool.

Place cream cheese, sour cream, and mayonnaise in a bowl and beat until smooth with an electric mixer. Add onions and mix well. Add additional salt and pepper to taste. Serve at room temperature with sturdy potato chips, vegetables, or Wheat Thins.

Hint: Can be refrigerated overnight; bring to room temperature before serving.

Yield: 10 to 12 servings

Rouxminations

Send In The Calvary

Willard P. Hall was in the Missouri Cavalry during the war with Mexico and was the second governor from St. Joseph in 1864. He was also a Lieutenant Governor. Silas Woodson was the last of the three governors from St. Joseph. He was elected to that office in 1872 as Missouri's first Democratic governor since the Civil War. He served until 1874.

Rouxminations

Hats Off To The Mail Service!

St. Joseph's first letters were delivered from a top hat. In 1840, the federal government opened the postal service in Joseph Robidoux's log warehouse. Because of the then- high cost of postage, 25 cents, the volume of mail was not large, and Postmaster Frederick Smith's top hat could easily hold the day's mail.

Salsarito

1	bunch fresh cilantro, chopped	1	(8 ounce) can whole black olives, drained and chopped
4	large ripe tomatoes, chopped		
10	large green onions, chopped	4	tablespoons white wine vinegar, or more to taste
2	(4 ounce) cans mild chopped green chiles, drained	4	tablespoons olive oil

Mix all ingredients together, cover and refrigerate at least 6 hours. Serve with corn chips.

Hint: Just right with your favorite margarita.

Yield: 12 servings

Roasted Garlic Dipping Sauce with Roquefort and Rosemary

6	whole heads garlic	2	teaspoons dried rosemary, chopped
3	tablespoons butter, cut into 6 slices	8	ounces Roquefort cheese, crumbled
¼	cup olive oil		Crusty bread, sliced
¾	cup chicken broth		
¼	cup dry white wine		

Preheat oven to 375 degrees. Cut ½ inch off top end of each garlic head, exposing tops of cloves. Remove any loose papery outer skin. Place garlic cut side up in a glass baking dish and top each head with a slice of butter. Pour oil over and add broth and wine to dish. Sprinkle rosemary over garlic. Bake, uncovered, until garlic is tender, about 1 hour and 15 minutes, basting every 15 minutes with pan juices. Add more broth if necessary to maintain some liquid in dish. Sprinkle with cheese and continue baking until cheese melts, about 10 minutes. Serve warm with bread.

Yield: 10 to 12 servings

White Bean Beer Dip

½ cup beer
1 teaspoon ground cumin
½ teaspoon dried oregano
½ teaspoon garlic powder
2 cups Refried White Beans
    (see recipe, page 192) or
    1 (16 ounce) can refried beans

½ cup chunky hot salsa
1 (16 ounce) package Velveeta
    cheese, cut into ½-inch
    pieces
    Jalapeño, finely chopped,
    optional

Combine beer, cumin, oregano, and garlic powder in a heavy medium saucepan. Bring to simmer and add beans and salsa. Stir until heated through. Add cheese and cook, stirring, until cheese melts, about 3 minutes. Transfer to a bowl and serve warm with tortilla chips.

Yield: 5 cups

Salsa Rojo for a Crowd

7 cups peeled and chopped fresh
    tomatoes
3 cups tomato juice
4 tablespoons crushed red pepper
½ cup chopped onion

½ tablespoon garlic powder
½ tablespoon salt
½ cup chopped fresh cilantro
1½ cups blended tomatillo
1½ cups diced mild green chiles

Combine all ingredients. If possible, allow a couple of hours before serving time for the flavors to combine. Serve with tortilla chips.

Yield: 12 cups

Rouxminations

Long Before FedEx and UPS

Captain Frederick Smith was St. Joseph's first postmaster. Due to the low volume of mail and because he knew everyone in town, Smith could leisurely stroll about town and stop at homes to deliver letters from his hat. This gave the city a free postal delivery service well before many larger cities had even heard of it.

Rouxminations

St. Joseph's
First Retirement Villa

St. Joseph once had a home for "aged and dependent" ex-slaves at 17th and Highland. Most of the slaves were centenarians and had no known living relatives and were therefore dependent on charitable causes. A report of the Census of the year 1860 showed that Buchanan County had "101 free Negroes and 2,011 Negro slaves."

Won Ton Crisps

4   tablespoons butter or margarine
5   egg roll wrappers
½   cup grated Parmesan cheese

Fresh or dried herbs, such as basil, parsley, oregano or thyme, optional

Preheat oven to 375 degrees. Melt butter in a small saucepan or in microwave. Brush a baking sheet or jelly-roll pan lightly with a small amount of melted butter. Brush egg roll wrappers on 1 side with remaining butter. Cut each wrapper into 4 squares, then cut each square in half, to make 8 rectangles. Place rectangles in a single layer on baking sheet. Sprinkle with cheese and herbs, if desired. Bake, uncovered, until golden, 5 to 6 minutes. Repeat process until all crisps are baked.

Hint: These work well as alternatives to both crackers and croutons!

Yield: 8 servings

Chili Cocktail Salsa Sauce

1   cup homemade or purchased salsa
1   cup bottled chili sauce
1½ tablespoons prepared white horseradish

1   tablespoon chopped chipotle chiles, or to taste
4   tablespoons chopped fresh cilantro

Mix salsa, chili sauce, and horseradish in a medium bowl. Add chiles and check for taste. Add more chiles, if desired. Sprinkle with chopped cilantro. If possible, allow flavors to blend for an hour. Serve with chilled boiled shrimp.

Yield: 2½ cups

Roquefort Grapes

1   (8 ounce) package cream
    cheese, softened
¼   pound Roquefort cheese
2   tablespoons heavy cream
1   pound red or green seedless
    grapes, washed and dried

10 ounces nuts - almonds, pecan,
    or walnuts, toasted*, or
    unroasted pistachio or
    macadamia nuts, coarsely
    chopped

Line a tray with wax paper and set aside. In bowl of electric mixer, beat together cheeses and cream until well blended. Drop grapes into mixture and stir to coat. Roll each cheese-dipped grape in nuts. Place on prepared tray. Chill in refrigerator. To serve, arrange grapes on serving tray to resemble a bunch of grapes.

*To toast nuts, cook in 350 degree oven for about 5 minutes. The nuts should smell toasted not burned.

Hint: This makes a beautiful addition to any buffet or holiday spread.

Yield: 12 servings

Rouxminations

The Mighty Missouri River Wreaks Havoc

In July 1993, the Missouri River crested at 32.63 feet, and ultimately left the city without drinking water for about a week. A levy break flooded Rosecrans Field, the National Air Guard field, portions of St. Joseph and the city of Elwood.

Cream Cheese Stuffed Strawberries

1   carton large fresh strawberries
6   ounces cream cheese, room
    temperature

½   teaspoon vanilla
4   tablespoons powdered sugar

Trim bottom of berries so each stands upright. Use melon baller to scoop out stems and tops.

Whip cream cheese until slightly fluffy, 2 to 3 minutes. Add vanilla and sugar. Transfer to a pastry bag fitted with a ½-inch star tip. Pipe into berries until cream cheese brims over top. Berries may be garnished with sliced toasted almonds, chocolate shavings, mint, etc.

Hint: You can use a ziplock bag to create a homemade pastry bag; just fill the bag and clip a small corner off to create your spout.

Yield: 6 to 8 servings

The Punch We Do

2	bottles champagne	1	cup peach or apricot brandy
1	(2 liter) bottle Sprite		

Mix and serve!

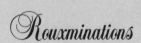

Best Bloody Mary

1	quart Clamato or Beefamato juice		Several heavy dashes of Worcestershire sauce
½	cup fresh lime juice	1	teaspoon celery seed
2	tablespoons horseradish, or to taste	1½	cups vodka
			Lime wedges for garnish

Mix juices, horseradish, Worcestershire, celery seed, and vodka in a large pitcher and stir well. Serve over ice garnished with lime wedges.

Hint: These Bloody Marys are lighter than ones made with tomato juice.

Triple Sec Limeades

1⅓	cups orange juice	¼	cup triple sec
1	(12 ounce) can frozen limeade	2	tablespoons fresh lime juice
¼	cup plus 2 tablespoons tequila	5¼	cups crushed ice

Place all the ingredients in a blender and mix well until desired consistency.

Hint: You may wish to put salt around the rim and garnish with a lime wedge.

Spirited Apricot Slush

1	(12 ounce) can frozen lemonade, thawed	1	cup gin
1	(12 ounce) can frozen orange juice, thawed	1	cup apricot brandy
		3	liters (12 cups) Sprite or 7-Up, divided

Combine all ingredients except 1 liter of Sprite in a large nonmetal container. Freeze 1 to 2 days. Remove slush from freezer 1 hour before serving. To serve, place slush in a punch bowl, pour remaining Sprite into the bowl, and stir gently.

Hint: It freezes well.

Yield: 34 (½ cup) servings

Citrus Almond Punch

3	large lemons	2½	cups pineapple juice
1⅔	cups sugar	1	teaspoon vanilla
1	quart water	1	teaspoon almond extract
2-3	slices fresh ginger	1	quart ginger ale, chilled
2	cups strong tea		

Squeeze juice from lemons into a small bowl. Set aside, reserving rinds. Place sugar, water, reserved rinds, and ginger slices in large saucepan or Dutch oven and mix well. Bring to boil and boil for 3 minutes. Add lemon juice, tea, pineapple juice, vanilla, and almond extract. Strain into a 4-quart bowl or container. Chill. Add ginger ale when ready to serve.

Hint: The base for this punch can be kept in the refrigerator for up to a week and be combined with ginger ale as needed.

Rouxminations

Those Were The Good Old Days

The Frog Hop Ballroom drew a crowd from all over St. Joseph and surrounding communities. One such patron of the Frog Hop, Dean Reese, recalls driving to St. Joseph from White Cloud, Kansas.
"We stopped at a bar called Murphy's just over the river bridge because the bartender would take out-of-town checks. We'd write a check for $5, buy a small bottle of whiskey, and go to the Frog Hop. We'd have money left over to go to the movie the next day."

✦ Flour Power ✦

John Corby was born in Limerick, Ireland. He once explained that as a boy he had played near a mill and had since wanted one like it. Upon his arrival in St. Joseph, Corby had the cash to make his dreams come true. It might have been the rhythmic sloshing of the water wheel or the peaceful surrounding he remembered that prompted John Corby to have a mill built on the 102 River.

Probably more than childhood memories prompted Corby to build the mill. He recognized the high cost of bringing flour to St. Joseph by steamboat and the economical sense of building a mill. Corby had already had a reputation of being a progressive thinker. After all, he built the first brick home in St. Joseph and had the first metal safe. Corby had the large, brick mill built on a stone foundation and the 102 River was dammed to furnish water power.

Today the mill is gone, destroyed by a tornado in the early 1900's. For a number of years, Kleinbrodt's restaurant flourished built on the stone foundation of the mill. Kleinbrodt's became a popular eating spot famous for roast beef sandwiches. Today, the only thing left of either the mill or the restaurant is the water sloshing onto the shores of the 102 River.

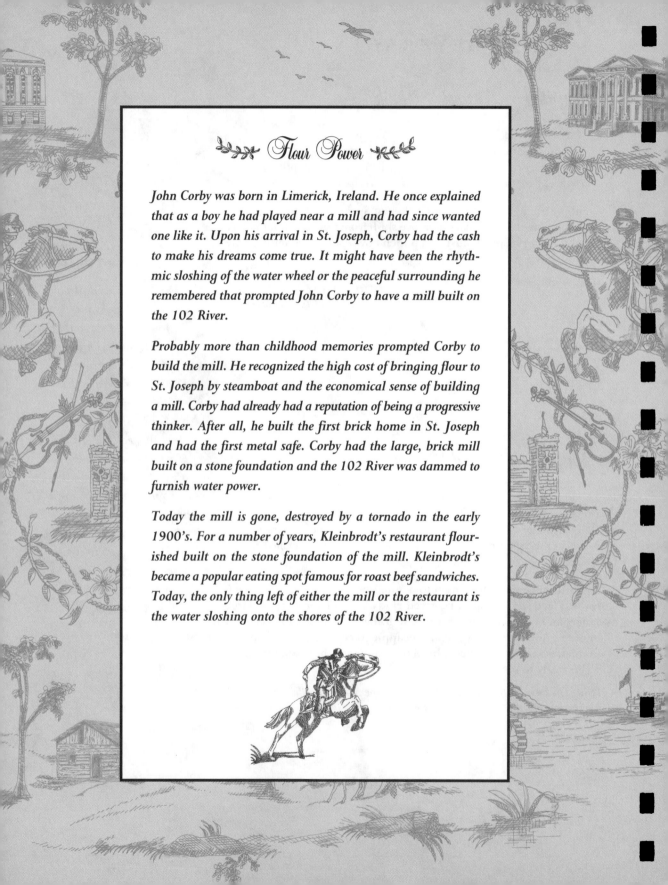

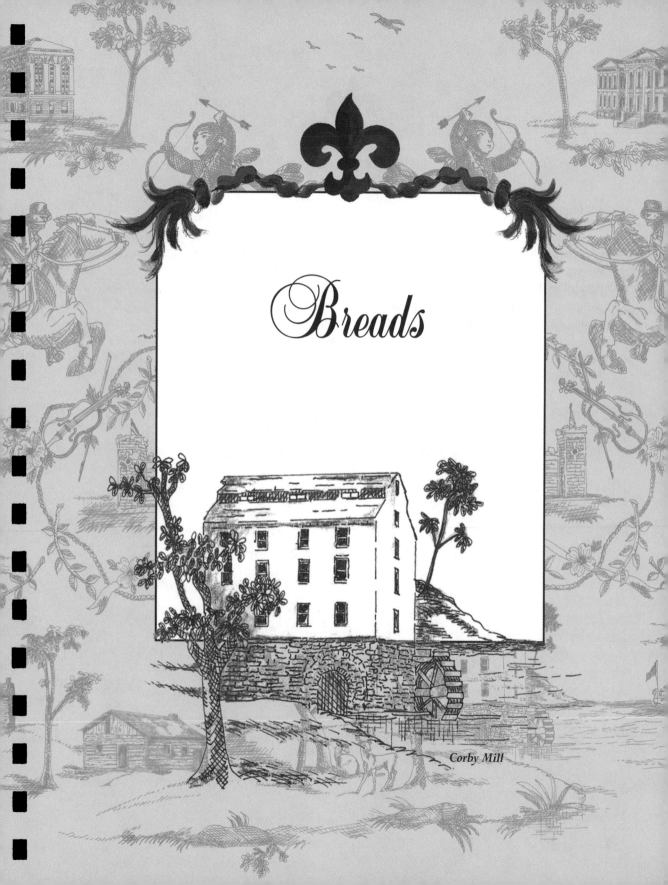

Breads

Corby Mill

Breads

Honey Wheat Bread

1	cup milk	2	packages active dry yeast
¾	cup shortening	3	eggs, slightly beaten
¾	cup honey	½	cup wheat germ
¼	cup firmly packed brown sugar	4½	cups all-purpose flour
2	teaspoons salt	1½	cups whole wheat flour
¾	cup warm water	1	teaspoon butter

In a small saucepan, heat milk until bubbles form around the edge of the pan. Remove from heat and add shortening, honey, and salt. Stir until blended. Cool to lukewarm. In a large mixing bowl, sprinkle yeast over warm water and stir. Let stand until dissolved, about 5 minutes. Stir in milk mixture. Add eggs and wheat germ and mix until blended.

Combine all-purpose and whole wheat flour in a medium bowl. Add two-thirds of flour mixture to yeast mixture. Mix with an electric mixer on low until well blended and smooth. Using a wooden spoon, gradually mix in remaining flour mixture. Turn out onto a floured surface and knead 5 to 6 minutes, until smooth and elastic.

Place dough in an oiled bowl, turning to coat, and cover with towel. Let rise in a warm place until doubled in size, about 1 hour. Punch down dough and divide into 2 pieces. Shape each piece into a ball. Place on a large greased cookie sheet, leaving about 5 inches between balls. Cover and let rise until doubled, about 45 to 50 minutes.

Preheat oven to 375 degrees. Bake until bread is golden brown and sounds hollow when tapped, 45 to 50 minutes. Remove from oven and rub butter over top. Cool on rack.

Hint: Best when served warm. For a crispier crust, use a baking stone.

Yield: 2 loaves

Rouxminations

Shave and A Hair Cut

In 1859, Abraham Lincoln got a shave at the Edgar House at the Northeast corner of Main and Francis.

CEO's of The USA

In 1879, President Rutherford B. Hays visited St. Joseph. Ronald Reagan had close ties to St. Joseph in his first wife, Jane Wyman, who was from St. Joseph.

Rouxminations

National Recognition

In 1987, The Junior League of St. Joseph's Health Education project with the Social Welfare Board received recognition as a Junior League model program and was highlighted at the Association's annual national conference.

Italian Herb Bread - Bread Machine Recipe

1½ cups warm water	1½ tablespoons dry milk
2 tablespoons butter or margarine	1½ tablespoons sugar
4 cups bread flour	1 tablespoon Italian seasoning
3 tablespoons freshly grated Parmesan cheese	1 teaspoon garlic salt
	2¼ teaspoons active dry yeast

Add water and butter to pan. Add dry ingredients except yeast and level pan to settle. Make a well in center of dry ingredients and add yeast. Lock pan in bread maker and set according to machine's directions.

Hint: This is for a large machine. This recipe can be halved for use in the smaller 1-pound machine. It is also wonderful as dough for rolls or pizza crust.

Yield: 1 loaf

Rosemary Kalamata Olive Bread

2½ teaspoons active dry yeast	5 cups bread flour, plus additional for dusting
2 cups warm water	1 cup whole wheat flour
½ cup pitted, chopped kalamata olives	2 tablespoons chopped fresh rosemary
2 tablespoons extra virgin olive oil	2½ teaspoons salt

In a bowl, sprinkle yeast over the warm water and let stand until bubbly, about 5 minutes. In bowl of an electric mixer, combine olives, olive oil, both flours, rosemary, salt and yeast mixture. Knead dough on medium speed until soft and smooth, about 10 minutes. Transfer to a lightly floured surface and shape into a ball.

Place dough in an oiled bowl, cover with a towel, and let rise in warm place until it doubles in size, about 1 hour. Punch dough down and let rise again until doubled, 45 to 50 minutes. Preheat oven to 400 degrees.

On a lightly floured surface, press dough flat and stretch sides down under to form a tight ball. Pinch seam underneath the bottom of loaf. Place dough on a baking sheet which has been lightly oiled and sprinkled with cornmeal. Dust dough with flour. Cover with a towel and let rise for only 4 to 5 minutes. Cut an "X" in top of loaf with a serrated knife. Bake until loaf is golden and sounds hollow, about 1 hour.

Yield: 1 loaf

Rosemary-Garlic Bread

1	cup warm water		1	tablespoon olive oil
2	teaspoons active dry yeast		1	cup whole wheat flour
½	teaspoon sugar		1½-2	cups unbleached flour, divided
1	teaspoon salt			
1	tablespoon fresh rosemary, minced		1-2	teaspoons kosher salt, optional
1½	teaspoons garlic powder			

Coat a large mixing bowl with olive oil spray and set aside. Pour water into bowl of a food processor fitted with a dough blade and stir in yeast and sugar. Let stand 5 to 10 minutes. Stir salt, rosemary, garlic, and olive oil into yeast mixture. Add whole wheat flour and pulse a few times to mix well. Add 1 cup unbleached flour and continue processing. Dough should begin to pull away from the sides to form a ball. Add more flour, a tablespoon or 2 at a time, processing in between, until dough forms a ball and begins to "clean" inside of processor.

Turn dough out onto a lightly floured surface, dust lightly with more flour, and knead 2 to 4 minutes until dough is elastic and not too sticky, adding more flour as necessary. Shape into a ball and place in prepared bowl, turning to coat with oil. Cover with plastic wrap and leave in a warm place to rise. Let rise until double, about 35 to 40 minutes. Punch down dough and turn out onto a clean surface. Knead a few times before shaping dough into a log 8 to 10 inches long.

Place on a baking sheet which has been coated with olive oil. Spray loaf with olive oil and cover lightly with plastic wrap. Preheat oven to 400 degrees while letting dough rise another 25 to 30 minutes or until almost double in size. Slash loaf lightly in a diagonal pattern with a serrated knife. Spray again with olive oil and sprinkle with kosher salt, if desired. Bake 25 to 30 minutes, until loaf is nicely browned and sounds hollow when tapped. Remove from oven and cool on rack. Allow to cool completely before slicing.

Yield: 1 loaf

Rouxminations

Good Clean Fun

Soap opera diva Ruth Warrick who plays Phoebe Wallingford on ABCs All My Children, is from St. Joseph. Warrick's character had a central role in the soap opera in the 1980's.

Rouxminations

Becoming Diversified

As the Junior League of St. Joseph entered the 1990s, community training events and community partnerships were often in the forefront of the League's activities. The League's projects in the early part of that decade included a Children's Museum Development project, the Woman to Woman project, and extension of the Social Welfare Board Health Education projects, and the Krug Park Zoo project.

Potato Egg Braid

3	medium red-skinned potatoes, peeled and diced		Pinch of sugar
¾	cup sugar	4	large eggs
6	tablespoons butter, softened	8-10	cups all-purpose flour, divided
4	teaspoons salt	1	egg beaten with 1 tablespoon water for wash
½	cup warm water		Sesame or poppy seeds for garnish
3	packages dry yeast		

Place potatoes in a large pot and cover with 5 cups warm water. Cover and boil until the potatoes are tender, about 35 minutes. Reserve 1¼ cups cooking liquid and cool until lukewarm. Drain potatoes and transfer to a large bowl. Mash until smooth. Add sugar, butter, salt and 1¼ cups reserved cooking liquid. Mix until well-blended and set aside.

In a small bowl, combine ½ cup warm water, yeast, and a pinch of sugar. Let stand for 5 minutes. Add yeast mixture to potato mixture and blend. Add eggs and beat well. Using a wooden spoon, mix in flour, 1 cup at a time, to form a soft dough.

Turn out onto a well-floured surface and knead until dough is smooth and elastic, adding more flour as necessary. Dough should be soft but not sticky. Knead 8 to 10 minutes. Place dough in an oiled bowl, turning once to coat. Cover with a towel and let rise in a warm area until doubled, about 1 hour. Punch down dough and divide into 4 equal pieces.

Divide 1 piece into 3 equal pieces and roll each of the 3 pieces into a rope about 15 inches long. Pinch the ends together and braid the 3 pieces together. Once the braid is formed, tuck the ends under and pinch ends together. Place braid on a lightly greased baking sheet and cover with a towel. Repeat process with the other pieces of dough. (You will have 4 braided loaves.)

Preheat oven to 400 degrees. Let dough rise until doubled, about 25 minutes. Brush loaves with egg wash and sprinkle with sesame or poppy seeds. Bake 15 minutes, then reduce heat to 350 degrees and continue baking 20 to 25 minutes longer, until loaves are golden brown and sound hollow when tapped. Pans may need to be switched half way through baking to insure even browning. Transfer to racks and cool completely.

Yield: 4 loaves

Basil, Sun-Dried Tomato, and Parmesan Focaccia

3 cups warm water, divided	¼ cup chopped fresh basil
2 tablespoons dry yeast	¼ cup chopped, softened sun-dried tomatoes
1 tablespoon sugar	
1 tablespoon balsamic vinegar	½ cup finely grated Parmesan cheese
5 tablespoons olive oil, divided	
2 teaspoons salt	1 teaspoon kosher salt
5 cups bread flour, divided	

Pour 1 cup warm water into large mixing bowl. Sprinkle yeast and sugar into water and let stand at room temperature for about 10 minutes, until yeast dissolves and starts to look foamy. Add 3 tablespoons olive oil, balsamic vinegar, remaining 2 cups water, and 2 cups flour. Stir until well blended. Add 2 teaspoons salt and remaining flour, 1 cup at a time, until it forms a soft, but not sticky, dough.

Turn out onto a floured surface and knead about 8 minutes, until smooth and elastic, adding a little flour if necessary to keep it from sticking. Place in an oiled bowl and let rise for 30 minutes in a warm draft-free place. Punch down and divide dough into 2 equal pieces. Place each piece on a separate greased round pizza pan and spread evenly in a circle to roughly fit the pans. Cover with a kitchen towel and let rest for 20 minutes.

Preheat oven to 400 degrees. Uncover and dimple the dough by pressing fingertips into it. Drizzle remaining olive oil evenly over each focaccia round and sprinkle each with half of sun-dried tomatoes, basil, and kosher salt. Bake until golden brown, about 25 to 30 minutes.

Yield: 2 loaves

Rouxminations

And That's The Way It Was

Walter Cronkite, famous broadcast journalist, was from St. Joseph. His niece, Kay (Cronkite) Barnes, mayor of Kansas City in the late 1990's and early 2000's, was born and raised in St. Joseph.

Be All That You Can Be

The 139th Airlift Wing of the Missouri Air National Guard is one of the first federally-organized air units, created in 1946. At the close of the second World War, Colonel John. B. Logan convinced his superiors to create the 180th Light Bombardment Squadron. The Guard's present day mission is to transport military personnel and goods using the C-130H model of the Lockheed Hercules.

Doubly Good Yeast Rolls

1	cup plus 1 teaspoon sugar	½	cup sugar
1	package active dry yeast	1	cup shortening, cut into small
½	cup warm water		pieces
2	eggs	2	cups warm water
1	teaspoon salt	7	cups all-purpose flour

Combine 1 teaspoon sugar, yeast and ½ cup of warm water in a small bowl. Stir to dissolve yeast and let stand 5 minutes. In a large bowl, mix eggs, salt, remaining sugar, shortening, and 2 cups warm water with an electric mixer on low. Slowly add yeast mixture and continue to mix on low just until blended. Add flour, 1 cup at a time, beating well with each addition. When all flour is incorporated, mix on medium for 3 minutes.

Transfer to an oiled bowl, turning once to coat. Cover with a towel and let rise in a warm place until double in size. Punch down dough, cover with plastic wrap, and refrigerate overnight.

Shape dough into 2-inch balls and place in a greased 9 x 13-inch pan. Cover with a towel and let rise 2 hours or until double in bulk. Preheat oven during this rising to 400 degrees. Bake rolls until golden brown, 10 to 12 minutes. If using a glass baking dish, lower temperature to 350 degrees and bake 12 to 14 minutes.

Yield: 4 dozen

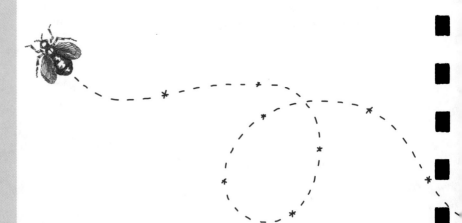

Refrigerator Crescent Rolls

2 envelopes dry yeast	1 cup mashed potatoes
½ cup warm water	1 cup scalded milk
⅔ cup shortening or butter	2 eggs, well beaten
1 teaspoon salt	7-8 cups all-purpose flour
¼ cup sugar	Melted butter

Dissolve yeast in warm water. Pour scalded milk over shortening. Add sugar and salt. Stir in potatoes and cool. Add eggs and yeast mixture and blend well. Gradually add 7 cups flour. Turn dough out onto a floured surface and knead until dough is smooth and elastic, incorporating more flour as necessary. Knead 7 to 8 minutes.

Place in a greased 3-quart bowl. Cover with wax paper and place in refrigerator. Let rise until double in size, 2 to 3 hours. Divide dough into 4 parts. Roll each part into a circle on a floured board. Spread melted butter over top. Cut dough into 16 wedges. Roll each 1 up, starting with wide end. Place on baking sheet, small tips down. Brush with butter and let rise 30 minutes. Preheat oven to 400 degrees during this rise. Bake rolls until brown, about 12 minutes.

Hint: Instant mashed potatoes can be used. This dough rises in the refrigerator and can be made 1 or 2 days ahead.

Variation: Roll into a long rectangle, spread with melted butter and sprinkle with a cinnamon and sugar mixture. Roll into a long roll and slice into ½-inch round rolls. Bake as above and frost with butter cream frosting when cool.

Yield: 64 rolls

Rouxminations

Play It Again, Sam

Coleman Hawkins was born in St. Joseph in 1904. He is considered to be the father of the jazz tenor saxophone and was an originator of bebop.

Jam Session

Coleman Hawkins traveled extensively and toured and recorded with the likes of Dizzy Gillespie, Miles Davis, and Louis Armstrong. In 1940, he recorded his signature tune, "Body and Soul."

Maple Sweet Rolls

Rolls

1	cup milk	1	egg, beaten
½	cup margarine, melted	2	packages active dry yeast
¼	cup sugar	¼	cup warm water
1	teaspoon salt	3½-4 cups all-purpose flour

Filling

½	cup margarine	1	teaspoon maple flavoring
⅔	cup sugar	2	teaspoons cinnamon
½	cup chopped pecans		

Glaze

1	cup powdered sugar	2	tablespoons margarine, room
1	teaspoon maple flavoring		temperature
			Milk

For Rolls: In a small saucepan, heat milk until bubbles start to form around edge of pan. Add margarine, sugar, and salt. Stir until mixed well and set aside to cool. In a large bowl, place yeast and warm water, stirring to dissolve. Let stand for 5 minutes. Pour cooled milk mixture into yeast mixture. Add egg and blend well. Beat in 1 cup of flour at a time, mixing well after each addition. Turn out onto a floured counter and knead 5 to 6 minutes, until dough is smooth and elastic. Place in an oiled bowl, cover with a towel, and let rise in a warm area until doubled in size, about 50 to 60 minutes. Punch dough down and let rest while making filling.

To make filling: Combine margarine, sugar, pecans, maple flavoring, and cinnamon. Mix well and set aside.

Divide dough into thirds. Flatten 1 piece of dough out with the palms of your hands onto a well-greased 12-inch round pizza pan. Spread evenly with half of filling. Top with another piece of dough and spread, using fingers, to cover first layer evenly. Spread with remaining filling and top with last piece of dough, once again using fingers to cover the layers below evenly.

Place a small drinking glass in the middle of the dough. Cut dough into 16 wedges starting from outside of dough up to the glass in the middle. Remove glass and twist each wedge 4 times, pressing down onto pan to keep the round shape. Dough should look like a flower with a solid middle. Cover with a towel and let rise 20 minutes in a warm area. Preheat oven to 350 degrees. Bake until golden, about 25 minutes.

Rouxminations

Uncle Jemima?

The Aunt Jemima pancake company originated here, and the Aunt Jemima house, located at the corner of 20th and Faraon streets in St. Joseph has been featured in Hallmark greeting cards and is still a single dwelling residence. By the way, the first Aunt Jemima was a man. Creator Chris Rutt found the image while at a minstrel show. One of the acts was a New Orleans style cakewalk to a song called "Aunt Jemima," and the performer was wearing an apron and a red bandanna.

(Maple Sweet Rolls continued)

While rolls are cooling, make glaze by mixing powdered sugar, margarine, and maple flavoring. Beat well, adding a little milk as needed to make glaze of a spreading consistency. Drizzle rolls with glaze and serve.

Yield: 16 servings

Grandma's Nut Rolls

4	cups flour		Powdered sugar for rolling out dough
1	cup margarine		
2	whole eggs	2	pounds walnuts, finely chopped
2	eggs, separated	1	cup sugar
1	package active dry yeast	½	cup milk
¼	cup warm water	1	teaspoon vanilla
½	pint sour cream	1	cup raisins

In a large bowl, cut margarine into flour with 2 knives, until pea-size crumbs are formed. Set aside. Dissolve yeast in warm water and let stand 5 minutes. Add 2 whole eggs, 2 egg yolks, and sour cream to yeast mixture and mix just until blended. Pour egg mixture into flour mixture and stir with a wooden spoon.

Turn out onto a well-floured counter and knead, adding additional flour as needed. Dough will be sticky to the touch. Place in an oiled bowl and cover with plastic wrap. Refrigerate overnight. When ready to bake, remove chilled dough from refrigerator and divide dough into 3 balls. Let dough stand while making the nut filling.

To make filling, beat 2 egg whites in a medium bowl until firm peaks form. Add nuts, sugar, milk, and vanilla, mixing with a spoon until well blended; set aside. Roll each ball of dough out on a counter heavily dusted with powdered sugar to a 10 x 14-inch rectangle. (Dough can be also rolled out in between 2 sheets of plastic wrap dusted with powdered sugar.) Spread evenly with a third of nut filling and sprinkle with a third cup of raisins. Roll dough up jelly-roll fashion, starting from the long side, and place seam side down on a greased cookie sheet. Let rise 1 hour. Preheat oven to 375 degrees after 30 minutes of rising time. Bake 45 to 60 minutes.

Hint: Great with honey butter.

Yield: 3 loaves

Rouxminations

Farewell Aunt Jemima

Over 75 years of history came to a halt in 2001 with the closing of Quaker Oat's cereal plant in St. Joseph. The plant, which was the original home of Aunt Jemima pancake mix, employed 600 people before its closing. The St. Joseph plant produced some of the country's most recognizable cereal products, including Quaker Oatmeal and Cap'n Crunch.

Rouxminations

A Glorious Run

The Pony Express, which operated for eighteen months, was soon overshadowed by the telegraph line which was installed from Omaha to Sacramento. The telegraph rendered the Pony Express obsolete.

Pumpkin Cornmeal Rolls

3	tablespoons yeast	¾	cup firmly packed dark brown sugar
¾	cup lukewarm water	3	tablespoons olive oil
1½	cups unseasoned canned pumpkin puree	7½-8½	cups all-purpose flour
1½	cups milk, plus more for brushing tops	1	cup cornmeal, plus more for dusting
		4	teaspoons salt

In a large bowl, stir together yeast and water. Let stand until bubbly, about 5 minutes. In a large saucepan, combine pumpkin, 1½ cups milk, brown sugar, and olive oil. Warm over medium heat, stirring frequently, until lukewarm, 3 to 4 minutes. Add to the yeast mixture, stirring until blended. Gradually add 7 cups flour, cornmeal, and salt, stirring to make a soft dough. Turn dough out onto a floured surface and knead until dough is smooth and elastic, incorporating more flour as necessary. Knead 7 to 8 minutes. Place dough in an oiled bowl, turning once to coat, cover with plastic wrap and let rise in a warm area until doubled in size, about 1 hour.

Lightly grease 2 baking sheets. Punch down dough, turn out onto a work surface, and knead lightly. Pinch dough off in 2-inch pieces and form each piece into a round ball. Place on baking sheet. Repeat process until all dough is used. Cover lightly with plastic wrap and let rise until doubled, about 45 minutes.

Preheat oven to 375 degrees. Brush tops of rolls with milk and sprinkle lightly with cornmeal. Bake until golden brown, 20 to 25 minutes, switching pans halfway through baking to insure even browning. Transfer to wire racks to cool.

Yield: 36 to 40 rolls

Pumpkinseed Crackers

1	cup lukewarm water	1	teaspoon salt
1	tablespoon sugar	1	cup finely chopped hulled
1	teaspoon active dry yeast		green pumpkin seeds
6	tablespoons cold butter	1	large egg
2½	cups all-purpose flour	2	tablespoons cold water
1	tablespoon chili powder		Kosher salt
⅓	cup cornmeal		

In a large bowl, stir together lukewarm water, sugar, and yeast. Let stand 5 minutes, until foamy. Cut butter into pieces and stir into yeast mixture. Add flour, cornmeal, chili powder, and salt. Stir until mixture forms dough.

Turn dough out onto a lightly floured surface and knead until smooth, about 5 minutes. Form into a ball and place in a lightly oiled bowl, turning to coat. Chill dough, covered with plastic wrap, for 1 hour or overnight.

In a small bowl beat together egg and cold water until combined well to make an egg wash.

Preheat oven to 400 degrees. Take dough from refrigerator and divide in half. On a lightly floured surface, roll out into a rough oval ⅛-inch thick and about the size of a large pizza. Sprinkle with half of seeds. Press seeds into dough with a rolling pin and roll as thin as possible. Roll until you don't think you can roll any more. The dough should be paper-thin. Brush dough with egg wash and cut as a pizza into irregular long wedges. Transfer wedges onto an ungreased cookie sheet and sprinkle with kosher salt. (Works best on a "good old" cookie sheet; does not work as well on teflon-coated sheets.) Bake until golden brown, about 8 to 9 minutes.

Hint: Sunflower seeds or dry roasted sunflower seeds may be substituted for the pumpkin seeds. Serve these alone or with a favorite spread; we like them with hummus. These are unique and always a hit!

Yield: 50 to 60 crackers

Rouxminations

The Great Pumpkin

The Pony Express Museum celebrates the spirit of the fall harvest with the Pony Express Pumpkinfest. This festival has been featured in Family Fun magazine, the Disney web site, and on HGTV. The festival features a spectacular Pumpkin Mountain of nearly 700 carved pumpkins with a lighting ceremony on Friday evening. It is believed to be the nation's only electrically-lit wall of pumpkins. Activities include live entertainment, arts, crafts, and children's events featuring a children's costume parade. The festival is held the second weekend in October.

Rouxminations

Hail To The Chief

Western Tablet was started in 1906 by William Albrecht. Westab, as it was know to St. Joseph residents, eventually merged with Mead Products. With every change and merger of the company, one product was a constant: the Big Chief Tablet, with its famous red cover. Albrecht's descendants gave his home on Frederick Avenue as a museum for art.

Crescent Caramel Swirls

½ cup margarine	2 tablespoons water
½ cup chopped pecans	2 (8 ounce) cans Pillsbury
1 cup firmly packed brown sugar	crescent rolls

Preheat oven to 375 degrees. Lightly grease 2 (8-inch) round cake pans. Heat margarine, pecans, brown sugar, and water in a heavy pan until margarine is melted. Remove crescents from can in rolled sections. (DO NOT UNROLL.) Cut each roll into 8 slices. Arrange 8 slices in each cake pan and top with half of pecan mixture. Bake for 10 to 15 minutes. Remove from oven and immediately invert onto serving platter.

Yield: 16 rolls

Sunflower Corn Muffins

1 cup sour cream	¼ cup sliced green onions
1 (15 ounce) can whole kernel corn, drained	¼ cup butter, melted
1 (15 ounce) can cream-style corn	1 egg, beaten
½ cup shredded Cheddar cheese	1 (8½ ounce) package cornbread mix
	3 tablespoons sunflower kernels

Preheat oven to 375 degrees. Combine sour cream, whole kernel corn, cream corn, cheese, green onions, butter, and egg in a bowl. Stir in cornbread mix and incorporate until just moistened. Spoon into greased miniature muffin tins and sprinkle with sunflower kernels. Bake until a tester inserted in center comes out clean, 20 to 25 minutes. Cool for 2 minutes before removing from pans to a wire rack. Serve warm.

Yield: 8 to 12 muffins

Pumpkin Apple Streusel Muffins

Muffins

2½ cups all-purpose flour
2 cups sugar
1 tablespoon pumpkin pie spice
1 teaspoon baking soda
½ teaspoon salt

2 eggs, lightly beaten
1 cup solid pack canned pumpkin
½ cup vegetable oil
2 cups peeled, finely chopped apples

Streusel Topping

2 tablespoons flour
¼ cup sugar

½ teaspoon cinnamon
4 teaspoons butter

Preheat oven to 350 degrees. In large bowl, combine flour, sugar, pumpkin pie spice, baking soda, and salt; set aside. In medium bowl, combine eggs, pumpkin, and oil, beating until well blended. Add to dry mixture and stir just until moistened. Stir in apples and set aside while making streusel topping.

To make topping, combine flour, sugar, and cinnamon. Cut in butter until mixture is crumbly. To assemble muffins, spoon batter into paper-lined muffin cups, filling three-quarters full. Sprinkle topping over batter. Bake until toothpick inserted in center comes out clean, 35 to 40 minutes.

Yield: 1½ dozen muffins

Rouxminations

Take Two Tablets and Call Me In The Morning

The Big Chief Pencil Tablet was patented in 1908 by Western Tablet Company in St. Joseph and featured a profile of a majestic Indian Chief on its cover. The keenest competition to the tablet came in the late 1970's when the Son of Big Chief tablet debuted, depicting a psychedelic, younger warrior wearing a headband, sunglasses, and a peace necklace.

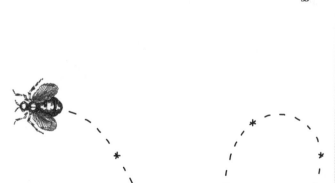

To Bees or Not To Bees

In an attempt to showcase the city for the 1904 World's Fair, St. Joseph sponsored the New Era Exposition in 1889. The World's Fair would have probably taken place in St. Joseph had it not been for two weeks of rain, a disastrous electrical fire that claimed a life of a night guard, the loss of a beekeeper's bees for a honey-making demonstration, and a musician losing all of his original musical manuscripts. These events not only ruined the Exposition, but also the city's chances for a World's Fair.

Cherry Cream Scones

¾ cup dried cherries	½ cup butter, softened
1 cup boiling water	1 egg, separated
3 cups all-purpose flour	½ cup sour cream
3 tablespoons sugar	¾ cup half-and-half
1 tablespoon baking powder	1 teaspoon vanilla
½ teaspoon salt	Additional sugar for sprinkling
½ teaspoon cream of tartar	

Soak cherries in boiling water for 10 minutes. Drain and set aside. Preheat oven to 400 degrees. In large bowl, combine flour, sugar, baking powder, salt, and cream of tartar. With pastry blender or 2 knives, cut in butter until crumbly in texture. Set aside. Combine egg yolk, sour cream, half-and-half, and vanilla in a small bowl. Add to flour mixture and stir until soft dough forms.

Turn out onto lightly floured surface and knead 6 to 8 times. Knead in drained cherries. Divide dough in half and shape into balls. Roll out each ball to a 6-inch circle and cut into 6 wedges. Place each wedge on a lightly greased baking sheet. Beat egg white until foamy and brush tops of scones. Sprinkle with sugar. Bake for 15 to 20 minutes. Serve warm.

Hint: Can substitute nonfat plain yogurt for sour cream. If this is done, add ½ teaspoon baking soda and reduce amount of baking powder to 2½ teaspoons.

Yield: 1 dozen

Maple Oatmeal Scones

Scones

3½ cups all-purpose flour
1 cup whole wheat flour
1 cup quick cooking oats, plus extra for sprinkling
2 tablespoons baking powder
2 tablespoons granulated sugar
2 teaspoons salt

1 cup chilled unsalted butter, diced
½ cup buttermilk
½ cup pure maple syrup
4 extra-large eggs, lightly beaten
1 egg beaten with 1 tablespoon milk for egg wash

Glaze

1¼ cups powdered sugar
½ cup pure maple syrup

1 teaspoon vanilla

Preheat oven to 400 degrees. In bowl of an electric mixer, using paddle attachment, combine flour, oats, baking powder, sugar, and salt. Blend cold diced butter in at the lowest speed just until butter is pea-sized pieces. In small bowl, combine buttermilk, maple syrup, and eggs, mixing well. Add to flour mixture and mix until just incorporated. Do not overmix. Dough may be sticky.

Turn dough onto a well-floured surface. Using a floured rolling pin, roll about 1-inch thick. (You will see lumps of butter in the dough.) Cut into 3-inch rounds using a plain or fluted biscuit cutter. Place on a lightly greased cookie sheet and brush tops with the egg wash. Bake 20 to 25 minutes, until tops are crisp.

Make glaze while scones are baking. Combine powdered sugar, maple syrup, and vanilla. Mix well. When scones have cooled 5 minutes, drizzle each scone with 1 tablespoon of glaze and sprinkle with some uncooked oats.

Yield: 14 large scones

Rouxminations

Playgrounds of Our Minds

The New Era Exposition was a test run of sorts for the Worlds Fair and was held in the valley just north of what is now Mark Twain and Truman Middle school area. The Expo was housed in the 990 foot-long Steel Car Plant. However, a disastrous fire two weeks after the Expo opened not only ruined the event, it also bankrupted the company.

Rouxminations

Say Cheese

Perhaps most notable in modern times for its famous cheesecake, was Ben Magoon's Delicatessen. Fondly know as "Benny Magoon's," it was an institution in St. Joseph for years. The deli stocked nearly everything imaginable from snail, to canned rattlesnake, to chocolate covered ants and grasshoppers.

Banana Bread with Chocolate Chips and Walnuts

1½ cups all-purpose flour	½ cup unsalted butter, room temperature
1 teaspoon baking soda	
1 teaspoon baking powder	1 cup sugar
¼ teaspoon salt	2 large eggs
¾ cup semisweet chocolate chips	1 cup mashed ripe bananas
¾ cup chopped toasted walnuts	2 tablespoons fresh lemon juice
	1½ teaspoons vanilla

Preheat oven to 350 degrees. Grease and flour a 9 x 5 x 2½-inch loaf pan. Combine flour, baking soda, baking powder, and salt in medium bowl; set aside. In a small bowl, place chocolate chips and walnuts; add 1 tablespoon of flour mixture and toss to coat; set aside.

Beat butter in a large bowl with electric mixer on high until fluffy, about 2 minutes. Gradually add sugar, beating well with each addition. Add eggs 1 at a time, beating well after each addition. With mixer on medium, beat in mashed bananas, lemon juice, and vanilla for 2 minutes. Add flour mixture and mix until incorporated.

Spoon a third of batter into prepared pan and sprinkle with half of chocolate chip and nut mixture. Spoon another third of batter into the pan and sprinkle with the remaining half of the chocolate chip and nut mixture. Spread remaining batter on top and run a knife through the batter in a zigzag motion. Bake bread until tester inserted in center comes out clean, 60 to 65 minutes. Let cool in the pan 10 to 15 minutes before turning onto a wire rack to finish cooling.

Hint: Mini-morsels work best.

Yield: 1 loaf

Citrus Streusel Quick Bread

1	(1 pound, 2½ ounce) box lemon cake mix	1	(3.4 ounce) package instant vanilla pudding mix
2	tablespoons brown sugar	4	eggs
1	teaspoon cinnamon	1	cup sour cream
1	tablespoon butter	⅓	cup oil
½	cup chopped pecans		

Glaze

2-3 tablespoons milk   1   cup powdered sugar

Preheat oven to 350 degrees. In a small bowl combine 2 tablespoons cake mix, brown sugar, and cinnamon. Cut in butter until mixture is crumbly. Stir in pecans and set aside. In a large mixing bowl, combine pudding mix, eggs, sour cream, oil, and remaining cake mix. Beat on medium speed with mixer for 2 minutes. Pour into 2 greased and floured loaf pans. Sprinkle each loaf with half of the pecan mixture. Bake until a tester inserted in center comes out clean, 45 to 50 minutes. Cool 10 minutes, then remove from pan.

For Glaze: Add enough milk to powdered sugar to reach desired consistency. Drizzle over tops of bread.

Yield: 2 loaves

Rouxminations

Real Business Savvy

In 1918, at the age of 13, Ben Magoon's Delicatessen was opened by the young Ben Magoon. Magoon once claimed that he made most of his money on whiskey, but that it was the food that brought his customers back. Magoon's changed hands over the years and is no longer in operation.

No Thanks, I'll pass

The strangest and most popular items at Ben Magoon's Delicatessen were sparrows on skewers, dried guava worms, tiger, elephant, rattlesnake, turtle soup, and chocolate covered caterpillars.

Cranberry Applesauce Bread

1½	cups all-purpose flour	2	eggs
2	teaspoons cinnamon	1	cup sugar
1	teaspoon baking soda	1¼	cups applesauce
½	teaspoon salt	½	cup chopped walnuts
½	teaspoon allspice	½	cup fresh whole cranberries
½	cup butter or margarine, melted		

Preheat oven to 350 degrees. Grease loaf pan and set aside. In a small bowl mix flour, cinnamon, baking soda, salt, and allspice, stirring until well blended. Set aside. In medium mixing bowl, mix margarine with eggs and beat until well blended. Add sugar and applesauce and mix well. Stir in flour mixture, mixing just until incorporated. Do not overmix. Fold in nuts and cranberries. Pour into prepared pan and bake until a tester inserted in center comes out clean, 55 to 60 minutes.

Yield: 1 loaf

Strawberry Nut Bread

3	cups all-purpose flour	1¼	cups vegetable oil
1	teaspoon baking soda	4	eggs
1	teaspoon salt	2	cups thawed frozen
1	tablespoon cinnamon		strawberries
2	cups sugar	1¼	cups chopped pecans

Preheat oven to 350 degrees. Grease 2 (9 x 5-inch) loaf pans. In a large bowl mix flour, baking soda, salt, cinnamon, and sugar. Add oil, eggs, strawberries, and nuts, blending well. Divide batter evenly in prepared loaf pans, and bake until a tester inserted in center comes out clean, 60 to 70 minutes.

Yield: 2 loaves

Rouxminations

Is there a doctor in the house?

Arriving in 1838, Dr. Silas McDonald was the first physician to practice medicine in Buchanan County. Some of his typical charges: $1 for a visit (within a mile) and a prescription, $5 for midwifery, $10 for twins, 50 cents to extract teeth, and from $5-25 for an amputation, depending on the part!

Blueberry French Toast Casserole

French Toast

12 slices day-old Texas toast, cut
       in 1-inch cubes
2   (8 ounce) packages cream
       cheese, cubed
1   cup frozen blueberries, thawed

12 eggs
2   cups milk
½   cup sugar
⅓   cup honey

Sauce

2   cups sugar
4   tablespoons cornstarch
2   cups cold water

2   cups frozen blueberries, thawed
2   tablespoons butter

Spread half of bread cubes in bottom of a 9 x 13-inch baking dish. Arrange cream cheese cubes evenly over bread and sprinkle with blueberries. Top with remaining bread cubes. In a medium bowl, beat eggs, milk, sugar, and honey with a whisk until well blended. Pour evenly over bread. Cover and refrigerate overnight.

Preheat oven to 350 degrees. Bake, covered, for 45 minutes then remove cover and continue baking for an additional 25 to 30 minutes.

Make the sauce while French toast is baking. Place sugar, cornstarch, and water in a small saucepan and bring to a boil. Boil for 3 minutes. Add blueberries and butter. Reduce heat to low and simmer 10 minutes. Serve over French toast.

Yield: 8 servings

Rouxminations

What's Up, Doc?

St. Joseph had a medical college called Samuel Ensworth Medical College located at Seventh and Jules. The last class to graduate was the class of 1914. The college was formed with the merger of the St. Joseph Medical College and the College of Physicians and Surgeons. Ensworth donated $100,000 to build the school and hospital.

Crème Brûlée French Toast

½ cup unsalted butter
1 cup firmly packed brown sugar
2 tablespoons corn syrup
1 (8 or 9-inch) round loaf country-style bread
5 large eggs

1½ cups half-and-half
1 teaspoon vanilla
1 teaspoon Grand Marnier or orange extract
¼ teaspoon salt

In a small heavy saucepan, melt butter with brown sugar and corn syrup over moderate heat, stirring until smooth. Pour into a 9 x 13-inch baking dish. Cut 6 (1-inch thick) slices from center portion of bread and trim the crust, reserving ends for another use. Arrange bread slices in a single layer over the brown sugar mixture. They should fit tightly. In a bowl, whisk together eggs, half-and-half, vanilla, Grand Marnier, and salt until well blended. Pour over bread. Cover and refrigerate at least 8 hours or up to 1 day.

Preheat oven to 350 degrees. Remove bread from refrigerator and allow it to warm to room temperature. Bake, uncovered, 35 to 40 minutes, until bread is puffed and the edges are golden. Serve immediately.

Yield: 6 to 8 servings

Caramelized Onion Flatbread

1 tablespoon butter
3 large yellow onions, thinly sliced
1 tablespoon minced garlic
¾ teaspoon salt
1 tablespoon dried Italian seasoning

¼ teaspoon dried crushed red pepper
1 thin Boboli crust
½ cup freshly grated Parmesan cheese

Preheat oven to 425 degrees. Melt butter in large skillet. Add onion and garlic and sauté until tender. Stir in salt, Italian seasoning, and red pepper. Spoon mixture over crust. Bake for 10 minutes; sprinkle with Parmesan cheese and bake for 3 more minutes. Cut into bite-sized squares.

Variation: Add Gorgonzola cheese.

Yield: 6 to 8 servings

Rouxminations

A Hilluva Ride

Devil's Back Bone, located behind the St. Patrick's church at 13th and Duncan is a popular sledding area for children because of the steep, rugged, spine-like bumps protruding throughout the hill.

From One Entrepreneur To The Next

Charles Geiger established one of the first grain businesses in St. Joseph called Geiger Grain Company. His home at the corner of Frederick Avenue and Noyes Boulevard, was built in 1924.

Garlic Bread with Pecorino Romano Butter

½ cup butter, softened
½ cup grated pecorino Romano cheese
¼ cup finely chopped fresh Italian parsley

2 cloves garlic, minced
Pepper to season, optional
1 (14-inch) loaf Italian or French bread, halved lengthwise

Preheat oven to 500 degrees. Mix butter, cheese, parsley, and garlic in medium bowl to blend well. Season with pepper, if desired. Place bread halves cut-side-up on a baking sheet. Spread evenly with butter mixture. Bake until topping is golden brown and bread is heated through, about 5 to 8 minutes. Cut bread crosswise into 2-inch pieces and serve immediately.

Yield: 1 loaf

Market Bread

1 loaf French or Italian bread, cut in half horizontally
5 tablespoons olive oil, divided
1 large onion, chopped
16 ounces Swiss cheese, sliced

1 large tomato, sliced
Fresh basil and oregano to taste or 1 tablespoon dried Italian seasoning
Salt and pepper to taste

Turn oven on broil to preheat. Broil bread 1 to 2 minutes, until starting to turn golden brown. Watch carefully to prevent burning. Remove from heat and drizzle each half with 2 tablespoons of olive oil.

Place onions in small skillet and sauté with remaining olive oil for 3 to 5 minutes. Sprinkle onions with basil and oregano or Italian seasoning. Sprinkle onion mixture evenly over bread. Top with cheese and tomato and sprinkle with salt and pepper to taste. Broil until cheese melts, about 5 minutes. Serve hot.

Hint: This is so good it is almost addictive.

Yield: 8 to 10 servings

Rouxminations

Westward, Ho!

Trails West! is St. Joseph's largest festival celebrating the city's unique cultural heritage. More than 150 years of history is condensed into three days of events for all ages. Fine art, folk art, dramatic stage performances, historical reenactments, musical entertainment and food are all a part of this weekend the third weekend in August.

"We've Come a Long Way, Baby"

"The handsome Club House of the Benton Club was open to visitors yesterday and a thorough inspection of the elegant house was made. The halls and billiard room have inlaid floors, easy couches, cozy arm-chairs, and everything for comfort. The culinary department is a trea-sure within itself. It is indeed a treat to the ladies to be allowed the privilege of visiting it once a week, every Thursday being given to them."

St. Joseph Daily News *November 11, 1887.*

Earlier that year letters had arrived in 125 St. Joseph homes. The envelope contained an invitation to join in the formation of a social club. Forty-one men accepted the invitation and became original stockholders and charter members by each subscribing $500. The Benton Club was reality.

The club's name honored Senator Thomas Hart Benton from St. Louis for his work in achieving statehood for Missouri in 1821 and in securing the Platte Purchase of 1836. The members purchased property at Seventh and Faraon and began remodeling. The news-paper again reported "it will be one of the most elegant private club houses in the West. Electric bells and speaking tubes will connect all the rooms."

The rooms of the Benton Club became a meeting place for some of the most prominent St. Joseph men and their families. There they could dine, entertain, play cards and visit with friends. Today the Benton Club still serves the same purpose for members at the original home purchased over a 100 years ago. Many of today's members can trace their family membership back to the charter members. And...the rule restricting ladies at the club to one day a week is no more.

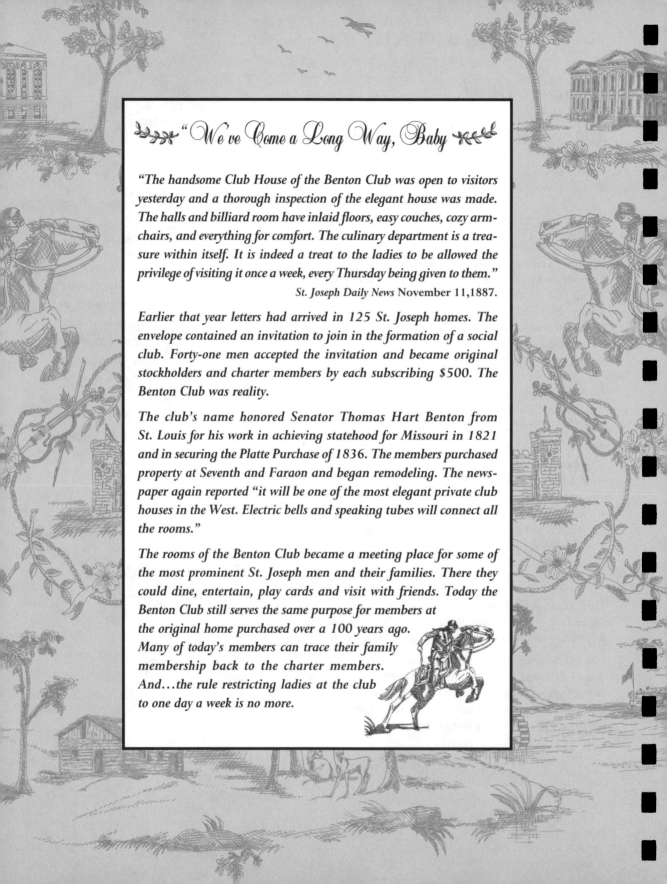

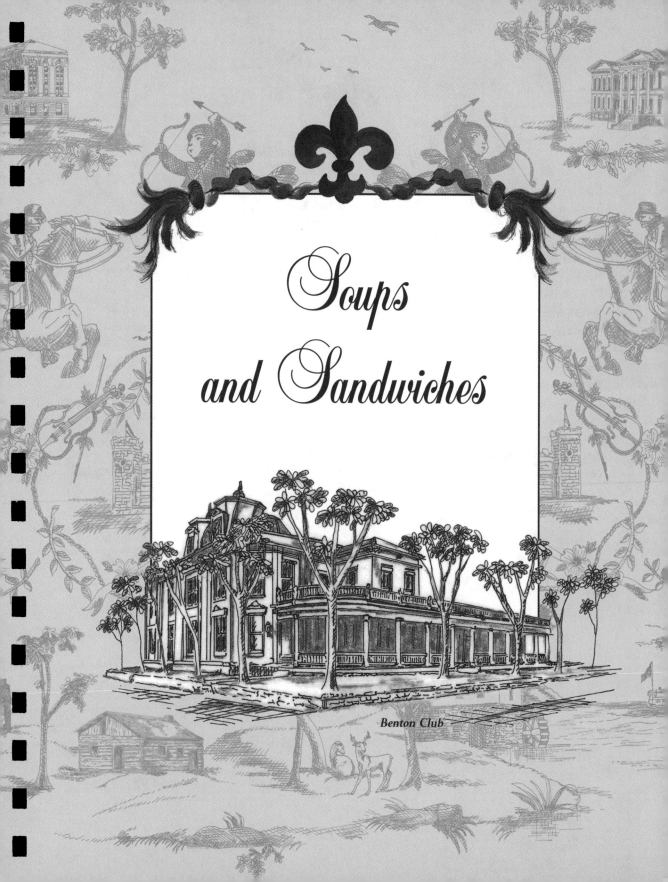

Soups
and Sandwiches

Benton Club

Soups and Sandwiches

Beef French Vegetable Soup

2 pounds stew meat, cut into bite-size pieces	1½ teaspoons salt
¼ cup vegetable oil	¼ teaspoon pepper
1 (10½ ounce) can French onion soup	8 carrots, sliced
5 soup cans of water	2 cups sliced celery
1 (6 ounce) can tomato paste	1 (16 ounce) can wax beans
1 tablespoon chopped fresh basil	1 (16 ounce) can kidney beans
	½ cup grated Parmesan cheese

Brown stew meat in hot oil in a stock pot over medium heat. Add soup, water, tomato paste, basil, salt, and pepper. Bring to a boil, reduce heat, cover, and cook 1½ hours. Stir in carrots, celery, wax beans, and kidney beans. Continue to cook for 30 minutes longer, uncovered. Stir in Parmesan cheese and serve.

Hint: Yummy and pretty!

Yield: 6 to 8 servings

Mexican Chicken Corn Chowder

3 skinless, boneless chicken breasts, cut into small pieces	2 cups shredded Monterey Jack cheese
3 tablespoons butter	1 (16 ounce) can cream-style corn
½ cup chopped onion	1 (4 ounce) can chopped green chiles, undrained
2 cloves garlic	
1½ cups chicken broth	1 teaspoon hot pepper sauce
1 teaspoon cumin	1 medium tomato, chopped
2 cups half-and-half	

Brown chicken in butter in a large pot with onion and garlic. Add chicken broth and cumin and bring to a boil. Reduce heat, cover, and simmer 5 minutes. Add half-and-half, cheese, corn, chiles, and pepper sauce. Cook and stir over low heat until cheese is melted. Stir in tomato and serve immediately.

Yield: 8 servings

Rouxminations

It's A Guy Thing

The Benton Club, at Seventh and Faraon Streets is the oldest club west of the Mississippi River. The club was named for Missouri statesman Thomas Hart Benton, and its name was chosen mainly for the role he played in securing statehood for Missouri in 1821. The Benton Club is still a popular meeting place today.

Black Bean Pumpkin Soup

3 (15½ ounce) cans black beans (about 4½ cups), rinsed and drained	½ teaspoon ground pepper (preferably coarse)
1 cup drained canned tomatoes, chopped	¼ cup unsalted butter (½ stick)
1¼ cups chopped onion	1 (16 ounce) can pumpkin puree
½ cup minced shallots	4 cups beef broth
4 cloves garlic, minced	½ cup dry sherry
1 tablespoon plus 2 teaspoons ground cumin	½ pound ham, cut into ⅛-inch cubes
1 teaspoon salt	3-4 tablespoons sherry vinegar
	Sour cream

Coarsely puree beans and tomatoes in a food processor. In a 5 to 6-quart heavy kettle, cook onions, shallots, garlic, cumin, salt, and pepper in butter over medium heat, stirring, until onion is softened and beginning to brown. Add bean puree. Stir in broth, pumpkin, and sherry until combined. Simmer, uncovered, stirring occasionally, until thick enough to coat back of spoon, about 25 minutes.

Just before serving, add ham and vinegar. Simmer soup, stirring, until heated through. Season with additional salt and pepper and garnish with sour cream. Serve with favorite bread or corn muffins.

Hint: If you like a more textured soup, leave 1 can of beans unprocessed. Substitute red wine vinegar for sherry vinegar.

Yield: 8 to 10 servings

Rouxminations

Living History

The Junior League of St. Joseph was part of the city's largest festival, Trails West!, in 1994 and 1995. The League staffed the Children's Art tent at the first and second festival. The Children's Art tent is one of the most popular features of the annual festival which highlights St. Joseph's rich history.

Happy Birthday To You

Thomas Hart Benton's grand nephew, the famous artist Thomas Hart Benton II, was honored when the Benton Club had its 75th birthday in 1962. A small sketch Benton drew of the occasion hangs still in the club.

Roasted Garlic Soup with Parmesan Cheese

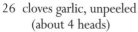

26 cloves garlic, unpeeled (about 4 heads)	18 cloves garlic, peeled
2 tablespoons olive oil	3½ cups chicken stock or canned low-salt chicken broth
Salt and pepper to taste	½ cup whipping cream
2 tablespoons butter	½ cup finely grated Parmesan cheese (about 2 ounces)
2¼ cups sliced onions	
1½ teaspoons chopped fresh thyme	4 lemon wedges

Preheat oven to 350 degrees. Place unpeeled garlic cloves in a small glass baking dish. Drizzle with olive oil and sprinkle with salt and pepper. Cover dish with foil and bake until garlic is golden brown and tender, about 45 minutes. Cool and squeeze pulp from skin with fingers into a bowl.

Melt butter in heavy large saucepan over medium-high heat. Add onions and thyme and cook until onions are translucent, about 6 minutes. Add roasted garlic and raw garlic cloves and cook 3 minutes. Add chicken stock, bring to a boil, reduce heat, cover, and simmer until garlic is very tender, about 20 minutes. Working in batches, puree soup in a blender or food processor. Return soup to saucepan; add cream and bring to simmer. Season with salt and pepper. Divide cheese among 4 bowls and ladle soup over it. Squeeze juice of 1 lemon wedge into each bowl and serve. It is also good topped with Won Ton Crisps, page 32.

Hint: Can be made 1 day ahead. Cover and refrigerate. Rewarm over medium heat, stirring occasionally.

Yield: 4 servings

Rouxminations

Equal Play For All

To help commemorate its 75th birthday in 1996, the St. Joseph League members donated money to build the city's first truly handicapped accessible playground in the center of the city in Barlett Park. The League coordinated donations and construction of the playground equipment with the city.

Rouxminations

Life Long Learning

Missouri Western State College in St. Joseph was originally Saint Joseph Junior College, and was founded in 1915, as an outgrowth of the St. Joseph school system. The school was transformed into a four-year college in 1969. The College has an enrollment of more than 5200 students and 190 faculty members.

Potato, Artichoke, and Leek Soup

2 tablespoons butter	2½ cups peeled, cubed baking potatoes
½ cup chopped onion	2 small thyme sprigs
1½ cups cleaned, chopped leeks, white and light green parts only	1½ cups milk
1 teaspoon minced garlic	¾ teaspoon Tabasco sauce
1 quart chicken broth	Salt and pepper to taste
1 (13¾ ounce) can artichoke hearts, well rinsed, drained, quartered	Fresh chopped parsley

Melt butter in a medium saucepan and sauté onion and leeks for about 10 minutes, until tender. Uncover and cook until the leeks are very soft, about 5 minutes, adding garlic for the last minute. Add broth, artichokes, potatoes, and thyme, and simmer 15 minutes longer. Remove from heat and discard the thyme. In a food processor or blender, puree soup until very smooth. Season with salt and pepper and garnish with parsley. Serve hot or cold.

Hint: This soup totally rocks and is great in winter or summer. It can be made ahead and freezes well.

Yield: 8 servings

Spinach Bisque

3 (10 ounce) packages frozen chopped spinach	1 (8 ounce) jar Cheez Whiz
4 cups chicken broth	½ cup shredded Parmesan cheese
2 onions (white or yellow)	½ cup shredded Cheddar cheese
4 tablespoons butter	1 pint half-and-half
	Cornstarch

Cook spinach in chicken broth in a large pot on medium heat for 5 minutes. In a large saucepan, sauté onions in butter until tender. Add to spinach. Add Cheez Whiz and stir until smooth. Add the other cheeses and cook, stirring, until melted. Add half-and-half and blend. If bisque is not thick enough, thicken with a thick mixture of cornstarch and a little warm water. Season with salt and pepper to taste and ENJOY!

Hint: Use Mexican Cheez Whiz for added kick. We love this with the Market Bread on page 59.

Yield: 6 or 8 servings

Red Pepper Soup

8	red bell peppers	1	tablespoon olive oil
3	carrots, peeled and thinly sliced	4	tablespoons unsalted butter
3	shallots, peeled and thinly sliced	1	quart chicken stock
1	clove garlic, peeled and thinly sliced	1	teaspoon crushed red pepper
1	pear, peeled, quartered, and thinly sliced		Dash of cayenne
			Salt and pepper to taste
			Fresh tarragon, to taste

Thinly slice 6 of the red peppers. Heat oil and butter in a large skillet and sauté sliced peppers, carrots, shallots, garlic, and pear over medium-low heat until tender, 8 to 10 minutes. Add stock, dried red pepper, cayenne, salt, and pepper. Bring to a boil, reduce heat, and simmer, covered, for 25 to 30 minutes.

While soup is cooking, roast remaining red peppers directly on gas flame or in broiler of oven, rotating with tongs until completely charred. Put in paper bag for 5 minutes to sweat. Wash off blackened skins under running water and remove seeds. Drain on paper towel.

Puree soup in blender, adding 1 roasted pepper. Return to pan and reheat over low heat. Julienne remaining roasted pepper and add to soup. Garnish with tarragon.

Hint: Simplify by using canned roasted red peppers. This is a little spicier than other red pepper soups.

Yield: 6 servings

Rouxminations

Anchors Away

W. True Davis and partner founded Anchor Serum in 1917. It became the largest producer of Hog Cholera serum in the world. St. Joseph was the ideal location for the business because of the availability of animals to produce the vaccine. The company changed hands several times and is currently part of the Boehringer-Ingelheim group which is one of the world's 20 leading pharmaceutical corporations.

Sassy Tomato Pasta Soup

1	pound ground beef	1	(15 ounce) can tomato sauce
1	small onion, diced (1 cup)	3	(12 ounce) cans V-8 juice
1	large carrot, julienned (1 cup)	1	tablespoon white vinegar
3	stalks celery, chopped (1 cup)	1½	teaspoons salt
4	cloves garlic, minced	1	teaspoon oregano
2	(14½ ounce) cans diced tomatoes	1	teaspoon basil
1	(15 ounce) can red kidney beans, undrained	½	teaspoon pepper
		½	teaspoon thyme
1	(15 ounce) can great Northern beans, undrained	½	pound small macaroni noodles

Brown ground beef in a large saucepan or pot over medium heat. Drain off most of fat. Add onions, carrots, celery, and garlic and sauté for 10 minutes. Add remaining ingredients except pasta and bring to a boil. Reduce heat and simmer for 1 hour.

About 50 minutes into simmer time, cook pasta in 1½ to 2 quarts boiling water over high heat. Cook 10 minutes, just until pasta is al dente, or slightly tough. Drain. Add pasta to soup, simmer for 5 to 10 minutes and serve.

Yield: 6 to 8 servings

Sunset Tomato Soup

1	pound bacon, diced and sautéed crisp, drippings reserved	1	tablespoon sugar
		1	tablespoon dried basil
1	large yellow onion, diced	1	tablespoon minced garlic
1	large green bell peppers, diced	2	chicken bouillon cubes
3	(14½ ounce) cans chopped tomatoes, undrained	1	quart whipping cream
			Fresh basil, optional

Dice 1 pound of bacon into ½-inch pieces, sauté in a skillet until crisp. Using a slotted spoon, remove bacon from pan and drain on a paper towel. Reserve 2 tablespoons of bacon grease and add to it the onions and peppers. Sauté until soft, about 5 minutes. Transfer the onions, peppers, and bacon to a stock pot. Add tomatoes, sugar, basil, garlic, bouillon cubes, and cream. Bring to a boil, reduce heat, cover, and simmer for 15 minutes. Garnish with fresh basil, if desired.

Hint: The Sunset Grill generously shared this recipe with us. Its location on the Missouri River, coupled with this incredible soup, makes the restaurant a local favorite.

Yield: 6 to 8 servings

Rouxminations

A Swedish Touch

St. Joseph residents could dine in a quaint Swiss setting in the early 1970's and 80's in the Swiss Chalet restaurant. The Chalet was originally built by the Swiss community as a meeting place and later became a restaurant. The restaurant featured a continental cuisine and an extensive wine list. The meals were served by waitresses in Swiss Alpine Dress. The exterior of the building was built to look like a Swiss Chalet and added a unique focal point to the St. Joseph horizon.

Tomato Garlic Soup

Soup

2 tablespoons olive oil	1 (46 ounce) can tomato juice
4-6 cloves garlic, minced or pressed	1 cup water
1 tablespoon paprika	¼ cup dry sherry

Herbed Croutons

4 cups small bread cubes	Pinch dried thyme
1½ tablespoons olive oil	Pinch dried marjoram
1½ tablespoons butter	

Topping

Grated Parmesan cheese	Chopped fresh parsley

Preheat oven to 350 degrees. Warm olive oil in a soup pot. Add garlic and sauté, stirring constantly, until sizzling and golden, 1 to 2 minutes. Sprinkle in paprika and cook 30 seconds more. Do not burn or scorch paprika or soup will be bitter. Add tomato juice, water, and sherry. Bring to boil, reduce heat and simmer for 15 minutes.

While soup simmers, make croutons. Spread bread cubes on ungreased baking sheet and bake until dry, 10 to 15 minutes. In microwave, heat olive oil, butter, thyme and marjoram until butter is melted. Pour butter mixture over toasted bread cubes and toss to coat.

Serve soup topped with croutons, Parmesan cheese, and parsley.

Rouxminations

Monet's Water Lilies, St. Joseph Style

The Lotus Club was originally built for $50,000 and was so named because of the many water lilies or lotus flowers that grew along side Lake Contrary. The lake is one of the largest ox-bow lakes in Northwest Missouri. The Lotus Club, built in the early 1900's, was famous for its fine food, and an early menu listed about eight pages of foods available. The most expensive meal was $1.50.

Tuscan White Onion Soup with Crostini

Soup

1	cup (2 sticks) butter	1	quart fresh chicken stock
4	large Spanish onions, sliced		Sea salt and fresh pepper, to taste
8	cloves garlic, shaved		Shaved Parmigiano-Reggiano cheese
3	shallots	1	cup whipping cream, whipped
1	fresh thyme sprig		
1	teaspoon cardamom		

Balsamic Reduction Sauce

1   bottle balsamic vinegar
    (size does not matter)

Crostini

1   baguette, cut in half lengthwise and sliced into ¼-inch thick slices

Extra virgin olive oil
Cracked black peppercorns and sea salt to taste
Grated Parmigiano-Reggiano cheese

Melt butter in a soup pot and sauté onions, garlic, and shallots until translucent. Add thyme and cardamom. Cover with chicken stock and bring to a boil. Season with salt and pepper, reduce heat, and simmer until tender. Transfer to a blender and process until smooth. Strain and return to pot. Adjust seasoning.

For Balsamic Reduction Sauce: In a saucepan over medium high heat, reduce balsamic vinegar until it is the consistency of syrup.

For Crostini: Preheat oven to 300 degrees. Line a baking sheet with parchment paper and brush paper with olive oil. Sprinkle with salt and pepper. Place bread slices on baking sheet. Brush the bread with olive oil and season with salt and pepper. Sprinkle with Parmesan cheese. Bake until golden, about 5 minutes.

To serve: Heat soup and whisk in whipped cream. Ladle into bowl and garnish with Balsamic Reduction, shaved Parmesan cheese and Crostini.

Hint: The Balsamic Reduction Sauce makes this special.

Yield: 8 servings

Wild Mushroom Soup

½ cup Madeira
2¾ cups chicken stock, divided
1 ounce dried morel mushrooms
4 tablespoons unsalted butter
3 leeks (white part only), well
     rinsed, dried, and diced
1 onion, diced

3 tablespoons all-purpose flour
2¼ cups beef stock
1 pound fresh button
     mushrooms, stems removed
Salt and black pepper to taste
2 tablespoons snipped fresh
     chives, for garnish

In a small saucepan, combine Madeira, ½ cup chicken stock, and the morels. Bring to a boil, remove from the heat and let stand for 30 minutes.

Melt butter in a large soup pot. Add leeks and onions and cook over low heat until wilted, about 10 minutes. Sprinkle with flour, and cook, stirring, an additional 5 minutes. Add remaining 2¼ cups chicken stock, beef stock, button mushrooms, morels and their soaking liquid, and salt and pepper. Simmer, uncovered, until the mushrooms are soft, 30 minutes. Allow soup to cool slightly. Puree soup in batches, in a blender or food processor. Return to pot and heat through over low heat. Serve garnished with snipped chives.

Hint: If morels are unavailable, substitute shiitakes or cèpes. Wonderful for fall or winter dish.

Yield: 6 servings

Rouxminations

This Place Is Rockin'

In its heyday in the early 1900's, the Lotus Club was among the greatest resorts of its kind in the Middle West. Many notables who visited St. Joseph were entertained there, including Theodore Roosevelt.

Worlds of Fun

St. Joseph's "Coney Island" could be found at Lake Contrary. It was also called "The Playground of the Central West," and Lake Park. All of the horses on the merry-go-round had glass eyes and real horsehair tails to make them seem more realistic. The horses even had wooden horseshoes on their feet.

Fall Fountain Stew

1	medium head garlic	1	teaspoon dried thyme
1	teaspoon olive oil	1	bay leaf
2	pounds beef chuck stew meat	6	cups beef broth
	Salt and pepper	3	medium potatoes, peeled and
2	tablespoons peanut oil		cut into 1-inch pieces
4-5	thick-sliced bacon strips, cut	6	medium carrots, peeled and
	into ½-inch pieces		cut in 1-inch pieces
3	cups chopped onions	1	(14½ ounce) can crushed
1	tablespoon minced garlic		tomatoes, undrained

Cut off top of garlic. Place garlic on a sheet of foil and drizzle with olive oil. Seal foil over garlic and bake in a preheated 400 oven for about 45 minutes, until soft.

Sprinkle beef with salt and pepper. Heat oil in large pot over medium-high heat. Working in batches, cook beef until well browned, stirring occasionally and scraping brown bits from pot as you go. Transfer meat to a plate and add bacon to same pot. Sauté until just crisp. Add onions, minced garlic, thyme, and bay leaf. Cover and cook until onions are tender, stirring occasionally, about 10 minutes. Add beef broth, then add potatoes and carrots and bring to a boil. Boil 5 minutes and reduce heat to medium. Add beef and accumulated juices. Squeeze roasted garlic head onto a plate and mash it with a fork. Stir garlic into pot along with crushed tomatoes. Cover and cook until beef is tender. Serve with hot crusty Parmesan bread or herbed biscuits.

Hints: Don't omit the thyme - it's essential. If you want a more stewish flare, toss beef with ¼ cup flour before browning. Great for cold fall and winter nights and smells delicious while simmering. The roasted garlic keeps in refrigerator up to a week, so do several at once.

Yield: 6 to 8 servings

Sirloin Stew with Roasted Garlic

2	pounds sirloin steak, cut into 1-inch strips	1	teaspoon sugar
1	cup red wine	1	can red beans, rinsed and drained
⅛	cup canola oil	1	(4½ ounce) can chopped tomatoes with chili seasonings, drained
2	cans black beans, rinsed and drained		
2	tablespoons Italian seasonings	1	(6 ounce) can tomato paste
½	teaspoon dried rosemary	1	(7 ounce) can salsa verde (do not substitute)
2	heads roasted garlic		
1	medium red onion	1	tablespoon chili powder
1	medium yellow onion	⅔	can beef broth
3	tablespoons olive oil		Salt and pepper to taste

Marinate sirloin in wine and oil for at least 2 hours or overnight.

Puree half of black beans in a blender. Add Italian seasonings, rosemary, and roasted garlic, and mix well. Set aside.

Sauté onions in olive oil in a soup pot. Sprinkle with sugar and cook until well softened, but not caramelized, stirring occasionally, about 20 minutes. Add beef and marinade. Cook, stirring, until beef is cooked through. Bring to a boil and boil for 5 minutes. Reduce heat to medium. Add puree, remaining black beans, red beans, tomatoes, tomato paste, salsa verde, chili powder, beef broth, and salt and pepper to taste. Cook over medium-low heat about 2 hours.

Hint: Ok, so lots of ingredients, but easy to do once you have everything together. Roasted garlic is key - don't substitute raw.

Yield: 6 to 8 servings

Rouxminations

Packing Up and Leaving

Following a riot and flag burning during the Civil War, the government moved the eastern terminus of the proposed Union Pacific Railroad from St. Joseph to Omaha. Consequently, St. Joseph lost its place as the metropolis of the Missouri River Valley.

No-Flag Chicken Chili

4-6 small chicken breasts
2 (1.2 ounce) packages chili seasonings
1 (8 ounce) jar mild banana peppers, undrained
2 (14 ounce) cans chili beans, undrained
1 (14 ounce) can pinto beans, undrained

1 cup chicken broth
1 (14 ounce) can kidney beans, undrained
1 (8 ounce) can tomato paste
1 (8 ounce) package Mexican Velveeta cheese
1 (14 ounce) can Mexican diced tomatoes

Preheat oven to 375 degrees. Place chicken in a baking dish and sprinkle with 1 package chili seasonings. Top with banana peppers and their juice. Bake until chicken is done, about 30 minutes.

While the chicken is cooking, combine remaining ingredients in a pot. Bring to a boil, reduce heat, and simmer for 30 minutes on a low-medium heat, stirring frequently to prevent sticking. When the chicken is thoroughly cooked, dice or shred and add it to chili and simmer for an additional 20 minutes. Serve with your favorite bread or with crackers. Make sure you have milk close by!

Hint: Kruner beans are the best, but any will do. This dish can be a little spicy, so make sure you use all the mild ingredients if you are not a fan of spicy food. Save a little of the banana pepper juice to pour into the chili mixture if it needs to be thinned.

Yield: 8 to 10 servings

Rouxminations

No Flags Here

Since Missouri was a border state during the Civil War in 1861, the city council passed an ordinance requiring citizens to cease flying either pro-Confederate or pro-Union flags. In defiance, a pro-Union postmaster hoisted a flag and a crowd immediately gathered to protest. The flag was ripped to shreds by a mob and an effigy of Lincoln was burned. A riot ensued. Stores were looted, and Negro shanties were burned. Federal troops stepped in to restore the peace. Another flag was saved during a similar incident at the "Cradle of Liberty" a meeting place for German-Americans with a fierce loyalty to the Union.

Spicy White Chili

1 cup chopped onion
1½ teaspoons minced garlic
2 cups chopped chicken
1 teaspoon olive oil
3 cups chicken broth
2 cans great Northern beans,
    rinsed and drained
1 can white corn, optional
2 tablespoons chopped cilantro

2 tablespoons lime juice
1 teaspoon cumin
½ teaspoon dried oregano
¼ teaspoon Tabasco sauce
¼ teaspoon salt
Corn chips
Salsa
Grated Cheddar cheese

Sauté onion, garlic, and chicken in olive oil in a soup pot until tender. Add chicken broth, beans, corn, if desired, cilantro, lime juice, cumin, oregano, Tabasco, and salt. Bring to a boil, reduce heat, and simmer for 20 minutes over very low heat. If desired, may transfer to a crock pot and cook slowly for 4 hours.

To serve, place a layer of corn chips in a soup bowl. Ladle chili over chips and top with salsa and cheese.

Hint: Great for crock pot and parties.

Yield: 6 to 8 servings

Rouxminations

Call The Fire Department

The first Sunday in March is the time for amateur and professional cooks from the region to cook some of the finest chili around for the Missouri State Championship Chili Challenge. Persons attending the event are treated to free chili samples and live musical performances.

Still Packing Them In

The Hoof and Horn restaurant catered to men working in the stockyards and to travelers. It was started in 1900 and is the oldest restaurant in St. Joseph. The original two-story building began as a saloon and brothel. A retired policeman bought the building in 1907, and it has been a restaurant ever since. Today the restaurant's specialty is the prime rib and outstanding steaks.

White Bean Verde Stew with Grilled Chicken

1	tablespoon vegetable oil	4	(7 ounce) cans salsa verde
2	cups chopped onions	1	cup chopped fresh cilantro
2	(4 ounce) cans diced green chiles, drained	5	cans Northern white beans, rinsed and drained
6	cloves garlic, minced	4	chicken breasts (1½ pounds)
1½	tablespoons dried oregano		Fresh cilantro, optional
1	tablespoon ground cumin		Grated Cheddar cheese, optional
1	tablespoon chili powder		
7	cups canned chicken broth		

Heat oil in 5-quart Dutch oven over medium heat. Add onions and sauté 5 minutes. Add chiles, garlic, oregano, cumin, and chili powder and sauté 5 minutes. Add chicken broth, salsa verde, 4 cans beans, and cilantro. Puree remaining can of beans and add to soup. Bring to boil and cook 20 minutes, stirring occasionally. Meanwhile grill chicken and cut into ½-inch cubes. Add to soup and cook for 30 minutes more on a low simmer. Serve topped with fresh cilantro and grated Cheddar cheese, if desired

Hint: A spicy low-fat dish that men love. Easy to prepare.

Yield: 8 to 10 servings

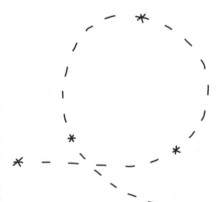

Chili Verde, Jesse James Style

3   pounds boneless pork
      (loin or butt)
2   tablespoons olive oil
1   large onion, chopped
1½ tablespoons minced garlic
3-5 canned or pickled jalapeños,
      cut into strips
2   (10 ounce) cans tomatillos,
      drained and juice reserved

½   cup loosely packed chopped
      cilantro, plus minced cilantro
      for garnish
1   (8 ounce) can mild green
      chiles, drained
    Salt and freshly ground pepper
      to taste
1   ripe avocado
1   tablespoon fresh lime juice

Cut pork into 2-inch cubes and trim any fat. Set aside. In a skillet, heat oil until it ripples. Add onions and garlic; sauté until limp. Add jalapeños, sauté 1 minute longer, and remove with slotted spoon to a heavy bottomed stew pot.

Puree tomatillos, ½ cup cilantro, and about half of the drained tomatillo liquid. Add mixture to stew pot along with chiles and pork. Season lightly with salt, as tomatillo juice is salty, and generously with pepper. Over high heat, bring mixture to a boil. Lower heat, cover and simmer slowly until pork is tender, about 2 hours. Let cool, cover, and refrigerate overnight.

Before reheating, skim congealed fat from stew. Reheat. Just before serving, peel and slice avocados and sprinkle with lime juice and minced cilantro. Float avocado slices on stew.

Hint: This is much better the second day. Cook it 1 day, refrigerate overnight, and serve the next day over rice or with warm tortillas.

Yield: 6 servings

Rouxminations

Ahoy, Matey

Lake Contrary was developed in the 1870's as a recreation area. In its heyday at the turn of the 20th century, the lake had an arcade, casino, theater, amusement park, race track and several hotels. Yacht races were one of the highlights of Lake Contrary with boats being shipped in by railroad cars.

Rouxminations

Where's The Popcorn

Yale's Electric Exposition, an attraction at Lake Contrary's amusement park, had mutoscopes which were the forerunners of the motion picture; pages of a book were flipped rapidly inside a machine, giving the illusion of movement.

Barbecue Cheddar Burgers with Barbecue Caramelized Onions

Burgers

3½ pounds lean ground beef
½ cup purchased barbecue sauce
1 teaspoon garlic powder
1 teaspoon salt
1 teaspoon ground black pepper

1 cup grated Cheddar cheese
12 sesame-seed hamburger buns, lightly toasted
Lettuce leaves
Tomato slices

Caramelized Onions

2 tablespoons olive oil
2 large onions, cut into ⅛-inch-thick slices
¼ teaspoon salt

⅛ teaspoon ground black pepper
½ cup purchased barbecue sauce
1 tablespoon apple cider vinegar or white vinegar

For Burgers: Mix ground beef, barbecue sauce, garlic powder, and salt in a large bowl until blended. Mix in pepper. Shape half of meat mixture into 8 (½ inch) thick patties.

Heat grill to medium-high heat. Cook patties to desired doneness, topping with cheese for last minute of cooking, about 4 minutes per side for medium-rare. Place burgers on bottom halves of buns. Top with lettuce, tomato, caramelized onion mixture and upper halves of buns.

Caramelized Onions: Heat oil in large skillet over medium-high heat. Add onions, salt, and pepper. Cook until onions begin to brown, stirring frequently, about 8 minutes. Add broth, barbecue sauce, and vinegar. Reduce heat to medium and simmer until sauce thickens, stirring occasionally, about 15 minutes. (Can be made 1 day ahead. Cover, chill. Rewarm before serving.)

Yield: 8 servings

Bucket Shop Beefburger

1½	pounds hamburger	2	tablespoons vinegar
½	cup chopped onion	1	tablespoon prepared mustard
2	teaspoons chili powder	½	cup water
½	pound brick chili		

Brown hamburger with onion and drain when no longer pink. Add remaining ingredients. Stir well and simmer at least 15 minutes and up to 1 hour, stirring occasionally.

Serve on a bun with, catsup, mustard, onion and/or relish. It is even better refrigerated overnight and reheated the next day.

Hint: May be frozen up to a month.

Yield: 6 to 8 servings

Cracker Bread Club Sandwich

1	(8 ounce) package cream cheese, softened	½	pound thinly sliced turkey breast
½	pound bacon, diced and cooked crisp	4	ripe tomatoes, halved, seeded, and thinly sliced
1	fresh lahvosh, softened dry lahvosh, or cracker bread*	1	teaspoon ground black pepper
1	medium red onion, very thinly sliced	8-10	soft lettuce leaves

In a small bowl, combine cream cheese and bacon; mix until well blended. Lay out cracker bread on plastic wrap. Spread evenly with cream cheese. Top with 1 layer each of onion, turkey, and tomatoes; arrange ingredients to cover previous layer completely. Sprinkle tomatoes with pepper and top with lettuce leaves.

Starting from 1 short side of cracker bread, tightly roll up bread and toppings, jelly roll fashion. Wrap in plastic wrap and refrigerate 2 hours or overnight. To serve, trim ends with serrated knife and slice sandwich crosswise into 8 pieces.

Hint: Use flavored cream cheese, any thin-sliced deli meat, or smoked salmon. Add relish and other sandwich ingredients that you like.

Yield: 4 servings

*Follow directions on package for softening.

Rouxminations

Honestly, Abe Was Here

Even Abraham Lincoln patronized the steamboat traffic on the Missouri River in St. Joseph. After he had been defeated by Stephen A. Douglas, Lincoln arrived in town on his way to Council Bluffs, Iowa to visit his former campaign manager who had requested a $3000 loan. A tract of land was offered as collateral for the loan, and Lincoln wanted to see the land for himself. So he took passage on a steamboat in St. Joseph to make the trip upriver.

Rouxminations

Hitting A Snag

The Missouri River is incredibly muddy, making it dangerous for steamboats and their captains. Trees were easily uprooted on the shore and sank into the river bed. Because the trees and their off-shoots were submerged under water, they were not always visible. The submerged trees were called "snags" and they often bore right through the hulls of steamboats. Because of snags and shifting sandbars, most riverboat captains did not operate at night.

Zesty Chicken Salad Sandwich

⅓ cup purchased olive oil vinaigrette	1½ cups diced seeded plum tomatoes
2 large cloves garlic, minced	½ cup diced salami
2 tablespoons chopped fresh oregano	½ cup chopped pimiento-stuffed olives
½ pound diced cooked chicken (about 2 cups)	Salt and pepper
	Kaiser rolls
	Sliced provolone cheese

Whisk vinaigrette, garlic and oregano in a medium bowl to blend. Mix in chicken, tomatoes, salami, and olives. Season salad with salt and pepper to taste. Mound salad on kaiser roll and top with a slice of provolone cheese.

Yield: 8 to 10 servings

7-Layer Taco Sandwich

½ cup coarsely chopped green and black olives	1 large tomato, sliced
½ teaspoon chili powder	1 pound thinly sliced deli turkey breast
½ teaspoon cumin	1 ripe avocado, peeled and sliced
¼ teaspoon salt	¾ cup (3 ounces) shredded Monterey Jack cheese
½ cup mayonnaise	Lettuce leaves
½ cup sour cream	Salsa
½ cup sliced green onions	
4 large oval slices French bread, about ½-inch thick	

Preheat oven to 350 degrees. Combine olives, chili powder, cumin, and salt in medium bowl; reserve 2 tablespoons. Stir mayonnaise, sour cream, and onions into remaining olive mixture. Using half of mayonnaise mixture, spread 1 side of each bread slice. Top with tomato and turkey. Spread remaining mayonnaise mixture on top of turkey. Top with avocado slices. Sprinkle with cheese. Transfer sandwiches to baking sheet and bake until hot, about 15 minutes. Top with reserved olive mixture. Serve on lettuce leaves with salsa.

Yield: 4 servings

Portobello Mushroom and Goat Cheese Sandwich

4	fresh portobello mushrooms, about 3 ounces each, stems removed	1	tablespoon chopped fresh rosemary
2	red or yellow bell peppers, 6-8 ounces each, halved lengthwise, seeded, and flattened	1	tablespoon finely chopped shallot
2	yellow squash, about 6 ounces each, ends trimmed, sliced lengthwise into ½-inch thick slices	½	teaspoon kosher salt
		¼	teaspoon freshly ground pepper
		3	tablespoons balsamic vinegar
1	large ripe tomato, about 8 ounces, sliced crosswise into ½-inch thick slices	8	ounces goat cheese
		8	(½-inch-thick) slices soft-crusted French or Italian bread or soft rolls
½	cup olive oil	12-16	fresh basil leaves

Put mushrooms, bell peppers, squash and tomato in a lock-top plastic bag large enough to hold them. In a small bowl, whisk together olive oil, rosemary, shallot, salt, and pepper. Add to vegetables. Allow vegetables to marinate at room temperature for 10 to 15 minutes.

Remove vegetables from bag and grill them directly over medium heat, turning once, until tender. The mushrooms will take 12 to 14 minutes, the bell peppers 10 to 12 minutes, the squash 8 to 10 minutes, and the tomato 3 to 4 minutes. Transfer to a large platter. Drizzle with balsamic vinegar and season with salt and pepper to taste.

Evenly spread goat cheese on 1 side of a bread slice. Build the sandwiches with the grilled vegetables, interspersing the basil leaves as you build. Place the remaining bread slices on top.

Serve warm or at room temperature.

Hint: May substitute provolone cheese for the goat cheese.

Yield: 4 servings

Rouxminations

Move Over, Rover

By 1889, St. Joseph became the first city in the nation to operate electric streetcars on a regular schedule. One of the early streetcars ran to the stockyards and Lake Contrary. Some of the streetcars were equipped with a fender which was lowered to push stray dogs and cats from in front of the streetcar.

Smoky Pulled Pork Sandwich

1 cup barbeque sauce	1 tablespoon granulated sugar
2 tablespoons paprika	2 teaspoons kosher salt
1 tablespoon packed brown sugar	1½ teaspoons black pepper
1 tablespoon chili powder	1 (4 to 5 pound) boneless pork shoulder roast (Boston butt)
1 tablespoon ground cumin	Hamburger buns

Coleslaw

1 (1½ pound) head red cabbage	1 teaspoon kosher salt
¼ cup cider vinegar	½ teaspoon black pepper
1 tablespoon sugar	¾ cup mayonnaise
1 teaspoon celery seeds	1 tablespoon Dijon mustard

Sauce

½ cup cider vinegar	½ teaspoon Tabasco sauce
2 tablespoons packed brown sugar	1 teaspoon kosher salt

Soak hickory or mesquite chips in water for at least 30 minutes.

For Pork: In a small bowl, mix together barbecue sauce, paprika, brown sugar, chili powder, cumin, sugar, salt, and pepper. Rub mixture into meat, wrap in plastic wrap, and refrigerate for at least 3 hours or as long as 24 hours.

For Coleslaw: Cut cabbage in half through the core. Remove core and slice cabbage as thinly as possible. In a large bowl, mix together vinegar, sugar, celery seeds, salt, pepper, mayonnaise and mustard. Add cabbage and toss to coat evenly. Cover and refrigerate for at least 1 hour or as long as 24 hours.

For Vinegar Sauce: Combine all ingredients in a small saucepan and heat, stirring, until blended.

Follow the grill's instructions for using wood chips. Grill pork, fat-side-up, indirectly over low heat until very tender but still juicy (the internal temperature should be 180 to 190 degrees), 3 hours or more. Remove pork from grill, cover loosely with aluminum foil, and allow to rest for 30 minutes. Remove any skin from the meat. Tear pork into shreds with 2 forks or your fingers. Put shredded meat in a large bowl and toss with the warm vinegar sauce. Pile pork on hamburger buns and serve topped with coleslaw.

Yield: 8 to 10 servings

Rouxminations

No City Slickers Here

Thorton Chisholm, founder of the Chisholm Trail, led the first longhorn cattle to St. Joseph in 1866. The ride took seven months and ten days to get to St. Joseph and included 1800 longhorns.

Stromboli

Italian Sausage Filling

1 pound mild Italian sausage
1 cup shredded provolone cheese
1 cup shredded mozzarella
   cheese
¼ cup freshly grated Parmesan
   cheese

Dash of dried basil
Dash of salt and freshly ground
   black pepper
Dash of dried rosemary

Spinach Filling

6 ounces center-cut bacon,
   chopped
½ cup chopped onion
1 (10 ounce) package frozen
   chopped spinach, thawed and
   squeezed dry

¼ teaspoon garlic salt
1 cup shredded Monterey Jack
   cheese

Sandwich

1 loaf frozen Rhodes bread
   dough, thawed

1 egg white, beaten

For Italian Sausage Filling: In medium skillet, brown sausage and drain. Combine sausage, cheeses, basil, salt, pepper and rosemary in a bowl and mix well.

For Spinach Filling: In medium skillet, cook bacon until almost crisp; drain grease. Add spinach and garlic salt and cook several minutes. Stir in cheese and mix well.

Preheat oven to 350 degrees. Roll out bread dough on floured counter to thickness of ¼ to ½-inch. Spread filling over dough. Roll up carefully so loaf looks like long loaf of French bread. Seal long edge and tuck under ends. Place on a greased cookie sheet, seam side down. Glaze with egg white. Bake for 30 to 40 minutes, until golden brown. Slice into ¾-inch slices and halve each slice.

Hint: A hearty appetizer for after skiing or a football game. Kids love it! Could easily double as a main dish if accompanied by a mixed green salad. Serve with prepared pizza sauce or favorite marinara sauce for dipping.

Yield: 4 servings

Rouxminations

**From Odd Fellow
To Guilty Fellow**

Among the actors who appeared at the Odd Fellows Hall located at 5th and Felix was the notorious assassin John Wilkes Booth.

A Human Skyscraper

*In 1939, 8'8" tall
Robert Wadlow visited
St. Joseph.*

Literally Speaking

Sara Bernhardt performed in 1881, and Oscar Wilde spoke at the Tootle Opera House in 1882.

Rouxminations

Flying High

In 1927, Charles Lindbergh stopped at Rosecrans airfield. Lindbergh was making a good-will tour of American cities to promote interest of aviation.

Boo Who

In 1868, Generals Grant and Sherman arrived in St. Joseph only to be booed by an angry crowd.

Stuffed Sandwich Crown

2 (12 ounce) jars roasted red pepper, drained
¼ cup olive oil
¼ cup balsamic vinegar
2 cloves garlic, minced
2 (1 pound) unsliced round bread loaves
12 hard salami slices
1 head red leaf lettuce
12 slices provolone cheese
12 slices red sweet onion
12 slices smoked turkey
  Honey mustard

Place peppers in a small bowl. Combine oil, vinegar, and garlic and pour over peppers. Stir to coat and allow to marinate for 1 hour at room temperature. Drain peppers from marinade and cut into ¾-inch strips.

Meanwhile, cut tops off loaves and reserve. Remove insides of loaves, leaving ½-inch-thick shell, reserving removed bread for another use. Spread insides of loaves and tops with a thin layer of mustard. Arrange half of salami in each loaf. Top with lettuce and add half of peppers. Layer with half of cheese and half of onion, then remaining peppers. Cover with half of turkey. Replace bread tops on loaves, wrap in plastic, and refrigerate. Cut each loaf into 6 wedges before serving.

Hint: Great for picnics or tailgating party.

Yield: 6 servings

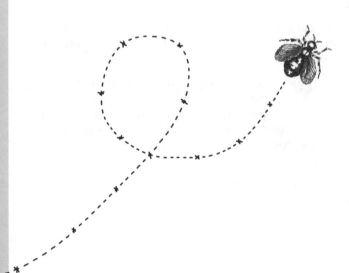

Tortilla Wraps

8	ounces lite cream cheese, softened	1	large red or yellow bell pepper sliced
1	tablespoon plus 1 teaspoon taco seasoning	1	large ripe avocado, sliced
6	large flour tortillas	1	cup sprouts
8	ounces or more grilled chicken breast, thinly sliced	1	cup fresh spinach or lettuce leaves, dried

Combine cream cheese and taco seasonings and spread evenly on 1 side of tortilla. Layer with chicken, bell pepper, avocado, sprouts and spinach, evenly dividing among the tortillas. Roll up and secure with toothpick. Cut into half.

Hint: Can be made several hours ahead. Individually wrap with plastic wrap and refrigerate. Can substitute shrimp for chicken. Great for lunch, tailgate or light supper. Can be made without chicken as a veggie wrap with favorite veggies.

Yield: 6 servings

Turkey Salad on Croissant

2	cups chopped deli turkey	½	cup chopped walnuts
1	Granny Smith apple, unpeeled, chopped		Mayonnaise
1	tablespoon minced celery		Salt and pepper
½	cup shredded Swiss cheese		Balsamic vinegar
		8	croissants

Preheat oven to 350 degrees. Combine turkey, apple, celery, cheese, and walnuts in a medium bowl. Add enough mayonnaise to moisten. Season with salt and pepper and balsamic vinegar.

Slice croissants and fill with salad. Wrap in foil and bake for 20 minutes or, if desired, freeze and bake later.

Hint: We love this recipe because it can be made in advance and is great for luncheons!

Yield: 8 servings

Rouxminations

Water, Water Everywhere

At one time, the Noyes swimming pool was the only pool in town. The original Noyes pool which opened in 1924 was larger than a football field and covered almost an acre of ground. The pool held almost 2,000,000 gallons of water—four times the amount of today's pools. It cost only $70 to fill the pool.

❧ Bank On It! ❧

If only those walls could talk! They might tell about the potential robbery of the bank by outlaw Jesse James. The walls were certainly privy to tales of going west and certainly heard gossip from the steamboat captains and passengers as well as from the wealthy patrons who utilized the bank's services. The walls were certainly knowledgeable of all of the tales of hardships and successes that were part of the growing pains of a young frontier city.

The Missouri Valley Trust is one of the architectural gems of downtown St. Joseph. The bank was furnished in lavish high Victorian style. The tellers worked behind hand-carved oak teller boxes, and the bank safe had painted decorations.

The elaborate lobby reflected the prosperous nature of the bank that had millions of dollars in assets in the 1870's. The painted cast iron columns stretched to the ceiling. The oak fireplace warmed the room and the light from its flames in turn reflected in the stained glass windows. The bank had its share of famous clientele.

In its later years, the bank was used for one of the sets for Paper Moon, *a film starring Ryan and Tatum O'Neal.*

Today the bank still stands as an example of the architecture of the period. The bank has been restored to its early grandeur. It is open daily to the public and group tours and houses the office of the St. Joseph Downtown Partnership.

Perhaps the walls are still collecting stories.

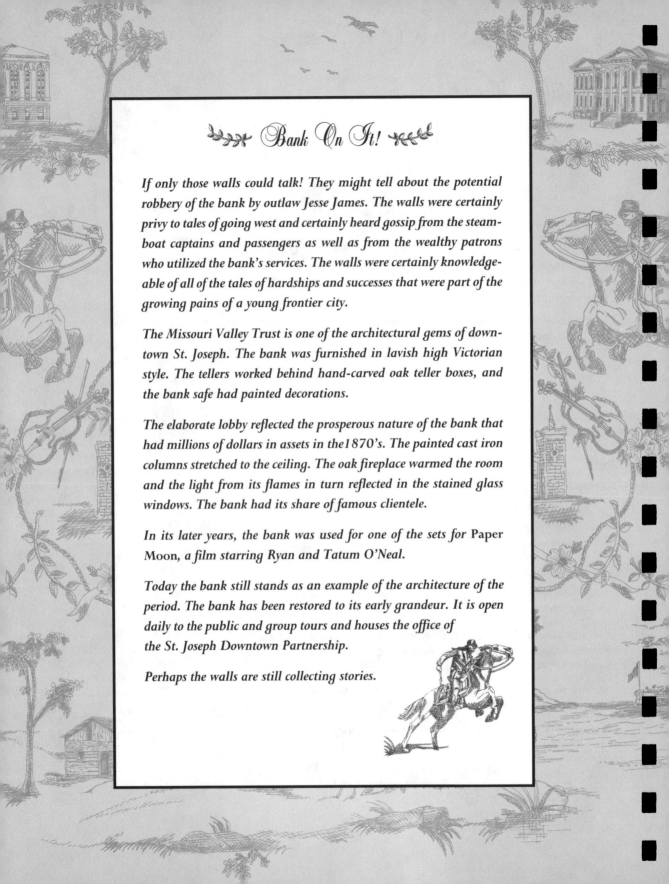

Salads

Missouri Valley Trust

Salads

Champagne Salad

Dressing

¼ cup olive oil
4 teaspoons minced shallots
2 teaspoons minced garlic
½ cup sherry wine vinegar
2 tablespoons freshly squeezed
   lemon juice

2 tablespoons Dijon mustard
10 ounces Brie cheese, rind
   removed, softened, and cut
   into small pieces
   Salt and pepper to taste

Salad

1 head romaine lettuce, torn into
   bite-size pieces
1 head curly endive, torn into
   bite-size pieces

1 head radicchio, torn into
   bite-size pieces
1 cup croutons

Warm olive oil in large skillet over low heat. Add shallots and garlic and cook for 2 to 3 minutes, until translucent. Add vinegar, lemon juice, and mustard, and mix until blended. Add cheese and stir until melted and smooth. Season with salt and pepper. Toss lettuces and croutons with hot dressing. Serve immediately.

Yield: 8 servings

Fall Salad

Salad

1 pound romaine lettuce
6 slices bacon, cooked and
   crumbled
⅓ cup thinly sliced red onion

1 Granny Smith apple, unpeeled,
   cut into small chunks
½ cup dried cranberries
½ cup walnuts

Dressing

3 tablespoons soy sauce (not lite)
½ cup canola oil

Combine salad ingredients in large bowl. In small bowl, combine oil and soy sauce. Pour over salad and serve immediately.

Yield: 6 servings

Seasonal Salad

Dressing

4 tablespoons cranberry juice concentrate
4 tablespoons rice wine vinegar
1½ teaspoons Dijon mustard

¼ teaspoon freshly ground pepper
½ cup canola or vegetable oil

Salad

8 cups mixed greens, cleaned and dried
1 avocado

½ cup thinly sliced red onion
½ cup pomegranate seeds or dried cranberries

Combine dressing ingredients in a jar with tight-fitting lid. Shake until well blended.

Place mixed greens in large bowl. Just before serving, slice and add avocado and onion. Drizzle dressing over salad and gently toss to coat. Sprinkle with pomegranate seeds and serve.

Hint: This salad can be made with whatever fruit is in season: apples or pears may be substituted for avocados in the fall; strawberries and blueberries in the summer.

Yield: 8 to 10 servings

Fig and Arugula Salad with Parmesan

2 tablespoons minced shallots
1½ tablespoons balsamic vinegar
1 tablespoon extra virgin olive oil
¼ teaspoon salt
16 fresh figs, halved lengthwise

6 cups trimmed arugula
¼ teaspoon freshly ground black pepper
¼ cup (1 ounce) shaved fresh Parmesan cheese

Combine shallots, vinegar, olive oil, and salt in a large bowl and stir well with a whisk. Add figs, cover, and let stand 20 minutes. Add arugula and pepper; toss well. Top with cheese. Serve immediately.

Yield: 6 servings

Rouxminations

Relive The Glory Days

The Missouri Valley Trust building is one of several locations in St. Joseph on the National Register of Historic Places, and visitors today can still tour the bank as it was in its heyday with its ornate carved oak woodwork, stained glass windows, cast iron pillars, tellers' cages and a vault reinforced with railroad rails.

Goat Cheese Salad with Garlic Dressing

4 ounces soft goat cheese	½ cup olive oil
¼ cup finely chopped hulled pumpkin seeds	10 large cloves garlic
1½ teaspoons dried chives	¼ cup red wine vinegar
½ teaspoon dried basil	1 teaspoon Dijon mustard
½ teaspoon dried thyme	½ teaspoon Worcestershire sauce
½ teaspoon dried rosemary	½ teaspoon Tabasco sauce
	4 cups mixed greens

Mix cheese, pumpkin seeds, and all dried herbs in small bowl. Spoon cheese mixture onto a piece of plastic wrap, forming a log. Roll log up in plastic and chill until firm, about 1½ to 2 hours.

Heat oil in heavy small saucepan. Add garlic and stir. Remove from heat and cool completely. Spoon garlic out of oil and transfer to food processor. Add vinegar and mustard to processor and blend well. Gradually add oil. Add Worcestershire sauce and Tabasco. Season with salt and pepper.

Preheat oven to 400 degrees. When ready to serve, unwrap cheese log and slice into ½-inch-thick rounds. Place on a baking sheet and bake until warm, about 3 minutes.

Toss greens with dressing to coat. Divide among plates and place cheese on top of greens. Serve immediately.

Hint: Cheese log may be made up to a week ahead.

Yield: 8 servings

Rouxminations

What Might Have Been

According to local legend, Jesse James cased the Missouri Valley Trust bank shortly before he was killed in 1882. James was recognized as the man who had recently called on the bank to change a $100 bill. This was, perhaps, his advance notice of another daring daylight robbery.

Hazelnut and Bleu Cheese Salad with Raspberry Vinaigrette

Raspberry Vinaigrette

½ cup vegetable oil
¼ cup raspberry preserves

½ teaspoon pepper
⅛ teaspoon salt

Salad

1 cup chopped hazelnuts
8 cups mixed greens
4 unpeeled pears, chopped

1 (4 ounce) package crumbled bleu cheese
Pepper, optional

Combine oil, preserves, pepper, and salt in a jar with a tight-fitting lid. Shake well and chill. Makes ¾ cup.

Place nuts on jelly-roll pan and toast in a 350 degree oven for 5 to 10 minutes, watching closely to avoid burning. Cool.

Combine cooled hazelnuts, mixed greens, pears, and cheese in a bowl. Add vinaigrette and toss gently. Sprinkle with pepper, if desired, and serve.

Yield: 8 servings

Rouxminations

We'll Leave The Light On For You

The Missouri Supreme Court once met upstairs in the Missouri Valley Trust building. Also, Pony Express riders, ox-wagon freighters, stagecoach passengers, French fur traders, steamboat captains, Union and Confederate soldiers, and gold miners all warmed themselves at the fireplace there before venturing out.

Mixed Greens with Spiced Pecans, Apples, and Hot Cider Dressing

Spiced Pecans

2 cups pecan halves	1 teaspoon ground cinnamon
2½ tablespoons vegetable oil	½ teaspoon ground ginger
¼ cup sugar	¼ teaspoon ground nutmeg
1 teaspoon salt	¼ teaspoon ground cloves
½ teaspoon dry mustard	

Hot Cider Dressing

2 cups apple cider	1 teaspoon ground cinnamon
8 slices bacon, cut into 1-inch pieces	1 tablespoon honey mustard
3 shallots, minced	½ cup olive oil
	Salt and pepper to taste

Salad

12 cups mixed greens	2 large McIntosh apples, cored and thinly sliced

For Spiced Pecans: Preheat oven to 300 degrees. Place pecans in small bowl, cover with boiling water, and let soak for 15 minutes. Drain well and pat dry on paper towels. Spread nuts on an ungreased cookie sheet and bake for 45 minutes, occasionally stirring. Remove nuts and increase oven temperature to 350 degrees. Whisk together the oil, sugar, salt, mustard, and spices in a bowl. Add hot nuts and toss to coat thoroughly. Spread nuts in a single layer on cookie sheet and bake 15 minutes more. Let cool and store in airtight container for up to 2 weeks.

For Dressing: Pour cider into a small saucepan and boil about 20 to 25 minutes, until reduced to ½ cup. Set aside. Sauté bacon in skillet over medium heat until crisp. Drain on paper towel and crumble. Save 3 tablespoons of bacon drippings and add shallots to the skillet. Sauté over medium heat for 3 minutes, until softened. Whisk in cinnamon and mustard and cook 1 minute. Add reduced cider and the olive oil. Season with salt and pepper. Keep dressing warm over low heat.

For Salad: Toss greens, apple slices, spiced pecans and bacon in large bowl. Toss with hot dressing and serve.

Hint: Mixed greens include leaf lettuce, romaine, endive, radicchio or watercress.

Yield: 6 servings

Rouxminations

It's Only A Paper Moon

The Missouri Valley Trust Company, built in 1859, was featured in Tatum O'Neal's Academy Award winning performance in Paper Moon.

Where's The ATM?

Brigham Young once did business at the Missouri Valley Trust before leading a group of Mormons to Utah.

Rouxminations

Passing The Torch

In 1996, the Olympic torched passed through St. Joseph on its way to Atlanta, Georgia, site of the 1996 Summer Olympics. Two St. Joseph natives, Wes Barnett and Pete Kelly, competed in Weightlifting at these Summer Games.

Northwestern Autumn Salad

Dressing

½ cup walnut or vegetable oil	1 tablespoon maple syrup
¼ cup cider vinegar	¼ teaspoon salt
2 tablespoons minced shallot	¼ teaspoon freshly ground pepper
2 tablespoons freshly squeezed lemon juice	

Salad

1 head red leaf lettuce	2 Red Delicious apples
1 head Bibb lettuce	¼ cup chopped glazed pecans or toasted walnuts
1 cup watercress leaves or arugula	¾ cup crumbled bleu cheese

For Dressing: Place oil, vinegar, shallots, lemon juice, maple syrup, salt, and pepper in a small jar with tight-fitting lid. Shake until evenly combined.

For Salad: Tear lettuces into bite-size pieces and place in a large salad bowl. Add watercress leaves. Cut apples into very thin wedges and arrange on top of greens. Sprinkle pecans and blue cheese evenly over salad. Drizzle dressing over salad. Toss gently and serve immediately.

Yield: 6 to 8 servings

Tomato, Cucumber and Avocado Salad

3 medium ripe tomatoes, halved and thinly sliced	1 small sweet red onion, thinly sliced
2 avocados, cut into chunks	2½ tablespoons olive oil
1 cucumber, halved and thinly sliced	2 teaspoons vinegar
	6-8 basil leaves, chopped
	Salt and pepper to taste

Combine all ingredients in serving bowl. Toss to mix, cover, and refrigerate an hour for flavors to blend.

Yield: 8 servings

Pear, Bleu Cheese, and Walnut Salad

Candied Walnuts

1	cup walnuts	2	tablespoons butter
½	cup sugar		

Pear Nectar Vinaigrette

½	cup white wine vinegar	1	teaspoon Dijon mustard
⅓	cup salad oil	¼	teaspoon salt
⅓	cup pear nectar	⅛	teaspoon pepper

Salad

3	medium pears	6	cups mixed greens
2	tablespoon lemon juice	½	cup crumbled bleu cheese

For Candied Walnuts: Line a baking sheet with foil and butter it. In a heavy skillet, combine walnuts, sugar, and butter, mixing well before heating. Cook over medium heat, shaking skillet occasionally, until sugar melts. Do not stir. Watch carefully. Reduce heat to low and cook until sugar is golden brown. Remove from heat and pour onto baking sheet. Cool completely and break into clusters.

For Pear Nectar Vinaigrette: Combine all ingredients in a jar with a tight-fitting lid. Shake well.

For Salad: Halve and core pears, thinly slice and brush with lemon juice. Line salad plates with mixed greens. Fan pear slices atop greens. Sprinkle with bleu cheese and candied walnuts. Drizzle vinaigrette over salad and serve.

Hint: Pecans can be substituted for the walnuts. Candied nuts may be prepared ahead and stored in an airtight container. If pears are underripe, thinly slice and sauté in butter.

Yield: 6 to 8 servings

Rouxminations

This Was No Petticoat Junction

In 1882, the First Union Depot was completed at Sixth and Mitchell. Curiously, on this same date in 1971, the last passenger train left St. Joseph.

Y Not?

Y-Fry, a men's cooking club, has 1600 "graduates." The club was started in the 1950's as a cooking class by Ethel Agenstein, a retired home economics teacher who thought it only fair that men be taught culinary skills. At the end of the session, each member is responsible for preparing a part of the graduation meal. No skill, but a little luck is required to get into the cooking class, as names are suggested by past graduates and then drawn from a lottery.

Rouxminations

Before The YMCA

St. Joseph had a popular health club resort called the St. Joseph Natatorium. The club opened in 1886. There was a swimming pool and several baths. An artist's rendition of the Natatorium shows several diving boards, slides, ladders and trapeze-like ropes and swings. The club was located at Fifth and Jules.

City Hall Salad

Salad

1	large red onion, sliced thin	1	(12 ounce) can artichoke hearts, drained and quartered
1	head iceberg lettuce, torn into pieces	1	(4 ounce) jar pimentos, drained
1	head romaine lettuce, torn into pieces	1	(12 ounce) can hearts of palm, drained and sliced

Dressing

1	cup extra virgin olive oil	½	cup balsamic vinegar
⅔	cup freshly grated Parmesan cheese		

Combine onion, lettuces, artichoke hearts, pimentos and hearts of palm in a large bowl. Toss well. Mix olive oil, Parmesan cheese, and vinegar to make dressing. Coat salad with dressing and refrigerate up to 2 hours to blend flavors. Serve cold.

Hint: The longer this salad is left in refrigerator the better the flavors blend together.

Yield: 10 servings

Strawberry Spinach Salad

2	bunches fresh spinach	½	cup mayonnaise
½	cup slivered almonds	2	cups sliced fresh strawberries
½	cup undiluted orange juice concentrate, thawed		

Preheat oven to 350 degrees. Tear spinach into bite-size pieces, removing the large stems. Place in glass serving bowl. Cover with plastic wrap and chill.

Spread almonds on an ungreased baking sheet and toast in preheated oven for 5 to 10 minutes, until browned. Watch carefully to avoid burning. Let cool completely.

Whisk together orange juice and mayonnaise. When ready to serve, pour dressing over spinach and toss until well coated. Top with almonds and strawberries.

Yield: 6 servings

Salad of Black Beans, Hearts of Palm, and Corn

1 (16 ounce) can black beans, rinsed and drained
1 (11 ounce) can corn, drained
1 (7½ ounce) jar hearts of palm, drained and cut into ¼-inch rounds
2 large tomatoes, seeded and diced
½ cup chopped red onion
½ cup chopped fresh cilantro
¼ cup olive oil
3 tablespoons fresh lime juice
  Salt and pepper to taste

In medium bowl, mix all ingredients. Cover and refrigerate before serving.

Hint: Salad may be prepared 1 day ahead.

Yield: 6 servings

Rouxminations

Buried Treasures

In 1940, the Junior League of St. Joseph opened a Thrift shop and operated it for 40 some years until the mid 1980's when the first Tossed and Found sale was held in the Kresge building, downtown. The Tossed and Found annual sale remains the League's biggest fund-raiser for community projects.

Tossed and Found Bean Salad

2 cups canned black beans, rinsed and drained
2 cups black-eyed peas, rinsed and drained
2 cups red beans, rinsed and drained
2 cups cooked Rosamirina pasta
2 cups frozen corn, cooked
3 cups vinaigrette dressing
1 cup salsa
½ cup sugar
½ cup chopped green onion
⅓ cup chopped fresh parsley
1 teaspoon cumin
  Lettuce
  Tortilla chips

Combine black beans, black-eyed peas, red beans, pasta, corn, dressing, salsa, sugar, green onion, parsley, and cumin in a large container. Cover and chill in refrigerator.

To serve, mound salad on a bed of lettuce. Place tortilla chips around perimeter of the plate.

Hint: To serve this as an appetizer, simply omit the bed of lettuce. This also makes a great side dish.

Yield: 8 to 10 servings

Corn Jumble

24	ounces frozen corn, thawed	2	tablespoons mayonnaise
¾	cup unpeeled, diced cucumber	1	tablespoon vinegar
¼	cup diced shallots	½	teaspoon salt
2	small tomatoes, chopped	¼	teaspoon dry mustard
¼	cup sour cream	¼	teaspoon celery seed

Combine corn, cucumber, onion, and tomatoes in a large salad bowl. Blend remaining ingredients in a small bowl and add to corn mixture. Toss to coat, cover, and chill.

Hint: Fresh or extra sweet corn enhances this summer dish.

Yield: 4 to 6 servings

Citrus Salad with Cilantro Vinaigrette

Cilantro Vinaigrette

¼	cup tightly packed cilantro leaves	1	teaspoon sugar
		¼	teaspoon dry mustard
¼	cup white wine vinegar	⅓	cup vegetable oil

Salad

2	red grapefruits	½	red onion, thinly sliced
4	large naval oranges	1	(6 ounce) package baby spinach

For Cilantro Vinaigrette: In work bowl of food processor fitted with steel knife blade, process cilantro until coarsely chopped. Add vinegar, sugar, and mustard. Pulse to blend. With machine running, gradually add oil. Makes ¾ cup.

For Salad: Peel grapefruits and oranges, removing white pith. Cut into cartwheel slices. Arrange fruit and onion in overlapping pattern around edge of flat plate. Drizzle with some of the Cilantro Vinaigrette. Mound spinach in center of plate. Serve remaining dressing on the side.

Hint: Even teachers don't always follow directions. Dressing may be made in advance, covered, and refrigerated for several hours or overnight. Whisk before serving. Can use olive oil instead of vegetable oil.

Yield: 8 to 10 servings

Applewood Fresh Fruit Salad

1	fresh pineapple, peeled, cored, and cubed	4	oranges, peeled and sectioned
1	quart fresh strawberries	2	bananas, sliced
½	cup fresh blueberries (may use frozen, thawed)	1	cup sugar
		1	teaspoon almond extract
½	cup fresh raspberries	1	teaspoon vanilla
2	cups chopped, unpeeled Red Delicious apples	2	cups orange juice

Place fruit in a large bowl. Combine sugar, almond extract, vanilla, and orange juice; stir until sugar dissolves. Pour over fruit mixture, tossing lightly. Cover and chill 2 to 3 hours before serving.

Hint: You can substitute other fresh fruit. This is great for a crowd, but can easily be halved.

Delicious Pasta Salad

1	(1 pound) bag rotelle pasta	4	green onions, chopped
¼	pound Monterey Jack cheese, cubed	3	tomatoes, chopped
¼	pound mozzarella cheese, cubed	1	(10 ounce) can black olives, drained
¼	pound summer sausage, cubed	1	(6 ounce) jar green olives, drained and sliced
¼	pound sliced pepperoni	1	tablespoon chopped fresh oregano
½	pound cooked and peeled small shrimp, optional	1⅓	cups safflower oil
1	green bell pepper, chopped	½	cup red wine vinegar
3	celery stalks, chopped		

Prepare pasta according to package directions, drain and cool. Add remaining ingredients in order given and toss well. Cover and chill before serving.

Hint: This is best when prepared ahead.

Yield: 25 to 30 servings

Rouxminations

From Opera House To Office Space

The Pioneer building, formerly known at the Tootle Opera House, was built for $165,000 and was once regarded as the finest theater west of Chicago. St. Joseph's social elite came here to see the leading theater companies of the day. The Tootle Opera House gave St. Joseph its early fame as one of the most cosmopolitan cities in the country. The building has since been remodeled into office space.

Couscous Salad

Couscous

1½ cups water
¼ teaspoon salt

1 cup uncooked couscous

Dressing

1 tablespoon chopped fresh basil
   or teaspoon dried
1 teaspoon chopped fresh
   oregano or ¼ teaspoon dried

¼ teaspoon salt
2 tablespoons balsamic vinegar
2 tablespoons olive oil

Salad

¾ cup chopped cucumber
¾ cup chopped green or yellow
   bell pepper
¼ cup sliced green onions

1 medium tomato, chopped
1 can garbanzo beans, rinsed and
   drained
⅓ cup crumbled feta cheese

Bring water and salt to boil in a medium saucepan. Remove from heat and immediately stir in couscous. Cover and let stand 5 minutes. Fluff couscous with fork and cool.

Combine basil, oregano, salt, vinegar, and olive oil in a small bowl. Blend well.

Place couscous in a large bowl. Add cucumber, bell pepper, green onions, tomato, and beans. Top with dressing and toss to coat. Cover and refrigerate for at least 1 hour. Sprinkle with feta cheese before serving.

Hint: Great substitute for potato or pasta salad.

Yield: 6 to 8 servings

Rouxminations

Hallowed Ground

Before any traces of white man came to the St. Joseph area, the ground was used for Indian Burial Grounds and Holy Land.

Bullseye!

In July of 1900, St. Joseph was the Geographical Center of the United States.

Midwest Pasta Salad with a Kick

Salad

8   ounces tricolor rotini
12 ounces mild breakfast sausage, diced and cooked
1   (15 ounce) can kidney beans, rinsed and drained
1   (8 ounce) can whole kernel corn, drained
2   medium tomatoes, chopped

1   small red or yellow bell pepper, chopped
½   cup sliced green onions
1   (2¼ ounce) can sliced black olives, drained
1   cup shredded low-fat Cheddar cheese

Dressing

1   (10 ounce) can diced tomatoes and green chiles, drained
½   cup reduced fat Italian dressing

2   teaspoons salt-free herb seasoning

Prepare rotini according to package directions and drain. In large bowl, combine all salad ingredients and mix well. In small bowl, combine dressing ingredients. Pour dressing over salad and toss to coat. Cover and chill up to 4 hours.

Yield: 8 servings

Mandarin Chicken Salad

3   cups diced cooked chicken
1   cup diced celery
2   tablespoons fresh lemon juice
1   tablespoon minced red onion
½   teaspoon salt
⅓   cup mayonnaise
1   cup seedless green grapes, sliced in half

1   cup seedless red grapes, sliced in half
½   cup slivered almonds, toasted
1   (11 ounce) can Mandarin oranges, drained
    Fancy leaf lettuce
    Grape clusters, optional

Combine chicken, celery, lemon juice, red onion, and salt. Stir well, cover, and chill 30 minutes. Add mayonnaise, grapes, and almonds; toss well. Gently stir in oranges. Serve on lettuce leaves, garnished with additional orange slices and grape clusters, if desired.

Hint: This salad is great with croissants.

Yield: 6 servings

Rouxminations

No Itsy Bitsy, Tweenie Weenie, Yellow Polka-Dot Bikinis Here

In 1851 St. Joseph City Ordinances declared that it was against the law to march or play in the streets to the sound of music on Sunday. It was also illegal to appear in clothing not belonging to one's own sex. People were not permitted to bathe in the rivers, lakes, and ponds one hour before sunrise and one hour after sunset.

Summer Salad

Salad

8	ounces colored spiral pasta	1	small onion, chopped
1	large cucumber, chopped	1	large tomato, chopped
1	head broccoli, chopped	1	small can sliced black olives, drained
1	medium green bell pepper, chopped		

Dressing

½	cups vegetable oil	2	tablespoons dry mustard
½	cup sugar	1	teaspoon salt
½	cup vinegar	½	teaspoon ground black pepper
3	tablespoons parsley flakes	1	teaspoon garlic powder

Cook pasta according to package directions. Rinse and drain. Place in a salad bowl and add cucumber, broccoli, green pepper, onion, and tomato. Toss well and add black olives.

Whisk together all the dressing ingredients until blended. Pour dressing over salad mixture, toss, and cover. Refrigerate overnight. Stir again before serving.

Yield: 10 servings

Mexican Chicken Salad

4	cups chopped cooked chicken	½	cup mayonnaise
2	cups shredded Cheddar cheese	1	envelope taco seasoning
1	(16 ounce) can kidney beans, rinsed and drained	2	tablespoons chopped green bell pepper
1	(4 ounce) can green chiles, drained and chopped	2	medium tomatoes, chopped
½	cup black olives		Corn chips or taco chips
½	cup sour cream		Shredded lettuce

In large bowl, combine chicken, cheese, beans, green chiles, olives, sour cream, mayonnaise, taco seasoning, bell pepper, and tomatoes. Cover and chill until ready to serve. Serve on a bed of chips and lettuce.

Yield: 6 to 8 servings

Wild Rice Chicken Salad

1 cup pecan halves	1 cup cooked wild rice
¼ cup rice wine vinegar	1½ cups cooked chopped or shredded chicken breast, in 1-inch pieces
2 cloves garlic, minced	
1 tablespoon Dijon mustard	
½ teaspoon salt	½ cup diced red bell pepper
¼ teaspoon sugar	½ cup snow peas, trimmed and cut into 1-inch pieces
¼ teaspoon pepper	
⅓ cup vegetable oil	3 green onions, chopped
3 cups cooked long-grain rice (preferably brown; white or Arborio may be used)	2 tablespoons lemon juice
	1-2 avocados, cut into 1-inch pieces Mixed greens

Preheat oven to 300 degrees. Spread pecan halves on a baking sheet and bake 5 to 10 minutes. Set aside.

Place vinegar, garlic, mustard, salt, sugar, and pepper in a blender. Cover and process on high for 10 seconds, until well blended. With blender still running, add oil in a slow steady stream; process until thickened, about 30 more seconds. Set aside.

Combine rice, chicken, red pepper, snow peas, green onions, and lemon juice in a large bowl. Toss. Pour dressing over chicken mixture and toss. Cover and chill 2 to 4 hours or longer. Stir in avocados and pecans just before serving. To serve, arrange chicken salad on mixed greens.

Yield: 8 servings

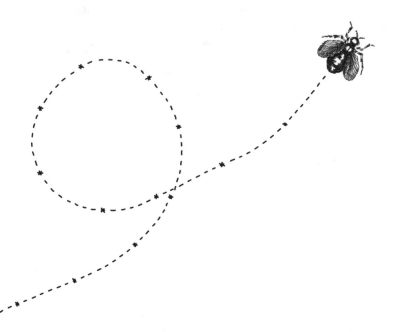

Rouxminations

History In The Making

The St. Joseph News-Press is the oldest family-owned newspaper west of the Mississippi. It started operations in 1845.

The Power of The Press

William Ridenbaugh came to St. Joseph with printing equipment rescued from the Missouri River after an angry Anti-Mormon mob had thrown it into the river. With this press, Ridenbaugh established the St. Joseph Gazette as a weekly newspaper in 1845. Through the years, this paper evolved into the modern day St. Joseph News-Press.

Shrimp and Artichoke Salad

4	whole artichokes, cleaned and chokes removed
2	lemons, cut in half
	Salt and freshly ground black pepper
¾	cup extra virgin olive oil
¼	cup balsamic vinegar
¼	cup chopped fresh mild herbs (such as tarragon, basil, parsley, chervil, etc.)
2	teaspoons minced garlic
4	dozen medium shrimp, cooked, peeled, and deveined
4	cups mixed greens
2	tablespoons grated Parmesan cheese
1	tablespoon chopped parsley
	Sprigs of fresh thyme

Place artichokes and lemons in a stockpot. Cover with water and season with salt and pepper. Bring liquid to a boil and reduce to a simmer. Submerge the artichokes in the water by laying a small cloth over the artichokes in the pan. Continue to cook for 18 minutes or until tender. Remove artichokes and place in a bowl of ice water for a couple of minutes, until chilled. Drain and pat dry. Season with salt and pepper.

In a mixing bowl, whisk oil, vinegar, herbs, and garlic together. Whisk until incorporated. Season with salt and pepper.

Combine greens and shrimp in a bowl and toss lightly with the vinaigrette. Season with salt and pepper. Mound a quarter of the shrimp mixture in the center of each artichoke. Garnish with Parmesan, parsley, and thyme sprigs.

Hint: Very nice presentation. Instead of the fresh artichokes, salad can also be made with a small jar of marinated artichokes. Simply drain the artichokes, chop into bite-size pieces, and add to rest of salad.

Yield: 10 servings

All-American Potato Salad

4 pounds large red potatoes, scrubbed	1 tablespoon Dijon mustard
½ cup cider vinegar	3 large celery stalks, diced (about 1½ cups)
3 tablespoons vegetable oil	½ cup finely chopped red onion
1½ teaspoons salt	2 tablespoons chopped parsley
¾ teaspoon freshly ground pepper	8 slices bacon, cooked crisp and crumbled
1½ cups mayonnaise	4 hard-cooked eggs, quartered
½ cup milk	Parsley sprigs, optional

Place potatoes in a saucepan and cover with water. Bring to a boil, reduce heat to medium, and cook 25 to 30 minutes, until tender. Drain and cool. Cut into ¾-inch cubes.

In large bowl, whisk together vinegar, oil, salt, and pepper. Add potatoes to vinegar mixture and gently stir to coat. Let cool to room temperature.

In small bowl, whisk mayonnaise, milk, and mustard until blended. Pour over potatoes. Add celery, red onion, and chopped parsley. Stir gently to mix. Cover and refrigerate for at least 4 hours to overnight.

Before serving, garnish with crumbled bacon, egg quarters, and parsley sprigs, if desired.

Yield: 10 servings

Rouxminations

The All-American Team

In 1997, St. Joseph earned the distinction of being an All-American city, an honored bestowed by the National Civic League. In its award winning presentation to the judges, St. Joseph leaders highlighted the economic recovery following the 1993 flood, the Patee Town rehabilitation, and the Healthy Communities Summit established by Heartland Health Systems.

Parmesan Walnut Salad Bowls

3 cups freshly grated Parmesan cheese	1 cup ground walnuts

Place a nonstick 9-inch sauté pan over medium-low heat. Sprinkle ½ cup Parmesan cheese over bottom of pan to cover surface. Cheese will begin to melt. Sprinkle the ground walnuts over the melted cheese and cook until the edges are golden brown. Peel away from pan with rubber spatula and place walnut side out over a 6-inch bowl to form a basket. Basket will be crisp within seconds. Repeat procedure for remaining baskets.

Yield: 8 bowls

Mixed Greens and Potato Salad

½	pound thick-sliced bacon, cooked crisp, drained, and crumbled	1	tablespoon Dijon mustard
2	bunches frisée or mixed salad greens	6	tablespoons olive oil Salt and freshly ground pepper
6-12	ounces blue cheese, crumbled	1	pound small red potatoes
		2	tablespoons unsalted butter
2	tablespoons red wine vinegar	2	cloves garlic, chopped

Combine bacon, salad greens, and Roquefort in a mixing bowl, reserving a little bacon and Roquefort for garnish. In small bowl, whisk together vinegar, mustard, oil, and salt and pepper to taste. Set aside.

Peel potatoes and cut into quarters. Rinse in several changes of water and dry thoroughly. In large sauté pan at medium heat, melt butter and skim foam. Add potatoes in 1 layer and brown thoroughly on 1 side before turning. (Potatoes may need to be cooked in 2 batches.) Cook until brown on all sides. Add garlic to pan and cook 1 minute longer.

Add enough dressing to the bowl of greens to dress lightly, reserving some for drizzling on potatoes. Divide salad among 6 plates and top each with some hot potatoes. Drizzle a little dressing over potatoes, and garnish each salad with the reserved bacon and cheese.

Hint: This is also good for picnics. Simply place dressed greens in a large bowl; put potatoes on top followed by bacon, then cheese. Toss before serving.

Yield: 6 servings

Rouxminations

Sacred Ground

The Indians who frequented Blacksnake Hills, where Joseph Robidoux established his trading post, consider the bluffs above the Missouri River sacred ground because of their unique fertile loess soil. Loess soil is extremely rare in the United States. No blood could be shed on the grounds.

Super Slaw

6 tablespoons rice vinegar	8 cups cabbage slaw mix
6 tablespoons vegetable oil	1 large red or yellow bell pepper, cut into matchstick-size strips
5 tablespoons creamy peanut butter	
3 tablespoons soy sauce	2 medium carrots, peeled, cut into matchstick-size strips
3 tablespoons golden brown sugar (packed)	8 large green onions, cut into matchstick-size strips
2 tablespoons minced peeled fresh ginger	½ cup chopped fresh cilantro
1½ tablespoons minced garlic	

Combine first 7 ingredients into a blender or food processor, on low speed, blend until creamy. (Dressing can be made 1 day ahead. Cover and chill. Let stand at room temperature 30 minutes before adding to slaw mix.)

Hint: This is a great alternative to traditional slaw. Great with Dickey's Ribs on page 130.

Yield: 4 to 6 servings

Rouxminations

The Spirit In The Sky

The Indians believed that from the bluffs along the Missouri River the souls of their departed would be carried to the Great Spirit on the rays of the setting sun. Their name for the place was "Wah Wah La No Wah," or the Sunbridge. Today, the Sunbridge area along the Missouri River Bluffs is a popular hiking site owned by the Missouri Department of Conservation.

And the money kept rolling in...

Cha ching. The sound of money passing hands resonated sweetly for the St. Joseph economy particularly during the pinnacle of the stockyards. The Livestock Exchange became a hotbed of activity when it was dedicated in 1899.

The buyers and sellers who came to the stockyards most likely returned to the Livestock Exchange building after doing business. The four-story brick building has 105 rooms, which at the time included the Stockyards offices, a bank, and a barbershop.

Back then, the St. Joseph Stockyards handled almost as many cattle, hogs and sheep as other notorious stockyards like Kansas City and Chicago. And, as the reputation of the stockyards grew, St. Joseph had become attractive to more than local meat packers when several railroads built connections to the city. Swift was the first major packer to come to St. Joseph with Armour following five years later. A whole community dedicated to meatpacking developed and the area around it thrived.

It was also a time when all that was needed to seal a deal was a gentleman's agreement and a shake of the hands; a far cry from the mountains of paperwork needed today.

The Hoof and Horn restaurant opened in the glory days of the stockyards and has been in almost continuous operation since. The Hoof and Horn has built a reputation for good food, especially steaks.

Like so many communities with large stockyards, as the meat packing industry became more automated and centralized the activity in them are slowed down. St. Joseph Foods is the only meat production plant still operating today.

Today there are only faint whispers of the cha chinging of money changing hands as the stockyards still operate for farmers to buy and sell cattle and hogs but at a much reduced volume.

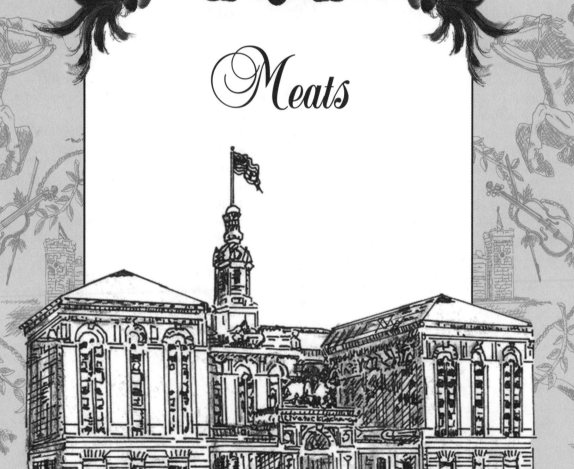

Meats

Livestock Exchange

Meats

Tenderloin with Roasted Shallots

1 whole tenderloin of beef
(3 to 4 pounds), trimmed
2 tablespoons melted unsalted
butter

2 tablespoons soy sauce
1 medium shallot, finely chopped

Roasted Shallots

18 large shallots, peeled, with tips
of root ends removed
1 tablespoon butter
½ cup whipping cream
2 tablespoons Madeira wine

1½ teaspoons chopped fresh
tarragon
¼ teaspoon salt
Finely ground white pepper, to
taste

Preheat oven to 400 degrees. Prepare the roast by tucking the tail under the meat so that roast is of uniform thickness. Tie meat tightly with heavy string, lengthwise and crosswise. Place on roasting rack and roast for 45 to 50 minutes, until a meat thermometer registers 140 degrees for rare or 160 degrees for medium. Check temperature after 25 minutes. Remove beef and let stand for 10 minutes. Leave oven on at 400 degrees.

Bring water to a boil in a medium saucepan, add shallots, and boil 2 minutes. Drain. Place shallots in a small baking dish and dot with butter. Place in oven and roast for 10 minutes.

In a small bowl, mix cream with Madeira, tarragon, salt, and pepper. Pour over shallots. Return shallots to oven and roast 30 to 35 minutes, watching carefully to see that cream does not separate. Stir gently and reduce heat, if necessary.

To serve, slice tenderloin diagonally and spoon 3 shallots with a little sauce onto each serving. Serve immediately.

Hint: Ask your butcher to tie the meat. Also, the shallots may be roasted and covered in cream mixture a day in advance. Allow to sit at room temperature for 30 minutes before proceeding.

Yield: 6 to 8 servings

Rouxminations

The Cow Palace

The Exchange Building, part of the St. Joseph Stock Yards, was home to the stock yards bank. The exchange building housed 32 firms to buy, sell, and handle the stock that was shipped daily.

Swift Move

Gustavus F. Swift came to St. Joseph in 1896 and purchased a majority of the property of the St. Joseph Stock Yards Company. In 1898, Swift and Company opened for business.

Rouxminations

Legally Speaking

The Junior League of St. Joseph provided financial assistance in cooperation with the local United Way to establish the Legal Aid Office in 1976. This agency was still under the United Way umbrella in 2001. The League received recognition in 1999 for its contribution in initiating this program.

Filet of Beef Balsamico with Red Onion Confit

¼	cup balsamic vinegar		Salt
2	tablespoons lemon juice	15	peppercorns, coarsely crushed
1	cup red wine	1	(3 to 3½ pound) filet of beef
¼	cup extra virgin olive oil	½	cup unsalted butter
¼	cup coarsely chopped fresh rosemary	1	cup sour cream
2	large cloves garlic, peeled and crushed	2	tablespoons prepared horseradish

Red Onion Confit

4	tablespoons extra virgin olive oil	¼	cup red wine vinegar
		¼	cup water
2	large red onions, sliced ¼-inch thick	2	teaspoons sugar
		¼	teaspoon salt
½	cup red wine	¼	teaspoon pepper

Whisk together vinegar, lemon juice, red wine, oil, rosemary, garlic, salt, and peppercorns in a large bowl. Add filet, turning to coat well. Cover and marinate overnight in refrigerator, turning meat several times.

Heat a grill until hot. Grill filet until medium rare, 145 degrees on a meat thermometer, about 30 minutes. If roasting in oven, heat to 450 degrees; heat a large heavy iron skillet until very hot. Place filet in pan and cook until brown on all sides, 5 to 10 minutes. Place skillet in oven and roast until meat is medium rare, about 20 minutes. Remove from pan and let cool to room temperature.

Combine sour cream and horseradish. Set aside.

For Red Onion Confit: Heat oil over low heat in a medium sauté pan. Cook the onions, stirring often, until very soft, 15 to 20 minutes. Add wine, vinegar, water, and sugar, and raise heat to medium. Cook uncovered for about 15 minutes. Season with salt and pepper.

To serve as a main course, slice filet and serve with horseradish sauce and confit on the side. To assemble as an hors d'oeuvres, slice filets into ¼-inch-thick slices. Slice 2 thin baguettes into 20 slices each, spread with butter, and lightly toast. Spread a little horseradish sauce on toast and top with a slice of beef. Garnish with red onion confit and additional rosemary.

Hint: This beef is especially delicious when grilled. This also works with pork tenderloin.

Yield: 6 entrée servings or 10 appetizer servings

Filet Mignon with Mushroom Wine Sauce

1	tablespoon margarine, divided	Cracked pepper
⅓	cup finely chopped shallots	4 (4 ounce) filet mignon steaks
½	pound fresh shiitake mushrooms, stems removed	1 tablespoon soy sauce
1½	cups dry red wine, divided	2 teaspoons cornstarch
1	(10½ ounce) can beef consommé, undiluted and divided	1 tablespoon fresh chopped thyme or 1 teaspoon dried

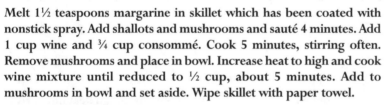

Melt 1½ teaspoons margarine in skillet which has been coated with nonstick spray. Add shallots and mushrooms and sauté 4 minutes. Add 1 cup wine and ¾ cup consommé. Cook 5 minutes, stirring often. Remove mushrooms and place in bowl. Increase heat to high and cook wine mixture until reduced to ½ cup, about 5 minutes. Add to mushrooms in bowl and set aside. Wipe skillet with paper towel.

Sprinkle pepper to taste on steaks. Grill to desired doneness, place on serving platter, and keep warm.

Combine soy sauce and cornstarch; stir well. Add remaining ½ cup wine and consommé to skillet, scraping skillet with wooden spoon to loosen browned bits. Bring to a boil and cook 1 minute. Add mushroom mixture, cornstarch mixture, and thyme. Bring to a boil and cook, stirring constantly, 1 minute. Serve with steaks.

Yield: 4 servings

Rouxminations

Meat Me in St. Joe

Meat packing has been active in St. Joseph from the early days. With the opening of the St. Joseph Stock Yards in 1887 and the opening of several new packing houses from then through 1923, St. Joseph became an important meat packing center. The industry provided a leading source of revenue for the City and its surrounding agricultural area.

Rouxminations

Building Community

The St. Joseph Junior League adopted the CASA (Court Appointed Special Advocate) Project, and also partnered with the YWCA to assist in the construction of an interview room used to tape testimony of abused children in the mid 1990s. Also, the PATHS (Preserving Architecture Through Historic Study) walking tour of historic downtown was implemented and recognized with a grant from the National Trust for Historic Preservation.

Smoky Bourbon Beef Filets de Robidoux

3 cups dry red wine	1 pound bacon, cut into ¼-inch pieces
6 cloves garlic, chopped	
3½ cups canned beef broth	2 tablespoons all-purpose flour
2½ cups low-salt chicken broth	2 tablespoons butter, divided
3 tablespoons tomato paste	8 (1-inch-thick) beef tenderloin steaks
2 bay leaves	
2 fresh thyme sprigs	2 tablespoons bourbon

Boil wine and garlic in heavy medium saucepan until reduced to 1 cup, about 25 minutes. (You certainly do not need to stand over it, just kind of keep an eye in that direction.) Add beef and chicken broth, tomato paste, bay leaves, and thyme; boil until reduced by half, again about 25 minutes. Set sauce aside. Sprinkle steaks with salt and pepper on both sides.

Cook bacon in heavy large skillet over medium-high heat until crisp, about 8 minutes. Using slotted spoon, transfer to paper towels. Pour off all but 1 tablespoon drippings from skillet and to this add 1 tablespoon of butter. Melt butter over medium-high heat. Add steaks to skillet and sauté until brown on outside with center raw. Remove steaks and arrange in 9 x 13-inch casserole.

Add remaining tablespoon of butter to skillet and scrape browned bits up (if skillet is really dry, add another tablespoon of bacon drippings). Add flour to skillet, whisking to blend. Cook 1 minute, whisking constantly. Gradually, whisk in sauce and bring to a boil. Reduce heat and simmer for about 5 minutes, until sauce thickens. Remove sauce from heat; remove bay leaf and thyme sprig. Stir bacon and bourbon into sauce and pour over steaks.

At this point, steaks may be covered and refrigerated overnight. Allow steaks to come to room temperature before cooking.

Preheat oven to 400 degrees. Bake steaks, uncovered, 15 to 20 minutes for rare, 20 to 25 minutes for medium to medium-well.

Yield: 8 servings

Perfect Prime Rib

1 standing rib roast   Seasoning salt
Garlic, minced   Ground pepper

Preheat oven to 400 degrees. Place beef in roasting pan. Rub with garlic, salt, and pepper. Place, uncovered, in oven for 1 hour. Turn oven off and DO NOT OPEN DOOR of oven at all. Let sit until ready for dinner. It is best to do this early in the morning and let it stay in oven all day.

Before mealtime, bring oven back up to 350 degrees. After the oven reaches 350 degrees, cook for 45 minutes for rare, 50 minutes for medium and 55 minutes for medium well. Remove from oven and let rest 15 minutes before slicing. That's all. Don't think. Just do it!

Hint: The classic, in case you haven't heard or have forgotten.

Rosemary Rib Roast

1 (5 pound) certified Angus beef rib roast
   Balsamic vinegar
2 tablespoons minced garlic
2 tablespoons fresh thyme or 2 teaspoons dried
1 tablespoon fresh rosemary or 1 teaspoon dried
2 tablespoons salt
1 tablespoon olive oil

Preheat oven to 450 degrees. Place roast fat side up on a rack in shallow roasting pan. Brush entire surface of roast with balsamic vinegar. Combine garlic, thyme, rosemary, salt, and olive oil to make a paste. Coat top, ends, and sides of roast with herb paste.

Place beef in the oven and roast for 15 minutes. Reduce heat to 350 degrees and continue roasting for 2 hours for a medium degree of doneness. Remove from oven and allow roast to stand for 5 to 10 minutes; slice across the grain.

Yield: 10 to 12 servings

Rouxminations

St. Joseph's Triple A

The headquarters of American Angus Association have been located in St. Joseph since 1956. As the world's largest beef breed organization, the American Angus Association provides programs and services for more than 35,000 members and thousands of commercial beef producers nationwide.

Stockyard Beef

4   cloves garlic, minced
½   cup grated Parmesan cheese
3   tablespoons butter, softened
1   tablespoon Marsala wine
1½ teaspoons brandy
1   teaspoon tomato paste
¼   teaspoon salt
½   teaspoon black pepper
1   (1½ to 2 pound) sirloin steak, 4 strip steaks, or 4 filet mignons

Combine garlic, Parmesan, butter, wine, brandy, tomato paste, salt, and black pepper in a food processor. Blend to a paste.

Grill steaks over medium-hot coals, almost to desired degree of doneness, turning once. Remove from grill and spread paste evenly over steak. Return to grill, paste-side-up and cook until mixture begins to bubble, about 1 to 2 minutes longer. Serve immediately.

Yield: 4 servings

Grilled Tequila Sirloin

1   (4 pound) sirloin tip roast
½   cup fresh lime juice
½   cup chopped fresh cilantro
½   cup olive oil
⅓   cup soy sauce
¼   cup tequila
7   cloves garlic, finely chopped
2   teaspoons grated lime peel
2   teaspoons ground cumin
2   teaspoons dried oregano
1   teaspoon ground black pepper

Pierce meat all over with a small knife and place in a large resealable plastic bag. Whisk together remaining ingredients and pour over meat. Seal bag and refrigerate at least 2 hours or overnight, turning bag occasionally.

Preheat barbecue to medium-high heat. Remove meat from marinade and grill to desired doneness, about 10 minutes per side for medium rare. Transfer to cutting board. Tent with foil; let stand 10 minutes. Cut diagonally across grain and serve immediately.

Hint: Serve this topped with Cherry Tomato Relish, page 131.

Yield: 8 servings

Sirloin Skewers with Peanut Sauce

2	cloves garlic, minced or pressed	1	teaspoon ground coriander
4	tablespoons soy sauce	1	(1½ pound) boneless top
2	tablespoons vegetable oil		sirloin, cut into 1-inch cubes
1	teaspoon ground cumin		Fresh cilantro, optional

Basting Sauce

3	tablespoons fresh lemon juice	¼	teaspoon ground cumin
2	tablespoons soy sauce	¼	teaspoon ground coriander

Peanut Sauce

1	cup water	1½	tablespoons fresh lemon juice
⅔	cup creamy peanut butter		
2	cloves garlic, minced or pressed	1	tablespoon soy sauce
2	tablespoons firmly packed brown sugar	¼-½	teaspoon crushed red pepper (to taste)

Combine garlic, soy sauce, vegetable oil, cumin, and coriander in a bowl. Whisk well. Add meat and marinate at least 2 hours or overnight.

For Basting Sauce: Combine all ingredients in a small bowl and whisk well. (This may be made up to 2 days in advance.)

For Peanut Sauce: In a 2-quart pan, combine water, peanut butter, and garlic. Cook over medium-low heat, stirring constantly, about 5 minutes, until mixture begins to thicken. Raise temperature to medium and bring to a boil. Remove from heat and stir in brown sugar, lemon juice, soy sauce, and red pepper. This should be served hot, but can be made ahead and refrigerated for up to 2 days. To reheat, stir over low heat until hot, adding a bit more water if necessary to restore to original consistency. Makes 2 cups.

Bring grill temperature to medium heat. Lift meat from marinade and drain briefly. Thread 4 to 5 pieces on each skewer. Arrange skewers on hot grill. Cook, turning often. After about the first 5 minutes, brush all over with basting sauce. Do this twice, if possible. Cook until well browned and done to your liking. Cut to test (about 8 to 10 minutes for medium rare). Remove from grill and serve with warm peanut sauce. Garnish with fresh cilantro.

Hint: To save time, use purchased peanut sauce. Look for it in the Oriental section of the supermarket. Chicken can be substituted for the sirloin for a variation.

Yield: 4 servings

Rouxminations

The Best of The Best

Angus beef is known worldwide as the best in beef, regarded for its tenderness and superior taste. For the best beef-eating experience, always look for the certified Angus Beef brand.

Flank Steak Three Ways

2   pounds flank steak

Rosemary Garlic Marinade

1   cup dry red wine
2   teaspoons chopped fresh rosemary or ½ teaspoon dried
2   teaspoons olive oil

1   teaspoon coarsely ground black pepper
½   teaspoon salt
4   teaspoons minced garlic

Southwestern Marinade

1   (10 ounce) can beer
¼   cup chopped cilantro
1   teaspoon minced garlic
¼   cup fresh lime juice
2   tablespoons red wine vinegar

1   tablespoon Worcestershire sauce
1   tablespoon grated lime rind
1   teaspoon cumin
1   tablespoon chili powder

Soy-Honey Marinade

¼   cup low-salt soy sauce
¼   cup rice vinegar
¼   cup honey

1   teaspoon minced garlic
1½ teaspoons dried ground ginger

Choose a marinade. Combine all marinade ingredients and mix well. Pour into a zip-top plastic bag. Add meat, seal bag, and refrigerate over night. Drain well and grill or broil until done. Do not overcook; this cut of meat is better when cooked to medium, about 4 minutes per side. Remove from heat and let stand for 5 minutes. Slice across grain into thin slices and serve immediately.

Hint: The rosemary garlic flank steak is great topped with caramelized onions (made with a touch of red wine vinegar and brown sugar), and the southwestern flank steak is perfect for fajitas.

Yield: 4 servings

Chicken-Fried Steak Strips with Milk Gravy

1	small onion	1	(1 pound) round steak, tenderized and cut into 4 x ½ x ½-inch strips
2	garlic cloves		Flour seasoned with salt and pepper
2	large eggs		Oil for frying
½	cup milk		

Milk Gravy

1 tablespoon all-purpose flour   Salt and pepper to taste
2 cups milk

In a food processor fitted with steel blade, chop onion and garlic until fine in texture. Remove from food processor and beat together with eggs and milk until well blended. Dip steak strips into egg mixture and dredge them in seasoned flour, shaking off excess.

Heat about ¼ inch of oil in a large skillet over medium-high heat. Fry steak in batches, turning until golden brown on all sides, about 2 to 3 minutes per side. Transfer to a paper towel and keep warm in a 200 degree oven.

For Milk Gravy: Pour off all oil and save 2 tablespoons of the drippings. Heat drippings over medium heat and add the flour. Cook, stirring, for 3 to 5 minutes. Add the milk in a stream, whisking. Simmer over low heat, whisking, until gravy is thickened, about 5 minutes.

Serve the strips with gravy on the side.

Yield: 4 servings

Rouxminations

What kind of kids like Armour hot dogs? (Sing along! Fat kids, skinny kids, kids who climb on rocks? Tough kids, sissy kids, even kids with chicken pox, like hot dogs, Armour hot dogs. The dogs kids love to bite.)

Amour and company purchased the Hammond plant in 1912, and with Swift became the two principal meat-packing plants in St. Joseph. Also doing a good business at the time was Seitz Packing Company.

Rouxminations

A Shooting Star

According the 1900 Journal of Commerce, "the career [of the Stock Yards] has been meteoric, and the continuous and phenomenal increase in receipts is but the brilliant tail of the 'new comet' in the live stock and packing firmament."

Brisket with Portobello Mushrooms and Dried Cranberries

1	cup dry red wine	1½	tablespoons chopped fresh rosemary
1	cup canned beef or chicken broth	1	(4 pound) trimmed brisket
½	cup frozen cranberry juice cocktail concentrate, thawed		Salt and pepper to taste
¼	cup all-purpose flour	12	ounces medium portobello mushrooms, dark gills scraped away, thinly sliced
1	large onion, sliced		
4	cloves garlic, chopped	1	cup dried cranberries (4 ounces) or Craisins

Preheat oven to 300 degrees. Whisk wine, broth, cranberry concentrate, and flour together in medium bowl. Pour into 15 x 10 x 2-inch roasting pan. Mix in onion, garlic, and rosemary. Season brisket on all sides with salt and pepper. Place brisket, fat side up, in roasting pan. Spoon wine mixture over top. Cover tightly with heavy-duty foil. Bake brisket until very tender, basting with pan juices every hour, about 3½ to 4½ hours.

Transfer brisket to plate and cool 1 hour at room temperature. Thinly slice brisket across the grain. Return slices to pan, overlapping slices slightly. (Brisket can be prepared 2 days ahead; cover and refrigerate.)

Preheat oven to 350 degrees. Place mushrooms and cranberries in sauce around brisket. Cover pan with foil and bake until mushrooms are tender and brisket is heated through, about 30 minutes, or 45 minutes if brisket has been refrigerated. Transfer sliced brisket to platter with all its trimmings and serve.

Hint: This is always better if prepared a day ahead.

Yield: 8 servings

Make Ahead Beef and Cheese Enchiladas

1 pound ground beef	12 (8 inch) flour tortillas
1 package taco seasoning mix	16 ounces Velveeta cheese, cut in
¼ cup plus 2 tablespoons	1-inch cubes
cornstarch	¼ cup dry onion flakes
4 tablespoons chili powder	¼ cup butter, divided

Brown ground beef, drain, and add taco seasoning. Mix until well combined, remove from heat, and set aside.

Put 4 cups water in a large skillet over medium-high heat (use a Dutch oven if you are doing more than 1 batch at a time.) While it is heating, combine ¾ cup of cold water and cornstarch in a small bowl. Stir vigorously with a fork until the mixture is completely blended and no lumps remain. Add to water in skillet. Stir to blend completely and then stir occasionally for about 10 minutes, until the sauce resembles thin gravy and coats a spoon, but will still pour off of it in a steady stream. Add chili powder and stir until well combined. Reduce heat to lowest setting.

To assemble enchiladas, drop a tortilla into sauce and coat both sides. Remove to a large plate. In center of tortilla, spread ¼ cup of beef mixture in a line, stopping ½ inch from each end. Place 3 to 4 cubes of cheese on top of beef and sprinkle about ¾ teaspoon of onion flakes. (Cheese and onion flakes are really to taste- strictly a matter of personal preference.) Roll up tightly and wrap in plastic wrap. Repeat procedure until all enchiladas are assembled. Place in freezer.

Before serving, thaw enchiladas on defrost setting in microwave. Heat enough butter in skillet to coat the bottom, add thawed enchiladas, and fry until golden brown on both sides.

Hint: Mass produce these with a friend. They are great to have on hand for kids and husbands to heat up for themselves. Teenagers love these!

Yield: 12 servings

Rouxminations

Certifiable

In 1978, the American Angus Association established Certified Angus Beef, which has grown to be the world's largest breed-specific branded beef program. Consumers around the world love the taste of certified Angus beef products.

Meatballs with Bell Pepper Sauce

½	pound ground beef	1	teaspoon minced garlic
½	pound Italian sausage	1	tablespoon Italian seasoning
4	slices white bread, toasted	1	teaspoon salt
2	eggs, lightly beaten	¼	teaspoon pepper
½	cup grated Parmesan cheese		Olive oil

Combine beef and sausage in a medium bowl and blend very well. Crumble toast, by hand or in food processor and add to beef mix. Add eggs, Parmesan, garlic, Italian seasoning, salt and pepper and combine well. Form meatballs, using about 1 tablespoon of mixture for each.

Preheat oven to 350 degrees. Coat a large cookie sheet with nonstick spray. Coat the bottom of a large skillet with olive oil and brown meatballs over medium-high heat. Cook, in 2 to 3 batches, until just browned. Using a slotted spoon, remove from skillet and place on prepared cookie sheet. Bake until just cooked through, about 10 to 15 minutes. Remove from oven and add to pot of bell pepper sauce, see following recipe. Simmer for at least 30 minutes, or up to 2 hours, on low.

Hint: These can be made a day in advance. Reheat before serving. They can also be frozen for up to a month.

Yield: 6 servings

Rouxminations

What's In A Name

Originally known as Blueside, Prime Tanning Corporation is one of the world's largest tanneries. After a several step process, including the application of numerous chemicals, the hides are ready for shipping. Before this point, the sides of leather turn a greenish blue color —a phenomenon from which Blueside derived its name. The color may be pretty, but the smell sure ain't!

Bell Pepper Tomato Sauce

3 tablespoons olive oil	4 tablespoons tomato paste
1 large onion, chopped	¼ cup chopped fresh parsley
4 cloves garlic, minced	½ teaspoon dried basil
1 large green bell pepper, seeded and cut into 1-inch cubes	½ teaspoon dried oregano
	½ teaspoon thyme
1 large yellow bell pepper, seeded and cut into 1-inch cubes	2 cups dry red wine, such as Cabernet Sauvignon
	1 teaspoon salt
2 (28 ounce) cans diced tomatoes with roasted garlic, onion, and oregano	½ teaspoon pepper

In Dutch oven, heat oil over medium high heat. Add onion, garlic, and bell peppers. Cook about 5 minutes, until vegetables begin to soften. Add tomatoes and cook 5 minutes. Stir in tomato paste, herbs, wine, salt, and pepper. Cook over medium heat, stirring occasionally, for 20 minutes. Serve over favorite pasta.

Hint: Shrimp, crab, and/or clams may be added to make a seafood stew. Simmer for a couple of hours for optimum flavor.

Grilled Pork Tenderloin with Plum Glaze

1 cup plum preserves	⅛ cup packed brown sugar
¼ cup Dijon mustard	¼ cup rice or other vinegar
⅛ cup honey	1 (1½ pound) pork tenderloin

Combine preserves, mustard, honey, brown sugar, and vinegar in a saucepan over low heat. Cook, stirring, until sugar and preserves melt.

Prepare grill. Dip pork in glaze and place on grill (this should use about half of the glaze). Grill for 13 to 15 minutes a side depending on your fire. Brush with remaining glaze when you turn the meat.

Yield: 2 servings

Rouxminations

Brain Freeze

Included among the popular eateries of modern St. Joseph was Miller's Grill, which was locally famous for its brain sandwiches and tenderloins. Another popular St. Joseph hang out was the Bucket Shop which served beef burgers and served several international beers. The recipe for the beef burgers was widely sought. Neither restaurant is open today.

Honey Hoisin Pork Tenderloin with Blue Cheese Cream Sauce

¼ cup hoisin sauce (sold in oriental section of grocery store)
¼ cup soy sauce
¼ cup honey

1 tablespoon minced garlic
1 tablespoon grated fresh ginger
2 (1¼ pound) pork tenderloins
Blue Cheese Cream Sauce (see following recipe)

Mix hoisin sauce, soy sauce, honey, garlic, and ginger in a small bowl with a whisk. Place tenderloins in a shallow dish or Ziploc bag. Pour marinade over meat and refrigerate. Marinate 6 hours or preferably overnight, turning tenderloin several times.

Preheat oven to 400 degrees. Remove pork from marinade and discard marinade. Place pork on a baking sheet which has been coated with nonstick spray. Roast in oven until juices run clear (about 18 to 20 minutes). Allow to rest 10 minutes before slicing. Slice and serve with Blue Cheese Cream Sauce.

Hint: To prepare ahead, make an extra batch of marinade, perhaps lighter on the garlic. Roast until meat registers 160 degrees with meat thermometer. Let cool for 10 minutes and slice. Arrange slices on foil-lined cookie sheet. Spoon some of the marinade over each slice, cover, and refrigerate. Reheat for about 15 minutes at 350 degrees.

Yield: 4 servings

Move Over Donna Karan

Sylvia Einbender, a St. Joseph fashion guru, created white shuttered changing rooms large enough for several women and shopping there was literally an all-day affair. Her maxim was "you can't sell a tired or hungry customer;" so she often had food and cocktails brought in for her clients. No wonder some ended up spending a small fortune for a day's shopping!

Blue Cheese Cream Sauce

¼ cup dry vermouth
    (or dry white wine-
    not cooking wine!)

½ cup whipping cream
¼ cup crumbled blue cheese
    (1 ounce)

In a small saucepan, over medium heat, simmer and reduce vermouth to about 2 tablespoons. Whisk in cream and reduce to about a third of a cup. (This should take about 10 minutes). Remove pan from direct heat and immediately whisk in blue cheese. Whisk until sauce is smooth. Keep warm by either putting saucepan in a skillet of hot water, in a thermos, or - our favorite - in a plastic squeeze bottle submersed three-quarters of the way up in warm water.

Hint: You can double and triple this. But, keep in mind that doing so will drastically increase the amount of time that it takes to reduce the sauce, and you MUST reduce. The reduction intensifies the flavor, and it is just not the same sauce at all if you don't reduce it enough. Also, the reduction of the vermouth in the first step is necessary to keep the cream from curdling in the second step. DO NOT use anything other than whipping cream. Milk and other lower-fat dairy products are not suitable for reduction sauces of this nature.

If you do decide to double the recipe, using half Gruyère cheese is great. (You can always add a little extra cheese if you desire to thicken the sauce a bit more.)

Yield: 1 cup

Rouxminations

Hot Diggity Dog

The meat processing tradition in St. Joseph continues today at Sara Lee Corporation's Seitz meat processing plant. The 250,000-square foot plant employs 400 who produce Hillshire Farm Deli Select, Hillshire Farm smoked sausage, Seitz hot dogs and luncheon meats and Ballpark franks. You can sample the famous Seitz hot dog at Kaufman Stadium, home of the Kansas City Royals baseball team.

Pork Tenderloin in Puff Pastry with Orange Balsamic Sauce

1   (1½ pound) trimmed pork tenderloin
1   tablespoon brown sugar
2   tablespoons brandy
½   sprig fresh rosemary, stemmed, chopped
¼   teaspoon ground pepper
2   tablespoons butter, divided
1   (6 ounce) package fresh spinach, rinsed, stems removed
1   clove garlic, minced
½   (17¼ ounce) box frozen puff pastry, thawed (1 sheet)
1   egg yolk, beaten with 1 teaspoon water
    Orange Balsamic Sauce (see page 127)

Place tenderloin in a glass baking dish. In small bowl, combine brown sugar, brandy, rosemary, and pepper. Rub over pork. Cover and marinate in refrigerator overnight.

In large skillet, over medium-high heat, melt 1 tablespoon butter. Add spinach and garlic; cook until limp. Drain spinach and set aside.

Remove tenderloin from marinade, discarding marinade. In same skillet over medium-high heat, cook pork in remaining 1 tablespoon butter until browned on all sides, about 10 minutes. Set aside to cool slightly. Reserve browned bits in skillet to make sauce.

Place puff pastry on lightly floured work surface. Roll dough length-wise until it is 2 inches longer than tenderloin. Place cooked spinach down center of pastry in a 2-inch wide strip. Place pork on top of spinach. Fold ends of pastry over pork, and tightly roll to completely enclose pork, pinching edges to seal. Place seam-side-down on parchment-lined shallow baking sheet. Use extra pastry to make a design on top. Brush with egg yolk. Refrigerate for 30 minutes to 1 hour.

While pork is chilling, preheat oven to 375 degrees. Bake tenderloin until pastry is golden brown and internal temperature is 155 degrees, about 23 to 25 minutes. Let stand 5 minutes before cutting into 6 slices. Serve immediately with sauce.

Yield: 4 servings

Orange Balsamic Sauce

10 tablespoons butter, divided	2 tablespoons balsamic vinegar
½ small yellow onion, diced	½ sprig fresh rosemary, stemmed and chopped
2 cloves garlic, minced	
1 teaspoon brown sugar	1½ tablespoons whipping cream
Grated peel and juice of 1 medium orange	1 teaspoon cracked black pepper Salt and pepper to taste

In the same skillet the pork was browned, melt 1 tablespoon butter, over medium-high heat. Add onion and garlic, sauté 3 to 4 minutes. Add brown sugar, cook 1 minute. Add vinegar, orange peel, orange juice and rosemayr. Reduce mixture to about half, stirring occasionally. Strain liquid into a small saucepan. Add whipping cream and pepper. Place over medium heat and whisk in remaining butter, 1 tablespoon at a time. Season with salt and pepper to taste. Serve immediately.

Yield: ½ cup

Pork Roast with Apples and Onions

1 (6 pound) pork loin	1 large onion, sliced thin
1 teaspoon sage	3 tablespoons brown sugar
1 teaspoon thyme	½ cup chicken stock or water
1 teaspoon marjoram	⅓ cup whipping cream
Salt and pepper to taste	1 pinch nutmeg
2 tart apples, peeled, cored, and sliced	

Trim the pork of any fat. Mix sage, thyme, marjoram, salt, and pepper, and rub into roast. Refrigerate for several hours.

Preheat oven to 325 degrees. Place pork on roasting rack in pan and roast for 1½ hours. Combine apples, onion, and brown sugar until well mixed. Spread evenly over pork and roast until meat thermometer reaches 170 degrees internal temperature, about 1 more hour.

Place roast on platter, spreading apples and onions around the pork. Carve the meat into ½-inch slices. Skim fat from pan juices, add chicken stock or water, cream, and nutmeg. Place over medium heat, bring to a boil, and cook until reduced by half and thickened. Serve sauce on side with pork roast.

Yield: 10 to 12 servings

Rouxminations

Cowboy Dome Home

John B. Stetson made St. Joseph the home for his famous business, Stetson Hats. John Wayne, the quintessential cowboy, Garth Brooks, George W. Bush and other celebrities and figureheads too numerous to name own Stetsons, because it is commonly regarded as THE cowboy hat to own.

No Chads On This Hat

Today the Stetson hat factory in St. Joseph is one of the largest in the country, and its adjacent outlet store is the number one tourist attraction in town. The local factory produces a line of hats in hundreds of styles and colors, including one owned by President George W. Bush.

Rouxminations

Where's The Beef

American Angus relocated their offices from Chicago to St. Joseph in the late 1950s. St. Joseph was chosen as its new headquarters because Missouri offered a central location, was home to a significant number of registered Angus breeders, and was the second largest beef cattle state in the nation.

Stuffed Pork Chops with Apple Bread Dressing

Stuffing

½	cup dry bread crumbs	3	eggs, beaten
1	cup coarse corn bread crumbs	¼	cup chopped walnuts
1¼	teaspoons salt	½	cup chopped apples
¼	teaspoon freshly ground pepper		

Chops

6	(10 ounce) center-cut pork chops, thick enough to cut a pocket in side		Salt and pepper to taste
		3	tablespoons butter

Tangy Sauce

¼	cup firmly packed brown sugar	¼	cup raisins, optional
¾	teaspoon prepared mustard	¼	cup red wine
1½	teaspoons flour	¾	cup water

Preheat oven to 325 degrees.

For Stuffing: Toss bread and corn bread crumbs together in a large bowl. Add salt, pepper, eggs, and walnuts. Dressing should be fairly fluffy. Add apples and mix well.

For Chops: Cut pockets in sides of chops, being careful not to cut clear through to the other side. Stuff each chop with dressing and skewer edges closed with toothpicks. Season with salt and pepper. Melt butter in a heavy skillet and cook chops about 6 minutes per side, until golden brown, turning carefully. Transfer to a baking dish and bake, uncovered, until juices run clear, about 30 minutes.

For Sauce: While chops are cooking, combine brown sugar, mustard and flour in a saucepan. Add raisins, if desired, wine, and water and bring to a boil. Lower heat and simmer about 10 minutes, stirring constantly.

To serve, remove toothpicks and spoon sauce over chops.

Hint: To soften and season the meat for this or any recipe calling for a savory chop, soak chops overnight in 2 cups of water mixed with ¼ cup brown or white sugar, ¼ cup salt, and a bit of crushed red pepper. The amounts can be adjusted; just be sure to use an equal amount of salt to sugar.

Yield: 6 servings

Marinated Mango Grilled Pork Chops with Mango Black Bean Salsa

1	cup red wine vinegar	1	large mango, peeled and pureed
1	cup sugar	4	(5 ounce) pork chops
1	tablespoon whole black peppercorns		Olive oil
			Salt to taste

Salsa

2	large mangoes, peeled and coarsely chopped	1	tablespoon seeded and finely diced serrano pepper
1	cup cooked black beans or canned beans, rinsed and drained	¼	cup fresh lime juice
		2	tablespoons olive oil
	Green onions, finely sliced	2	tablespoons honey
		¼	cup chopped cilantro
			Salt and pepper to taste

Place vinegar, sugar, and peppercorns in a saucepan. Bring to a boil and reduce until thickened, stirring occasionally. Whisk in mango puree and cook 1 minute. Strain into a bowl and set aside.

Preheat grill. Brush pork chops with olive oil on both sides and season with salt. Grill for 5 minutes on each side for medium doneness. Remove and brush liberally with the mango glaze.

For Salsa: Combine all ingredients in a medium bowl. Let sit 30 minutes before serving.

To serve, top each pork chop with generous serving of salsa.

Hint: Recipe may be doubled. This is very easy, but looks and tastes gourmet. Don't be scared off by the mangoes; grocery stores routinely stock them these days.

Yield: 4 servings

Rouxminations

Mutton Bustin' Included

St. Joseph celebrates the Southside Fall Festival every year on the third weekend of September. It features a professional rodeo in the Stock Yard Arena, parade, booths, crafts, entertainment and of course, food.

Dickey's Ribs

1	cup paprika	1	cup black pepper
1	cup Lawry's seasoned salt	½	cup lemon pepper
½	cup garlic salt	¼	cup red pepper or to taste
½	cup onion salt	1	slab pork spareribs
½	cup cumin		Honey

Mix dry ingredients well. Do not trim fat from ribs. Sprinkle mix evenly over ribs and pound into meat. Cover and refrigerate for 1 day.

Start grill, beginning with charcoal, then add hickory or apple wood. Using a rib rack, place ribs on grill, meat-side-up. Cook over a water pan, 3 to 5 hours, without allowing temperature to exceed 250 degrees.

When meat is pink, usually after it has cooked about 4 hours, baste with honey. Cook another 30 to 45 minutes. Remove from fire, baste with your favorite sauce, slice the ribs, and baste again. Serve.

Hint: Store extra dry rub in an airtight container for up to a year.

Easy Barbecue Ribs

1-2	baby back pork ribs (about 4¼ pounds)	2-3 teaspoons Chef Paul's seasonings or your favorite seasoning mix
2	cans beer	KC Masterpiece BBQ sauce

Preheat oven to 250 degrees. Place ribs in a roasting pan. Pour beer over ribs and sprinkle liberally with Chef Paul's seasonings or Magie's Pepper Sauce. Bake in oven for 3 hours.

Bring grill temperature to medium-high heat. Remove ribs from oven and transfer to grill. Sear both sides on grill. Brush with sauce and allow sauce to then sear onto meat. Remove from grill and serve with extra sauce, if desired.

Yield: 6 servings

Bed and Breakfast Bake

2 cups seasoned croutons	6 eggs
1 cup shredded Cheddar cheese	2½ cups milk, divided
1 (4 ounce) can mushroom pieces, drained	½ teaspoon salt
	½ teaspoon pepper
1½ pounds bulk fresh country sausage, crumbled	½ teaspoon dry mustard
	1 (10¾ ounce) can cream of mushroom soup
½ cup chopped onion	

Place croutons in greased 9 x 13-inch baking pan. Top with cheese and mushrooms. Brown sausage and onion. Drain and spread over cheese. Beat eggs with 2 cups milk and seasonings; pour over sausage. Cover and refrigerate overnight. (May be frozen at this point.) Mix soup with remaining milk until smooth. Spread over dish. Bake in 325 degree oven until a knife inserted in center comes out clean, about 1 hour.

Yield: 12 servings

Cherry Tomato Relish

¼ cup balsamic vinegar	⅔ cup drained canned diced mild green chiles
4 teaspoons chopped fresh oregano	4 green onions, finely chopped
¾ cup olive oil	4 cups halved cherry tomatoes
	Salt and pepper

Whisk vinegar and oregano in medium bowl to blend. Gradually whisk in oil. Mix in green chiles and green onions. (Can be made to this point up to a day ahead. Cover and chill.) Just before serving, add tomatoes and toss to coat. Season with salt and pepper

Hint: Great on top of grilled meats.

Yield: 5½ cups

Rouxminations

Before Power Tools

The Wyeth Hardware and Manufacturing Company of St. Joseph was incorporated in 1880 and became the largest wholesale hardware, saddlery, and tinware house west of the Mississippi River. The five story office building which housed the different operations was built in 1890 on North Second Street.

Ham with Grits and Greens Stuffing

1   pound greens (spinach, mustard, collard greens, kale, or turnip greens), washed, deveined, and stemmed
5   tablespoons unsalted butter, plus more for baking dish
1   cup finely chopped yellow onion
4   cloves garlic, finely chopped
½   cup dry white wine
3   cups milk
1   cup whipping cream

1   cup quick grits
1½   cups freshly grated Parmesan cheese, divided
½   teaspoon fresh thyme leaves
2   tablespoons chopped fresh parsley
    Coarse salt and pepper
1   (10 pound) bone-in ham, preferably Smithfield
2   large eggs, well beaten
    Cheesecloth and twine

Stack several greens on top of 1 another, roll tightly, and cut into thin strips. Continue with all the greens. In a large sauté pan, heat butter over medium heat. Add onion and garlic and cook until translucent, about 10 minutes. Add wine and greens. Partially cover, reduce heat to a simmer, and cook until greens are very tender, 40 to 45 minutes. Remove greens to a bowl and allow to cool completely.

Wrap greens in several layers of cheesecloth and squeeze, removing excess moisture.

Meanwhile, combine milk and cream in medium saucepan over medium heat until simmering. Stir in grits. Cook 5 minutes, stirring frequently to prevent bottom from burning. Remove from heat and stir in 1 cup Parmesan, thyme, salt, pepper, and parsley. Spread mixture on a cookie sheet to cool. Add cooled grits to the greens. Stir in eggs and mix well.

Preheat oven to 350 degrees. Remove bone from ham. With a sharp knife, remove fat and enough meat (about 2 cups) to create a pocket for stuffing. Dice meat and stir into stuffing. Spoon about 1½ cups stuffing into the cavity, or as much as it will hold, reserving any extra.

Rub outside of ham with black pepper. Using a small knife, make slits at 1-inch intervals on outside surface along the length of the ham. Tie the ham with kitchen twine, using the slits to secure the twine. Place a double layer of cheesecloth over the ham and tie it closed at the narrow end. Place ham, stuffing-side-up, on a V-shaped rack set in a roasting pan to prevent stuffing from leaking out. Bake about 12 minutes per pound, 2 to 2½ hours.

Remove ham from oven and cool slightly. Transfer to a baking sheet and remove twine. Turn oven to broil and broil ham until browned, about 10 minutes. Remove from oven and let rest 10 to 15 minutes before slicing.

(Ham with Grits and Greens Stuffing continued)

Preheat oven to 400 degrees. Spoon leftover stuffing into a buttered 8-inch square shallow baking dish and sprinkle with remaining Parmesan. Bake until bubbly, about 20 minutes. Serve with favorite vegetables and biscuits.

Hint: Have the butcher remove the ham bone. Remember to save any meat off the bone.

Yield: 8 servings

Spiced Bacon Twists

1	cup packed light brown sugar	¼	teaspoon cayenne pepper
2	tablespoons dry mustard	1	pound sliced peppercorn
½	teaspoon cinnamon		bacon (about 23 to 25 strips)
½	teaspoon nutmeg		

Arrange oven racks in middle and bottom positions of oven. Preheat oven to 350 degrees. Line bottom of a broiler pan or large cookie sheet with aluminum foil. Place broiler rack or another metal cooling rack over aluminum-lined sheet. Set aside.

In a small bowl, using a fork, combine brown sugar, dry mustard, cinnamon, nutmeg, and cayenne until evenly blended. Transfer mixture to a large sheet of wax paper. Dip bacon strips into sugar mixture to coat evenly. Twist each strip several times. Place 12 coated strips on prepared pan rack. Bake approximately 30 minutes. (You may want to do 2 pans at a time; if so, reverse pan positions in oven halfway through baking time). Remove from oven when almost crisp and sugar is bubbly. (In some ovens, this may take as long as 45 minutes.) Transfer strips to clean aluminum foil surface.

Hint: May be prepared a day or 2 ahead of baking; refrigerate then bake; or bake, refrigerate, and reheat in microwave. This is perfect on a breakfast buffet.

Yield: 4 to 6 servings

Rouxminations

Waiting On You Hand and Foot

At Einbender's store, only about five percent of the merchandise was displayed on the showroom floor. Most of the inventory, some 10,000 garments, was held in a stockroom. The customer described what she was looking for, and the salesperson would bring in several selections at a time.

❧❧❧ Steamboat Olympics ❧❧❧

"Keep the steam coming, boy," he yelled. The shrill, haunting whistle sounded, announcing the arrival of the Polar Star in the record time of two days and 20 hours.

During the trip, Captain Tom Brierly looked up the river keeping an experienced eye out for snags and sandbars as the Polar Star steamed past Atchison, Kansas on his way to St. Joseph.

As Brierly approached the wharf, he knew he owned the new record for traversing the Missouri River from St. Louis to St. Joseph.

While there wasn't a gold medal ceremony, there were cheers from the crew and those on the wharf. In fact, the next day the Robidoux Greys, a uniformed military company, presented Captain Brierly with a set of silver mounted elk horns. Brierly responded in kind and threw a champagne reception to entertain the Greys and the cream of St. Joseph society. Unfortunately, a Missouri downpour came sweeping in from the west and prevented many ladies from attending the festivities.

Steamboats played a significant role in the development of young cities because the river was the fastest way to travel. When the railroads arrived, steamboat traffic slowed to a trickle.

Today, the Spirit of St. Joseph, a replica steamboat, reminds citizens of their riverboat heritage. While today's steamboat no longer brings settlers up river, citizens and visitors can still have a sense of the power of the Missouri by dining on the Spirit as it makes its way up river during the summer months. If you cup your hand to your ear and lean to the river, you can almost hear that shrill haunting whistle of the Polar Star's ghost.

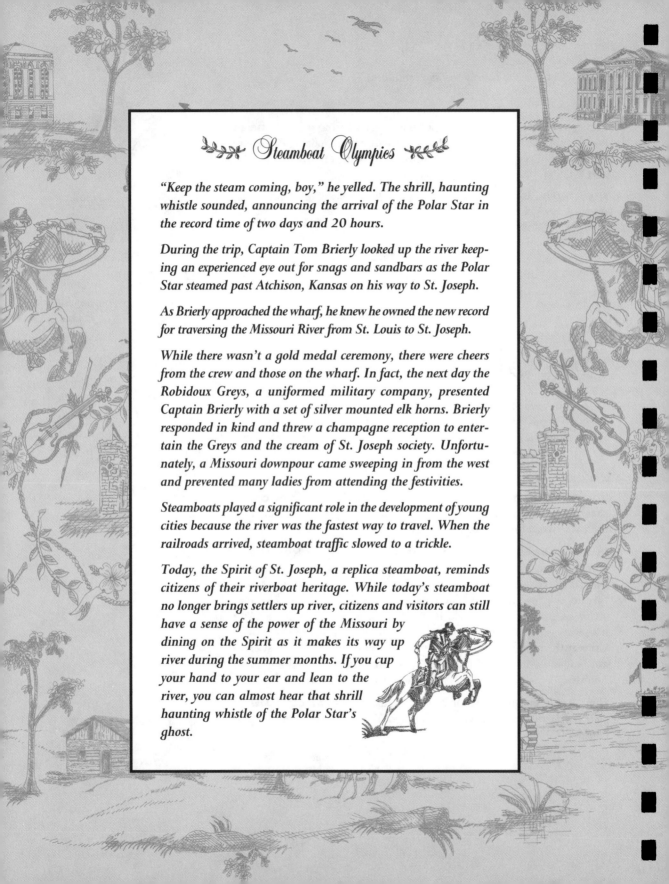

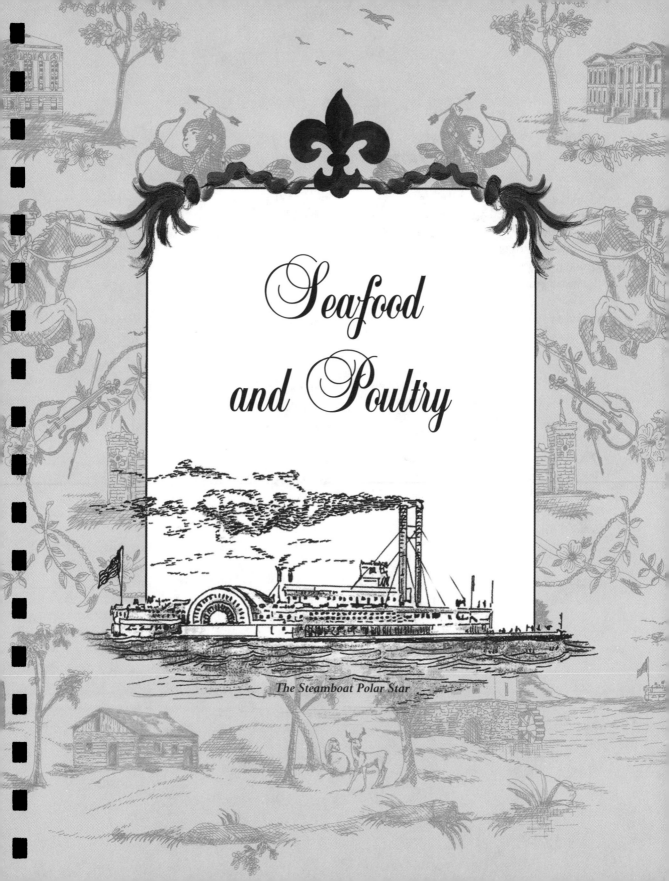

Seafood and Poultry

The Steamboat Polar Star

Seafood and Poultry

Classic Crab Cakes with Chili-Lime Mayonnaise

Crab Cakes

12 ounces lump crabmeat, picked over to remove cartilage
2 slices white bread, broken into small crumbs
1 tablespoon Dijon mustard
1 teaspoon Worcestershire sauce
2 teaspoons Old Bay seasoning
2 medium jalapeño peppers, seeds and ribs removed, minced

3 tablespoons finely chopped cilantro
1 large egg, lightly beaten
1 large shallot, minced
2 tablespoons mayonnaise
Grated zest of 1 lemon
Pepper
3-4 tablespoons canola oil
Cilantro sprigs, optional

Chili-Lime Mayonnaise

1 clove garlic, minced
1 teaspoon kosher salt
Grated zest of 1 lime
2 tablespoons fresh lime juice

1 hot chili pepper, seeds and ribs removed, minced
2 cups mayonnaise

Preheat oven to 400 degrees. Line a 12 x 17-inch baking sheet with parchment paper, or lightly coat with nonstick cooking spray. Combine crabmeat and bread crumbs in a medium bowl. In another medium bowl, mix mustard, Worcestershire sauce, Old Bay seasoning, jalapeños, cilantro, egg, shallot, mayonnaise, and lemon zest. Add mixture to crabmeat and stir to combine well. Add pepper to taste. Using your fingers, shape about 1½ tablespoons of crab mixture into half-dollar sized rounds. Continue with remaining mixture.

Heat oil in a large skillet over medium heat. Working in batches of 6 to 8, cook crab cakes in skillet until golden brown on the bottom, 30 seconds to 1 minute. Turn and cook about 1 minute more. Transfer cakes to a paper towel to drain. Transfer to prepared baking sheet. Bake in oven for 10 minutes, or until golden brown.

While these are baking, mix all the ingredients for the chili-lime mayonnaise. Whisk well to combine and refrigerate until ready to use. Serve crab cakes warm, topped with a dollop of chili-lime mayonnaise. Garnish with small sprig of cilantro, if desired.

Hint: Crab cakes may be held in a warm oven for 30 minutes, or cooled, refrigerated and then reheated at serving time.

Yield: 4 servings

Rouxminations

River Traffic Jam

The population of St. Joseph more than doubled during the 1850's. Most of the newcomers came by steamboat since the railroad did not arrive until 1859. At least one steamboat arrived every day, and at times, five or six. At times, the St. Joseph riverbank would be packed with as many as 25 steamboats. Steamers paid a $5 wharfage fee in St. Joseph to unload.

Rouxminations

A Card Carrying Member

The Junior League of St. Joseph formed the Allied Arts Council with other member organizations in 1964 and is still a member today. Among agencies belonging to the Allied Arts Council are the St. Joseph Symphony, the American Guild of Organists, the Robidoux Resident Theater, the Performing Arts Association, the Creative Arts Production, and the St. Joseph Community Chorus.

Halibut with Tomato Tarragon Cream Sauce

Sauce

½	yellow onion, cut in ½-inch slices
3	plum tomatoes, cored and cut in ½-inch slices
1	tablespoon olive oil
	Kosher salt and freshly ground pepper

3	dry pack sun-dried tomatoes
½	cup boiling water
¼	cup heavy cream
1	tablespoon sherry vinegar
1	tablespoon roughly chopped fresh tarragon

Halibut

4	(7 to 8 ounce) halibut filets, about 1-inch thick
2	tablespoons olive oil

Kosher salt and freshly ground pepper

For Sauce: Brush onion and tomato slices with olive oil and season with salt and pepper to taste. Grill onion slices directly over medium heat, turning once, until soft, 12 to 14 minutes. Grill tomato slices directly over medium heat, turning once, until grill marks are clearly visible, 8 to 10 minutes.

Place the sun-dried tomatoes in a bowl and add boiling water. Soften for about 15 minutes. Remove sun-dried tomatoes, reserving water. Place sun-dried tomatoes in a food processor along with grilled onions and tomatoes. With processor running, add cream, vinegar, and tarragon. Add enough of reserved water to make a smooth sauce. Season with salt and pepper to taste. Transfer to a small pan and keep warm.

Brush halibut filets with olive oil and season with salt and pepper to taste. Grill directly over medium heat, turning once, until the flesh begins to flake when tested with a fork, about 8 minutes total. Do not overcook. Serve warm with the sauce.

Hint: Salmon or orange roughy may be substituted for the halibut.

Yield: 4 servings

Leaf-Wrapped Stuffed Salmon

Lemon Almond Stuffing

1	cup fine fresh bread crumbs made from French bread
1	cup unblanched almonds
1	cup fresh parsley sprigs
1	tablespoon fresh tarragon or thyme leaves

3	tablespoons freshly grated lemon zest
¼	cup freshly squeezed lemon juice
¼	pound unsalted butter, softened Salt, freshly ground black pepper, cayenne pepper

Salmon

3	heads butter lettuce
1	(5 to 8 pound) whole salmon, boned

Caviar for garnish

For Stuffing: Combine bread crumbs, almonds, and parsley in food processor and process until coarsely chopped. Add tarragon or thyme, lemon zest, juice, and butter. Mix thoroughly. Add to taste: salt, pepper, and cayenne. Set aside.

For Salmon: Preheat oven to 350 degrees. Dip lettuce leaves in boiling water just until wilted, about 10 seconds. Plunge into ice water, drain, and blot dry on paper towels. Rinse salmon and pat dry. Stuff cavity of salmon with bread crumb mixture. Place fish on a baking sheet and wrap with the lettuce leaves, overlapping them as you work. Cover fish completely with several layers. Bake about 10 minutes per inch of thickness.

To Serve: Cut fish crosswise into 1-inch thick slices. Garnish with caviar and serve immediately.

Hint: Can make individual servings by using 6 (1 pound) salmon filets. Divide stuffing and wrap each 1 individually. If dividing a whole filet into individual servings, cut pieces on diagonal to balance thin tail section with fleshier center portion.

Yield: 6 servings

Rouxminations

Not Quite Breaking The Sound Barrier

In 1854, Captain Thomas H. Brierly with his new steamer, Polar Star, broke the record for upriver trips from St. Louis to St. Joseph by making the 500-mile trek in two days and 20 hours. Two years later, another boat in which Brierly had a part-ownership made the fastest run in the history of the river, 59 hours and 22 minutes from St. Louis to St. Joseph.

Pistachio Crusted Salmon with Madras Curry and Orange Sauces

Madras Curry Sauce

2	tablespoons Madras curry powder	¼	cup rice vinegar
½	cup peanut oil	1	tablespoon lime juice
1	teaspoon minced shallots	½	teaspoon soy sauce
1	teaspoon minced fresh ginger	1	tablespoon honey
			Salt and pepper to taste

Orange Sauce

2	cups orange juice	2	teaspoons red wine vinegar
2	tablespoons finely chopped jalapeño peppers	2	teaspoons rice vinegar
2	tablespoons minced shallots	1	tablespoon peanut oil
2	tablespoons minced fresh ginger	2	teaspoons olive oil
1	small navel orange, peeled and cut between membranes to release sections	¼	teaspoon sesame oil

Salmon

3	tablespoons olive oil	2	medium carrots, julienned
6	(6 ounce) salmon filets, skinless	2	medium leeks, white and tender green part, julienned
¾	cup finely chopped unsalted pistachio nuts	1	medium red bell pepper, julienned
4	cups fresh spinach	1	tablespoon sesame seeds

For Madras Curry Sauce: In small skillet, stir curry powder over moderate heat until fragrant, about 2 minutes. Transfer to a bowl and add peanut oil; let stand overnight. In small bowl combine shallots, ginger, rice vinegar, lime juice, soy sauce, and honey. Whisk in curry oil in a thin stream until well blended. Salt and pepper to taste.

For Orange Sauce: In saucepan combine orange juice, jalapeños, shallots, and ginger. Boil over moderate heat until reduced to ½ cup, about 30 minutes. Let cool. Add orange sections, red wine vinegar, and rice vinegar. Whisk in peanut oil, olive oil, and sesame oil and season with salt and pepper. Both sauces can be made up to 3 days ahead. Refrigerate and return to room temperature before serving.

Rouxminations

United We Stand

The Junior League of St. Joseph in conjunction with the United Way of Greater St. Joseph, formed the Volunteer Action Center and Leadership St. Joseph in the early 1980s. These two organizations are instrumental in finding and training volunteers for the city. The League still supplies a delegate on the board of Leadership St. Joseph.

(Pistachio Crusted Salmon with Madras Curry and Orange Sauces continued)

For Salmon: Preheat oven to 350 degrees. Lightly brush cookie sheet with olive oil. Heat 3 tablespoons olive oil in large skillet. Press 1 side of salmon into chopped pistachios. Put salmon in skillet, pistachio-side-down, and cook over high heat until lightly golden, about 2 to 3 minutes. Transfer salmon to cookie sheet, nut-side-up, and bake 8 minutes, until slightly opaque in center. Let rest on baking sheet about 5 minutes.

To Serve: Heat ⅓ cup of Madras curry sauce in small saucepan. In large bowl combine spinach, carrots, leeks, and red peppers, and toss with warm curry sauce. Divide mixture onto 6 plates and top with salmon. Drizzle each plate with 2 tablespoons of orange sauce and sprinkle with sesame seeds.

Yield: 6 servings

Grilled Salmon Salad

2 pounds salmon fillets	2 tablespoons minced fresh dill
Good olive oil, for grilling	2 tablespoons drained capers
Kosher salt	2 tablespoons raspberry vinegar
Freshly ground black pepper	2 tablespoons good olive oil
1 cup diced celery (3 stalks)	½ teaspoon kosher salt
½ cup diced red onion (1 small onion)	½ teaspoon freshly ground pepper

Cut the salmon fillets crosswise into 4-inch-wide slices. Marinate in olive oil, salt, and pepper for up to an hour.

Prepare grill with hot coals. Brush salmon fillets with olive oil. Grill for 5 to 7 minutes on each side. Salmon should still be rare on inside. Remove to plate, cover with plastic wrap, and chill in refrigerator until firm. Remove skin, break fillets into large pieces, and put into a salad bowl. Add remaining ingredients and mix well. Serve cold or at room temperature.

Hint: Light and fresh.

Yield: 4 servings

River War Zone

When the Missouri River opened for navigation in 1849, several thousand adventurers, ready to seek gold in California, streamed into St. Joseph from all parts of the northern United States, from the south by way of Panama, and many from Europe. The steamboats stopped on St. Joseph's riverbank and unloaded passengers, mules, horses, cattle, vehicles, and commodities. Because housing was scarce, it made for an action-packed scene with many people pitching tents on both sides of the river. St. Joseph often looked as though it was besieged by an army.

Rosemary Roasted Salmon

2	large bunches fresh rosemary		Salt and pepper
1	large red onion, thinly sliced	2	large lemons, thinly sliced
1	(2 pound) center-cut salmon filet with skin	⅓	cup olive oil

Preheat oven 500 degrees. Arrange half of rosemary sprigs in single layer in center of heavy baking sheet. Arrange onions on top of rosemary. Place salmon, skin-side-down, on onions. Sprinkle with salt and pepper. Cover salmon with remaining rosemary sprigs. Arrange lemon slices over rosemary and drizzle with olive oil. Sprinkle lemon slices with salt. (Can be prepared to this point 8 hours ahead. Cover and refrigerate.) Roast salmon until just cooked through, about 20 minutes. Transfer to plates. Serve with roasted onions and lemon slices.

Yield: 4 servings

Salmon Bake with Pecan Crunch Coating

4	(1½ inch thick) salmon filets	1½	tablespoons honey
¼	teaspoon salt	¼	cup soft bread crumbs
⅛	teaspoon pepper	¼	cup finely chopped pecans
2	tablespoons Dijon mustard	1	tablespoon chopped fresh parsley
2	tablespoons butter or margarine, melted		

Preheat oven to 450 degrees. Sprinkle salmon with salt and pepper; place skin-side-down on lightly greased baking dish. Combine mustard, butter, and honey. Brush over salmon. Combine bread crumbs, pecans, and parsley; spoon evenly over salmon. Bake, uncovered, for 12 to 15 minutes, until fish flakes easily when tested with a fork.

Yield: 4 servings

Tangy Grilled Salmon

2 tablespoons butter, melted	1 tablespoon Worcestershire
2 tablespoons vinegar	sauce
2 tablespoons ketchup	1 (1 pound) salmon steak
	Lemon wedges

Combine butter, vinegar, ketchup, and Worcestershire sauce. Place fish on a hot grill and brush with sauce. Grill 6 inches from heat about 15 minutes, brushing often with sauce. Serve with lemon wedges.

Hint: Quick, simple and good.

Yield: 2 servings

Rouxminations

150,000 and Counting

Historians estimate that between 1843 and 1859, 300,000 pioneers attempted to make the journey across the Plains to the western frontiers. Historical records also indicate that as many as half of those travelers passed through St. Joseph on their way out West.

Shrimp De Jonghe

1¼ pounds large (20 to 24 per pound) shrimp, shelled and deveined	2 tablespoons medium dry sherry
	½ cup fine dry bread crumbs
	¼ cup finely chopped fresh parsley
½ cup unsalted butter, softened	¼ cup sliced almonds, lightly
2 medium cloves garlic, minced and mashed to a paste with a pinch of salt	toasted
	Lemon wedges for garnish

Preheat oven at 400 degrees. Blanch shrimp in boiling salted water 30 seconds, then drain in a colander and rinse under cold water until cool. Pat dry and arrange in 1 layer in a buttered 1-quart gratin dish or other ovenproof dish.

Stir together butter, garlic paste, and sherry until blended. Stir in bread crumbs, parsley, and salt and pepper to taste. Dot shrimp with crumb mixture and sprinkle with almonds.

Bake shrimp until just cooked through and topping is lightly browned, about 15 minutes. Garnish with lemon wedges.

Yield: 4 servings

Rouxminations

There's A Train Comin'

The influence of steamboat traffic on St. Joseph was short-lived. The reason for the decline was the completion of the Hannibal-St. Joseph railroad which made St. Joseph the western terminus for the great American railroad system. The train cut the distance from the Mississippi to the Missouri by half. However, a steamboat played a critical role in the railroad's arrival in St. Joseph. A steamboat arrived in St. Joseph in 1857, carrying tons of rails and the locomotive that would pull the first train across the Missouri.

Pecan Crusted Snapper with Lemon Sauce and Crabmeat Relish

Crabmeat Relish

½ pound fresh lump crabmeat, drained	2 tablespoons minced roasted red bell peppers
½ cup pecan halves, toasted	1 tablespoon lemon juice
4 green onions, chopped	¼ teaspoon salt
	½ teaspoon pepper

Spicy Mix

5 tablespoons sweet paprika	2 tablespoons onion powder
¼ cup salt	2 tablespoons cayenne
¼ cup garlic powder	2 tablespoons dried oregano
2 tablespoons freshly ground black pepper	2 tablespoons dried thyme

Lemon Sauce

1 cup dry white wine	⅛ teaspoon Worcestershire sauce
3 lemons, peeled and quartered	⅛ teaspoon hot sauce
6-8 cloves garlic, minced	½ cup whipping cream
1 teaspoon salt	¾ cup unsalted butter, sliced
½ teaspoon freshly ground pepper	1 tablespoon chopped fresh parsley

Snapper

4 (5 to 6 ounce) red snapper filets	2 large eggs
2 cups all-purpose flour, divided	1 cup milk
½ cup toasted ground pecans	½ cup olive or canola oil

For Crabmeat Relish: Toss together all ingredients. Cover and chill for up to 8 hours.

For Spice Mix: Combine all ingredients in a resealable plastic bag.

For Lemon Sauce: Cook white wine, lemons and garlic in a non-aluminum saucepan over medium-high heat 5 minutes, whisking to mash lemons. Stir in salt, pepper, Worcestershire, and hot sauce, and cook until texture of syrup, about 10 minutes. Stir in whipping cream; cook 1 minute. Reduce heat to low, and gradually whisk in butter. Pour through a wire-mesh strainer, discarding pulp. Stir in parsley, and keep warm.

(Pecan Crusted Snapper with Lemon Sauce and Crabmeat Relish continued)

For Snapper: Preheat oven to 375 degrees. Sprinkle filets evenly with 1 tablespoon spice mix and set aside. Combine 1 cup flour and 1 tablespoon spice mix; set aside. Combine 1 tablespoon spice mix, remaining 1 cup flour, and pecans. Stir together eggs and milk until well blended. Dredge filets first in flour mixture; dip in egg mixture, and dredge in pecan mixture, shaking off excess. Fry filets in hot oil in a large ovenproof skillet, about 3 minutes each side. Place skillet in oven and bake 8 minutes, until filets are browned and crisp. Spoon lemon sauce evenly on individual plates; add filets and top with Crabmeat Relish. Serve immediately.

Yield: 4 servings

Diablo Shrimp and Angel Hair Pasta

½ cup unsalted butter	1 pound jumbo shrimp, deveined but not peeled
1 tablespoon finely chopped garlic	½ teaspoon kosher salt
1 teaspoon cayenne pepper	8 ounces angel hair pasta
½ cup dry white wine	¼ cup extra-virgin olive oil
4 tablespoons finely chopped fresh parsley, divided	⅓ cup freshly grated Parmesan cheese
	1 lemon

In a saucepan over medium heat, combine butter, garlic, and cayenne pepper. Cook until the garlic is soft, about 5 minutes. Add wine, raise heat to high, and cook until reduced by half. Allow to cool. Stir in 2 tablespoons parsley.

Place shrimp in a medium bowl. Pour butter mixture over shrimp. Add salt and toss to coat shrimp thoroughly. Place shrimp directly over high heat and grill, turning once, until just opaque, about 3 to 4 minutes. Meanwhile, cook pasta in boiling salted water, until al dente. Drain and mix with olive oil, cheese, and remaining parsley. Transfer shrimp to a bowl and squeeze lemon juice over them. Toss well and serve immediately with the pasta.

Hint: Grilling with the shells on captures the natural moisture of the shrimp.

Yield: 4 servings

Rouxminations

Let's Go To The Hop

The Frog Hop Ballroom, or the "Hop," as it was affectionately known to its regulars, hosted many popular swing masters including Benny Goodman, Harry James, Duke Ellington, Glen Miller, the Tommy Dorsey band, and Lawrence Welk. The love of dance is what inspired Frank Frogge to build the first Frog Hop in St. Joseph, in 1928.

Rouxminations

Leaf Your Worries At Home

The Frog Hop changed owners and locations several times throughout the years, but became known for its 10,000 aluminum leaves that covered the entire ceiling and the birch trees which were painted on the walls and the support posts. The leaves rustled as dancers swooshed by, but today the leaves and trees are long-gone. Currently the ballroom is a carpet and home improvement store.

Spicy Coconut Beer-Battered Shrimp

Seasoning Mix

2	tablespoons cayenne pepper	2	teaspoons salt
1	tablespoon paprika	1	teaspoon onion powder
1	tablespoon freshly ground pepper	1	teaspoon thyme
		1	teaspoon oregano

2½ teaspoons garlic powder

Shrimp

1½	cups all-purpose flour, divided	5	cups grated coconut, in medium bowl
2	eggs, lightly beaten	2	cups vegetable oil
1	cup beer		
1	tablespoon baking powder		
2	pounds uncooked shrimp (medium to large), cleaned, deveined, tail on		

Blend seasoning mix ingredients in a small bowl. Combine 1 cup flour and 1 tablespoon seasoning mix in a medium bowl. Combine remaining flour, eggs, beer, baking powder, and 2 teaspoons seasoning mix in a medium bowl. Stir until blended. Dip shrimp in seasoning mixture, and dredge in flour mixture. Dip all but the tail in batter mixture. Coat with coconut. Pour vegetable oil into skillet, until about 1 inch deep. (Use remaining oil to replenish later, as needed.) Heat over medium-high heat. Fry shrimp until nicely golden, about 1 minute per side.

Hints: Try it with the Zucchini Linguine, page 172. It is a labor of love and worth the effort. Use with Horseradish Marmalade recipe below.

Yield: 6 servings

Horseradish Marmalade

1	(18 ounce) jar orange marmalade	2-3	tablespoons prepared horseradish
3-4	tablespoons Creole or brown mustard		

Mix all ingredients, cover and store in refrigerator. May be prepared ahead.

Market Seafood

Sauce

2 (28 ounce) cans diced tomatoes in tomato juice, undrained	1 tablespoon chopped sun-dried tomatoes
1 cup whipping cream	1 teaspoon nutmeg
1 cup grated Parmesan cheese	2 tablespoons granulated garlic
	Salt and pepper to taste

Seafood

2½ pounds favorite combination of seafood: shrimp, scallops, salmon, and/or tuna	1 pound favorite pasta, cooked according to package directions
¼ cup olive oil	Chopped fresh basil, optional
1 tablespoon granulated garlic	Grated Parmesan, optional
Salt and pepper to taste	

For Sauce: Combine all ingredients in a large saucepan. Simmer gently, stirring occasionally, until all ingredients combine when stirred, 30 to 40 minutes.

If using fish, cut in cubes. Heat oil in a large skillet. Add garlic, salt and pepper, and seafood. Cook over medium heat until seafood just changes color, about 5 minutes. Watch closely and do not overcook. To serve, arrange seafood over pasta and top with sauce. Garnish with basil and Parmesan, if desired.

Yield: 6 servings

Rouxminations

Compromising Position

On February 8, 1820, Henry Clay of Kentucky addressed the House of Representatives resulting in the adoption of the Missouri Compromise, allowing Missouri to enter the Union as a slave state.

Fried Feathered Friends

St. Joseph citizens cross town to South 22nd Street to eat chicken at Galvins. When the restaurant first opened, patrons could buy chicken by the bucketful. Other homestyle dishes including mashed potatoes, corn, green beans and homemade pies are still a mainstay at this popular family-style restaurant today.

Rouxminations

Queen For A Day

Authentic Mexican food can be found at the St. Patrick's Fiesta held the first weekend in August. The Fiesta begins with a queen coronation dance, and activities during the weekend include activities for children and food booths.

Seafood Bake

2 cups uncooked shell macaroni	¼ teaspoon garlic powder
3 ounces Neufchâtel cheese, softened	1 (2 ounce) jar diced pimentos, undrained
½ cup plain low-fat yogurt	½ pound imitation crab, flaked into pieces
½ cup lemon yogurt	
1 cup part skim milk ricotta cheese	½ pound peeled cooked shrimp
	½ cup shredded Monterey Jack cheese
⅓ cup chopped green onions	
1 teaspoon dried whole basil	

Cook macaroni according to package directions, omitting salt and fat. Drain and set aside.

Preheat oven to 350 degrees. Combine Neufchâtel, yogurt, ricotta, green onions, basil, garlic powder, and pimentos, stirring well. Coat a 2-quart baking dish with nonstick spray. Place half of macaroni in baking dish. Sprinkle half of imitation crab and half of shrimp over macaroni. Top with half of cheese mixture. Repeat layers with remaining ingredients. Bake for 30 minutes. Sprinkle with Monterey Jack cheese and bake until cheese melts, about 5 more minutes. Let stand 10 minutes before serving.

Yield: 6 servings

Artichoke Stuffed Chicken Breasts with Lemon Wine Sauce

1	medium onion, finely chopped	½	cup slivered almonds, toasted
6	shallots, minced	1	tablespoon minced fresh
3	tablespoons unsalted butter		tarragon or 1 teaspoon dried
1	can artichoke hearts, drained		Salt and pepper to taste
1	can black olives, drained	8	chicken breasts with skin

Sauce

1	tablespoon olive oil	1	tablespoon lemon juice
1	teaspoon minced garlic	¼	cup cream
¼	cup white wine	3	tablespoons butter

Preheat oven to 350 degrees. Brown onion and shallots in butter. Add artichoke hearts, olives, almonds, tarragon, salt, and pepper. Loosen skin of chicken breasts, season with salt and pepper, and place artichoke mixture between skin and meat. Refrigerate until ready to bake. Bake, uncovered, for 45 minutes. Serve cold or hot with sauce.

For Sauce: Combine olive oil, garlic, white wine, and lemon juice in a saucepan. Bring to a boil and cook until reduced to 2 tablespoons. Add cream, whisk, and reduce by half. Whisk in butter and keep warm.

Yield: 8 servings

Robidoux Chicken

½	cup peanut or vegetable oil	2	tablespoons vinegar
¼	cup bottled lemon juice	1	teaspoon salt
2	tablespoons Worcestershire sauce	2	teaspoons sugar
1	tablespoon paprika	2	teaspoons garlic powder
6	dashes Tabasco sauce	10-12	chicken breasts

In a medium bowl, completely mix all ingredients except chicken. Transfer to a heavy-duty zip-lock bag and add chicken. Marinate in refrigerator overnight.

Preheat grill to medium. Discard marinade and cook chicken 8 minutes per side. Do not overcook.

Yield: 10 to 12 servings

Rouxminations

It Was In The Cards

Legend has it the Joseph Robidoux had a penchant for cards. One story suggests that the fate of St. Joseph was dealt at the poker table. Apparently in 1839, three businesses from Independence, Missouri, proposed to buy Robidoux's land for $16,000 with the intent of establishing a town. The terms were agreed to and the exchange was to be made the next day. That evening, a card game turned into a quarrel, and Robidoux accused the three of cheating him. Whether the charge was valid, or merely an excuse Robidoux used after changing his mind about the sale, no one knows. But, because of it, the deal was off, and Robidoux retained the land that is now St. Joseph.

B B Q Chicken

1½ cups chopped yellow onion
3 cloves garlic, minced
¼ cup vegetable oil
1 cup tomato paste
½ cup cider vinegar
1 cup honey
½ cup Worcestershire sauce
1 cup Dijon mustard
½ cup soy sauce
1 cup hoisin sauce
2 tablespoons chili powder
1 tablespoon ground cumin
½ teaspoon crushed red pepper flakes
2 (2½ to 3 pound) chickens, quartered and backs removed or an equivalent amount of breasts

In large saucepan over low heat, sauté onion and garlic in vegetable oil for 10 to 15 minutes, until translucent but not browned. Add tomato paste, vinegar, honey, Worcestershire, mustard, soy sauce, hoisin, chili powder, cumin, and red pepper. Bring to a boil, reduce heat and simmer 30 minutes. Use immediately or store in refrigerator.

Using two-thirds of sauce, marinate chicken overnight, if possible, or at least a few hours. Grill chicken until done, about 45 minutes, turning once or twice. Serve with extra sauce on the side.

Hint: The sauce may be stored in refrigerator for up to a month.

Yield: 6 to 8 servings

Garlic Chicken

8 boneless chicken breasts
¾ cup butter
2 cloves garlic, minced
¾ cup Italian bread crumbs
½ cup grated Parmesan cheese
1½ tablespoons chopped fresh parsley
1 teaspoon salt
Pepper to taste

Preheat oven to 350 degrees. Place chicken breasts in a zip-lock bag and flatten with a meat cleaver until ½-inch-thick. Melt butter, add minced garlic, and stir. Dip chicken in garlic mixture. Mix together bread crumbs, cheese, parsley, salt, and pepper. Place a spoonful of bread crumb mixture on each chicken breast. Roll up and secure with toothpick. Place in a baking dish and drizzle with any remaining butter and crumbs. Bake for about 15 to 20 minutes, until done. Do not overbake or chicken will dry out.

Yield: 8 servings

Chicken Chalupas

12 ounces Monterey Jack cheese, grated
12 ounces sharp Cheddar cheese, grated
2 bunches green onions, tops included, chopped and divided
2 (10¾ ounce) cans cream of chicken soup
1 (4 ounce) can green chiles, drained and chopped
1 pint sour cream
1 cup pitted black olives, sliced
4 large chicken breasts, poached, skinned, boned, and cut into 1-inch pieces (about 6 cups)
12 (6 inch) flour tortillas

Combine cheeses and divide in half. Divide green onions into 2 equal portions. Combine half the cheeses, half the onions, soup, chiles, sour cream, and olives in a large bowl. Set aside 1½ cups of mixture for topping. Add chicken to remaining filling and mix well.

Place 3 heaping tablespoons of filling on each tortilla and roll up. Place rolls seam-side-down on a lightly oiled shallow baking dish. Arrange in a single layer, using 2 baking dishes if necessary. Spread reserved topping over tortillas. Sprinkle with remaining cheese and onions. Cover and refrigerate overnight.

Preheat oven to 350 degrees. Bake, uncovered, for 45 minutes. Let stand a few minutes before serving.

Hint: This recipe may be frozen for future use. Defrost completely before baking.

Yield: 12 servings

Rouxminations

Dust In The Wind

On the evening of January 29, 1976, the Hotel Robidoux opened its doors to more than 500 guests assembled to bid farewell to "the handsomest hotel West of New York." Nostalgic speeches recalled the impressive list of national celebrities from politics, sports, and entertainment who visited the hotel. The implosion of the building in June of 1976 was featured on a national television beer commercial. Bank offices now stand in place of the grand old hotel.

Chicken Fabu

1	cup olive oil	2	tablespoon Italian seasonings
1½	cups white vinegar		Salt and pepper to taste
4	cloves garlic, minced	6-8	chicken breasts, deboned
¼	cup lemon juice	½	cup Italian-flavored croutons
½	cup white wine		Cooked fettuccine

Combine olive oil, vinegar, garlic, lemon juice, white wine, Italian seasonings, and salt and pepper in a zip-lock bag. Add chicken, seal, and refrigerate overnight, turning occasionally.

Remove chicken from marinade, reserving marinade. Place chicken between 2 pieces of plastic wrap and pound to about ½-inch thick. Slice flattened breasts into 1 to 2-inch strips. Add croutons to marinade and spoon over 1 side of strips. Roll up strips as tightly as possible with the bread crumb mixture on the interior of the rolls. Skewer rolls lengthwise with shish-kabob skewers and cook on a hot grill for about 25 minutes. Serve with fettuccine.

Hint: If unable to grill, skewers may be cooked in preheated 350 degree oven for 40 to 45 minutes.

Yield: 6 to 8 servings

Lime-Salsa Grilled Chicken

	Juice of 2 fresh limes	1	cup salsa
½	cup olive oil	2	tablespoons fresh lime juice
8	pieces chicken	2-4	teaspoons chili powder

Combine lime juice and olive oil in a zip-lock bag. Add chicken, seal, and marinate for 1 to 2 hours.

Combine salsa, 1 tablespoon juice, and chili powder. Remove chicken from marinade and place on a hot grill. Cook until done, basting with salsa mixture when turning.

Hint: Serve with shredded lettuce and Tossed and Found Bean Salad on page 97.

Yield: 8 servings

Chicken Yucatan

3   tablespoons fresh orange juice
3   tablespoons canned
      unsweetened pineapple juice
3   tablespoons fresh lime juice
2   tablespoons chopped fresh
      oregano or 2 teaspoon dried
1   tablespoon olive oil
1   teaspoon ground cumin

1   teaspoon chili powder
1   clove garlic, finely chopped
½   teaspoon salt
4-6 dashes Tabasco sauce
6   bone-in chicken thighs, skin
      and fat removed
Salt and pepper to taste

Preheat oven to 375 degrees. In a food processor or blender, combine juices, oregano, olive oil, cumin, chili powder, garlic, salt, and Tabasco. Puree until smooth. Arrange chicken in a baking dish and brush with some of the citrus-herb mixture. Roast chicken for 30 to 35 minutes, turning once. Brush with remaining citrus-herb mixture throughout roasting. Season with salt and pepper.

Hint: Can be cooked 1 day ahead. Cover and store in refrigerator. Serve hot or cold.

Yield: 6 servings

Parmesan Chicken

1   cup grated Parmesan cheese
½   cup Italian bread crumbs
¼   cup chopped fresh parsley
1   clove garlic, minced

½   teaspoon dried oregano
½   teaspoon fresh ground pepper
8   boneless chicken breasts
8   tablespoons butter, melted

Preheat oven to 350 degrees. Coat a baking sheet with nonstick spray. Combine Parmesan, bread crumbs, parsley, garlic, oregano, and pepper in a shallow bowl. Dip chicken in butter, then in Parmesan mix. Arrange on prepared baking sheet. Cover and bake until cooked through, about 45 minutes.

Hint: For a kid pleasing variation, omit oregano, reduce Parmesan to ¾ cup, and replace Italian bread crumbs with 2 cups crushed cornflakes.

Yield: 8 servings

Rouxminations

Jacks Of All Trades

The St. Joseph Kicks Band with their 30's and 40's style music helped continue the mystic appeal and popularity of the Frog Hop. The group was comprised of an eclectic group of St. Joseph business men and educators including the executive vice president of Hillyard Chemical Company, a weight inspector for the St. Joseph Grain Exchange, a high school student, an ophthalmologist, an attorney, and the owner and president of an insulation firm, Neale Dillon. Dillon later managed a dance club in the early 1980s at the Frog Hop location and brought back several ghost bands of the swing era.

Rouxminations

**His Face
Sure Rings A Bell**

Twin Spires, with its two 146 foot towers, is the stunning downtown landmark which was the former Immaculate Conception church designed by E. J. Eckel in 1910. The north tower houses a 60 inch diameter bell, estimated to weigh between six to eight thousand pounds; and the south tower houses four additional bells. The church also has twelve breath-taking stained glasses portraying the life of Mary.

Chicken Caprese with Tomato Basil Cream

⅔ cup soft bread crumbs
⅓ cup crumbled feta cheese
1 tablespoon chopped fresh basil or 1 teaspoon dried
¼ teaspoon salt
¼ teaspoon pepper
3 tablespoons olive oil
2 tablespoons lemon juice
4 boneless, skinless chicken breasts

Tomato Basil Cream

1 cup spaghetti sauce
2 tablespoons whipping cream
1 tablespoon chopped fresh basil or 1 teaspoon dried

Preheat oven to 375 degrees. Stir bread crumbs, feta, basil, salt, and pepper together in a shallow bowl. Whisk together olive oil and lemon juice until blended. Dip chicken into oil mixture and dredge in bread crumb mixture, pressing to coat. Place in lightly greased 11 x 7-inch baking dish. Bake for 30 minutes.

For Tomato Basil Cream: Cook all ingredients in a small saucepan over low heat, stirring often, until thoroughly heated, about 5 minutes. Serve over chicken.

Yield: 4 servings

Chicken in Lemon Cream Sauce

6   boneless, skinless chicken breasts
Salt and pepper
¼   cup butter
2   tablespoons dry vermouth
2   tablespoons fresh lemon juice
2   teaspoons grated lemon peel

¾   cup whipping cream
½   cup canned low-salt chicken broth
½   cup freshly grated Parmesan cheese, divided
Chopped fresh parsley
Lemon wedges, optional

Lightly pound chicken between sheets of wax paper to ½-inch thickness. Season with salt and pepper. Melt butter in large, heavy skillet over medium-high heat. Add chicken and sauté just until cooked through, about 3 minutes per side. Transfer to platter, cover with foil, and keep warm.

Pour butter from skillet. Add vermouth, lemon juice, and lemon peel to same skillet. Boil 1 minute, scraping up browned bits. Add cream, broth, and any juices from chicken. Boil until reduced to sauce consistency, about 8 minutes. Mix in ¼ cup Parmesan, season with salt and pepper and pour around chicken. Sprinkle with remaining Parmesan and parsley; garnish with lemon, if desired. Serve immediately.

Yield: 6 servings

Rouxminations

Torah, Torah, Torah

One of the most important objects housed in the Twin Spires Museum is the Malvazinka Torah which contains the first five books of the Old Testament as delivered with the Ten Commandments to Moses. The scrolls are handwritten in Hebrew. The Malvazinka Torah was plundered by the Nazis and later recovered.

Cilantro Pesto Goat Cheese Stuffed Chicken Breasts

¼ cup finely chopped cilantro	Salt and pepper to taste
¼ cup chicken stock	4 chicken breasts, boned but
2 tablespoons olive oil	skin left on

Stuffing

2 cloves garlic, peeled	2 tablespoons grated Parmesan
1 serrano chili, stemmed	cheese
2 cups cilantro leaves	3 ounces goat cheese
2 tablespoons olive oil	¼ cup ricotta cheese
	Salt and pepper to taste

Preheat oven to 375 degrees. Mix chopped cilantro, chicken stock, oil, and salt and pepper in a medium bowl. Add chicken and marinate for 15 minutes. Drain, reserving marinade. Place chicken on grill skin-side-down. Cooking 3 minutes per side, brushing with reserved marinade. Remove from grill and set aside.

For Stuffing: In a blender or food processor, puree garlic, chili, cilantro, oil, Parmesan cheese, goat cheese, and ricotta cheese. Season with salt and pepper and transfer to a pastry bag. Pipe stuffing directly under skin of chicken, piping an even layer. Place breasts in a baking pan and pour some of reserved marinade over them. Bake for 12 minutes and serve.

Hint: Stuffing may be prepared up to 2 days in advance.

Yield: 4 servings

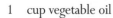

Grilled Herb Chicken with Tomato Mustard Sauce

1 cup vegetable oil	1 tablespoon fresh basil, chopped
½ cup red wine vinegar	1 teaspoon black pepper
1 tablespoon Dijon mustard	½ teaspoon salt
1 tablespoon brown sugar	4 (8 ounce) boneless, skinless
1½ tablespoons fresh thyme leaves or 2 teaspoons dried	chicken breasts, pounded to ½-inch thickness
1 tablespoon fresh rosemary or 1 teaspoon dried	

Tomato Mustard Sauce

1 ripe tomato, cored and finely chopped	1 tablespoon white wine vinegar
1 tablespoon Dijon mustard	1 tablespoon dry white wine
1 tablespoon olive oil	Salt and pepper to taste

Combine vegetable oil, vinegar, mustard, brown sugar, herbs, pepper, and salt in a medium bowl. Add chicken, cover, and refrigerate 2 to 4 hours, stirring after 1 hour.

For Tomato Mustard Sauce: Combine all ingredients in a small bowl and set aside.

Remove chicken from marinade, discarding marinade. Grill chicken on oiled grill over white-hot coals, 5 to 7 minutes per side. Serve with sauce.

Yield: 4 servings

Rouxminations

The Hall of Fame

The 1880s and 1890s were the Golden Age of prosperity for St. Joseph. As businesses flourished, many of the residents built decadent homes complete with spectacular stained glass windows, turrets, and towers. Many of these elaborate homes stand today and can be found on historic Hall Street. Several have been restored to their grandeur and are bed and breakfast businesses.

Herb Crusted Chicken Pot Pie

4 pounds bone-in chicken breasts with skin	2 tablespoons minced fresh thyme or 1 tablespoon dried
4-6 cups chicken broth	½ head roasted garlic
3 large carrots, peeled, cut into ½-inch pieces	½ cup all-purpose flour
1 pound red potatoes, peeled, cut into ½-inch pieces	½ cup dry white wine
¼ cup butter	½ cup whipping cream
1 small onion (yellow or white), roughly chopped or 3 medium leeks, sliced, and 2 to 3 large shallots, chopped	Salt and pepper
	Herb crust (see following recipe)

Butter 2 (9-inch) glass pie plates or 1 (4-quart) oval baking dish.

Place chicken in a heavy large pot and add just enough broth to cover. Bring broth to a boil; reduce heat to low, cover and simmer until chicken is just cooked through, about 20 minutes. Do not over-cook. Transfer chicken to a plate and cool. Add carrots and potatoes to broth. Simmer, uncovered, until vegetables are just tender, about 10 minutes. Using slotted spoon, transfer vegetables to prepared baking dish. Strain broth and reserve 4 cups.

Remove skin and bones from chicken. Cut or tear meat into ½ to ¾-inch pieces. Add chicken to vegetables. Melt butter in same pot over medium heat. Add onions. Sauté until tender, about 8 minutes. Add roasted garlic and stir to combine. Add flour and stir 2 minutes. Stir in reserved broth and white wine. Increase heat to high and bring to a boil, stirring constantly. Add cream and boil until sauce thickens enough to coat the spoon, whisking frequently, about 6 minutes. Season with salt and pepper. Pour gravy over mixture in dish. Stir to blend and cool for 45 minutes. (Filling can be made 1 day ahead. Cover and refrigerate until ready to use.)

Position rack in top third of oven and place baking sheet on bottom rack of oven; preheat to 400 degrees. Roll out crust dough on wax or parchment paper. (If you are doing 2 pies, separate dough into 2 portions before rolling). Using paper as an aid, turn dough over onto filling. Tuck dough edge inside dish. (Optional: Roll out scraps of dough to ¼-inch thickness and cut into leaf shapes. Brush bottoms of cutouts with water and arrange on crust.) Cut slits in crust to allow steam to escape.

(Herb Crusted Chicken Pot Pie continued)

Place pie on top rack in oven and bake until crust is golden and gravy is bubbling, about 50 minutes. Let stand 10 minutes before serving

Hint: It is the perfect dish to take new parents. Comfort food at its best!

Herb Crust

2½ cups all-purpose flour	½ cup (1 stick) chilled unsalted butter, cut into ½-inch pieces
2 tablespoons chopped fresh parsley	½ cup chilled solid vegetable shortening, cut into ½-inch pieces
1 tablespoon chopped fresh thyme	6½ tablespoons ice water, approximately
1 teaspoon salt	
1 teaspoon sugar	

Blend first 5 ingredients in a food processor until herbs are very finely chopped. Add butter and shortening. Blend (using a fork or pulse in food processor) until mixture resembles coarse meal. Transfer mixture to a large bowl. Using fork, mix enough ice water into flour mixture to form moist clumps. Gather dough into a ball, flatten into rectangle. Cover and chill 30 minutes.

Hint: This can be made 2 days ahead. Keep chilled. Let dough soften slightly before rolling out.

Rouxminations

You Can't Judge A Book By Its Cover

Under the alias of Mr. Howard, Jesse James and his family moved to St. Joseph in 1881. In St. Joseph, James was a quiet, churchgoing man who could quote scripture with the best of them. James' charmed life of crime came to an abrupt end in 1882 when he was shot by Bob Ford, a man whom James had befriended and a member of his gang.

Roasted Chicken with Herbs and Madeira

1	small onion, finely chopped	1	(4½ to 5 pound) chicken
1	carrot, finely chopped		Salt and pepper
1	celery stalk, finely chopped	1½	cups dry Madeira, divided
3	tablespoons olive oil, divided	1	tablespoon butter, room
6	cloves garlic		temperature
6	fresh rosemary sprigs	1	tablespoon all-purpose flour
6	fresh sage sprigs		

Preheat oven to 350 degrees. Sprinkle onion, carrots, and celery in a large roasting pan. Drizzle with 2 tablespoons olive oil. Place garlic and herbs in chicken cavity. Place chicken on vegetables in pan. Rub remaining oil over chicken and season with salt and pepper. Roast chicken 1 hour and 20 minutes, basting occasionally with pan juices.

Pour ¾ cup Madeira over chicken. Increase oven temperature to 400 degrees. Continue roasting chicken until golden brown and juices run clear when the thickest part of the thigh is pierced, about 15 minutes. Transfer chicken to serving platter.

Strain contents of roasting pan into heavy medium saucepan. Add ¾ cup Madeira and boil 1 minute. Mix butter and flour in small bowl. Whisk butter mixture into sauce and simmer until thickened, about 3 minutes. Season with salt and pepper. Serve chicken, passing sauce separately.

Yield: 4 servings

Tequila Jalapeño Chicken

4	boneless, skinless chicken breasts		All-purpose flour
	Teriyaki sauce	½	cup butter, divided
2	eggs beaten with a little milk	8	ounces mushrooms, sliced
		½	cup tequila

Jalapeño Sauce

1	cup whipping cream	1	teaspoon juice from jalapeño jar
½	cup sour cream		
½	teaspoon chicken base	1	jalapeño, minced
1	tablespoon butter	2	ounces shredded Monterey Jack cheese
2	teaspoons flour		

Cover chicken with teriyaki sauce and marinate for 1 hour. Remove from marinade and dip into egg mixture. Dust with flour. Melt 2 to 3 tablespoons butter in a sauté pan. Sauté chicken over medium heat until almost done (8 to 10 minutes). In another pan, place remaining butter, tequila, and mushrooms. Sauté over medium heat for 1 minute. Add chicken to pan and cook until done. Transfer chicken to individual plates or serving platter. Top with mushrooms and warm jalapeño sauce.

For Sauce: Heat cream in heavy saucepan over high heat. When ready to boil, add sour cream and stir. Reduce heat to medium. Stir in chicken base and jalapeño juice and simmer. While cream is heating, melt butter and make roux by adding flour, mixing with wire whip until mixture starts to turn pale gold. Add roux to cream mixture, whisking briskly and constantly until sauce is thickened. Remove from heat, add jalapeño and cheese, stirring until cheese is melted.

Yield: 4 servings

Rouxminations

Bad Boys

According to **St. Joseph: A Pictorial History,** *a book published in 1981 and compiled by Mildred Grenier, "Few men [as Jesse James] achieved more widespread fame for less praiseworthy accomplishments." The James brothers, Jesse and Frank robbed banks, railroad trains, and stage coaches in Iowa, Kansas, Minnesota, and Kentucky, and, of course, Missouri.*

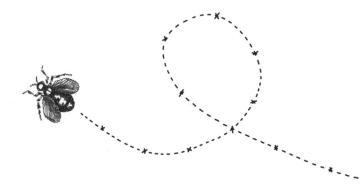

Silent Vigil

Jesse James' two children, Mary and Jesse Edwards, slept on the funeral train to Kearney, Missouri while relatives kept watch over the coffin bearing James for fear the body would be stolen.

The Buck Doesn't Stop Here

The house where Jesse James was shot and killed has been open for tours almost since the day he died. At the time, there was a 10 cents charge for admission and a tour. Today an adult tour costs two dollars.

Sesame Lemon Chicken with Crisp Phyllo Crust

6	(6 ounce) boneless, skinless chicken breasts	2	teaspoons minced fresh ginger
			Pinch of cayenne pepper
3	tablespoons fresh lemon juice	½	teaspoon ground black pepper
2	tablespoons soy sauce	1	egg white
3	tablespoons honey	4	sheets phyllo dough
2	tablespoons vegetable oil	4	tablespoons melted butter
1	clove garlic, minced	½	cup sesame seeds, toasted

Rinse chicken breasts and pat dry. Make a few slashes in each breast. Combine lemon juice, soy sauce, honey, vegetable oil, garlic, ginger, cayenne, black pepper, and egg white in a non-reactive dish. Add chicken, cover the dish tightly, and refrigerate for at least 4 hours, but preferably overnight.

Preheat oven to 450 degrees. Coat baking sheets with nonstick spray. Remove breasts from marinade and allow to drain on a plate. Set aside.

Brush a sheet of phyllo with melted butter, top with another sheet, butter second sheet, and repeat with remaining sheets. Cut phyllo stack into 6 equal strips. Lay 1 piece of chicken at the end of 1 strip of phyllo and roll it up, leaving the ends exposed. Dip each exposed end into toasted sesame seeds, fully coating with seeds. Place chicken, phyllo-seam-down, on prepared baking sheet. Repeat procedure with the other 5 pieces of chicken. Brush the tops of phyllo with melted butter before cooking. Bake until crisp and brown, about 25 to 30 minutes.

Hint: Serve with the following recipe, Creole Mustard Sauce.

Yield: 6 servings

Creole Mustard Sauce

1 cup mayonnaise	½ teaspoon cayenne pepper
¼ cup Creole or Dijon mustard	½ teaspoon salt
1 tablespoon yellow mustard	1 tablespoon minced green onion
1 tablespoon horseradish	1 tablespoon minced garlic
½ teaspoon cider vinegar	1 teaspoon finely chopped green bell pepper
¼ teaspoon Worcestershire sauce	1 teaspoon finely chopped celery
1 teaspoon red wine vinegar	1 teaspoon finely chopped onion
1 teaspoon water	

Mix all ingredients together.

Hint: Great dipping sauce for sirloin skewers, chicken strips, or shrimp.

Rouxminations

The Proof Is In The Pudding

Modern day science has helped solve an age-old question about the end of Jesse James' life. There has been much debate, resulting in the exhumation of James' body in 1997, as to whether or not Jesse James escaped and lived to be a ripe old age. The DNA testing proved to a 99 percent certainty it was James who was killed in St. Joseph.

Sautéed Chicken with Fresh Thyme and Roasted Garlic

1 teaspoon salt	8 tablespoons unsalted butter, divided
1 teaspoon pepper	18 cloves garlic, peeled
1 cup all-purpose flour	1 teaspoon chopped fresh thyme
1 (3 pound) chicken, cut up, or a like amount of boneless chicken breasts	1 teaspoon chopped fresh parsley
	3 ounces dry white wine
	6 ounces chicken bouillon

Preheat oven to 325 degrees. Combine salt, pepper, and flour in a shallow bowl. Dredge chicken in flour mixture. Melt 4 tablespoons butter in an ovenproof skillet. Add garlic and chicken pieces. Brown chicken for 3 minutes on each side.

Place pan in oven and bake for 20 minutes, until chicken is just cooked through. Remove from oven. Using a slotted spoon, remove chicken from pan to a plate. Carefully drain off fat from skillet and return it to the burner over medium heat. Add thyme, parsley, and white wine to pan drippings. Bring to a boil, constantly scraping bottom of pan. Add bouillon and reduce liquid by half. Add remaining butter while gently stirring. Return chicken to pan and heat through. Season with additional salt and pepper, if desired.

Yield: 4 servings

Mochila Mail

Wanted: Young, skinny, wiry fellows. Not over 18. Must be expert riders. Willing to risk death daily. Orphans preferred. Wages twenty five dollars a week.

So read the want ad for Pony Express riders, and young men clamored to the Pony Express headquarters at Patee House to join the fraternity of mail carriers.

The Pony Express originated in St. Joseph as a business idea of a group already hauling freight overland to California. And, while the idea of using horses to deliver mail wasn't new (Ghengis Kahn, emperor of China in 1203-1277, was thought to have used horses to deliver mail to remote areas), the discovery of gold in California in 1848 prompted the need for better communication with the young and vast country. Enter Russell, Majors & Waddle who were the major financial backers of the Pony Express.

The riders carried parcels in the mochila, a pouch with a removable leather cover, placed over the saddle. They rode to fulfill the promise of quicker mail service because railroad and telegraph did not reach that far. But technology was not far behind. By the end of 1860, the telegraph had reached coast to coast and the need for the Pony Express came to an end.

During its brief romantic history, the express made 308 runs each way from St. Joseph to Sacramento. The riders covered a distance equal to 24 times around the earth. Neither rain, nor snow, nor sleet, kept the mail from being delivered. The Pony Express closed a colorful chapter in the history of communication.

Today, the Pony Express Museum is a national treasure. There are Pony Express organizations and enthusiasts as far away as the Czechoslovakian Republic. Each year in June, riders recreate the Pony Express route to relive that brief, romantic era of mail delivery. Pony Express.net is one of St. Joseph's internet service providers, and it brings yet another chapter to the history of mail delivery.

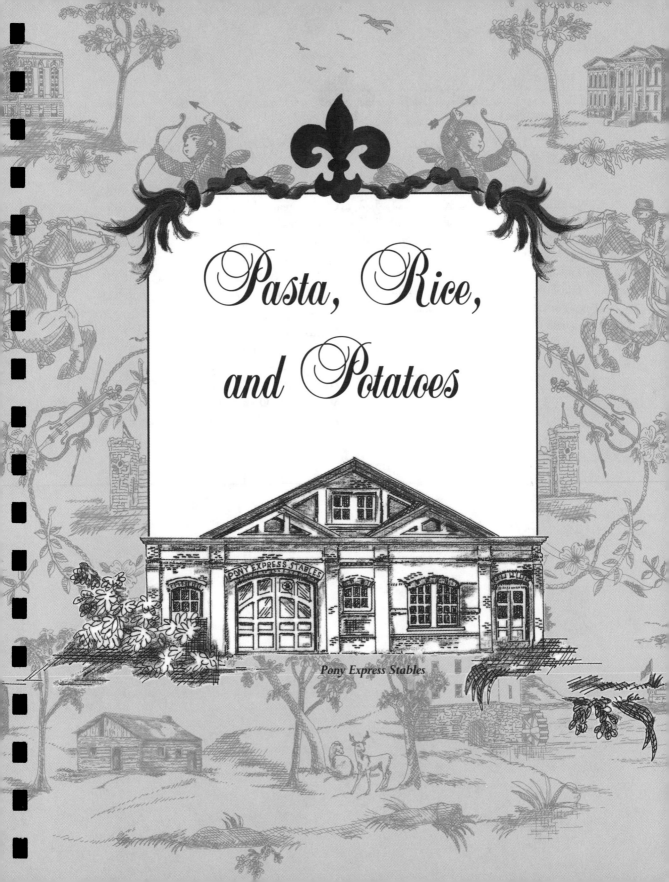

Pasta, Rice, and Potatoes

Pony Express Stables

Pasta, Rice, and Potatoes

Bow Tie Pasta with Creamy Shallot Sauce

¼ cup olive oil
1 large red pepper, seeded and sliced
1 large yellow pepper, seeded and sliced
4 shallots, finely chopped
8 ounces mushrooms, sliced
½ cup dry white wine

2 cups chicken broth
1 cup whipping cream
1 tablespoon chopped fresh parsley
12 ounces bow tie pasta, cooked
½ cup grated Parmesan cheese
Salt and pepper to taste

Heat olive oil in a large sauté pan. Add peppers, shallots, and mushrooms and sauté until tender. Remove from pan. Add wine, chicken broth, and cream, and simmer until thickened. Add vegetables, parsley, salt, and pepper. Pour sauce over cooked pasta and sprinkle with Parmesan.

Yield: 6 servings

Goat Cheese Ravioli with Basil

1 large clove garlic
1 (5½ ounce) log soft fresh goat cheese
⅔ cup fresh ricotta cheese
½ cup chopped fresh basil
Salt and pepper

2 large egg yolks
24 egg roll or spring roll wrappers
1 egg, beaten
Extra-virgin olive oil
Parmesan cheese, shaved
Fresh basil sprigs

Finely chop garlic in food processor. Add goat cheese, ricotta, and basil and blend until smooth. Season with salt and pepper. Blend in egg yolks. Using 4-inch round cookie cutter, cut out 1 round from each egg roll wrapper. Place scant tablespoon of filling in center of each round. Brush edge of wrappers with beaten egg. Fold in half and press edges to seal. (These can be made up to 6 hours ahead.) Arrange on floured baking sheet, cover with plastic, and chill. Working in batches, cook ravioli in large pot of boiling water until just tender, stirring occasionally, about 2 minutes per batch. Using slotted spoon, transfer ravioli to large shallow bowl. Drizzle with oil. Sprinkle with Parmesan and garnish with basil sprigs.

Yield: 6 servings

Rouxminations

Under The Microscope

Practically the whole western world had its eyes on St. Joseph on April 3, 1860, as the first Pony Express rider left the stables carrying mail from the Hannibal and St. Joseph Railroad train. The destination was nearly 2000 miles away in Sacramento, California.

Old and Fat Need Not Apply

The first Pony Express ride was April 3, 1860. Riders responded to an ad which read: "Wanted: Young, skinny, wiry fellows." Riders were paid $125 per month.

Reading Rainbow

The Junior League of St. Joseph with the Public Library helped bring the Reading Is Fundamental (RIF) program to St. Joseph in 1980. Throughout the League's existence, it has partnered several times to bring many literacy projects to St. Joseph.

Chicken Spinach Lasagna

2 tablespoons butter	¼ teaspoon pepper
1 cup chopped pecans	1 tablespoon soy sauce
6 lasagna noodles, uncooked	1½ (10¾ ounce) cans cream of mushroom soup
1 (10 ounce) package frozen spinach, thawed	1 (8 ounce) carton sour cream
2 cups chopped cooked chicken	1 (4½ ounce) jar sliced mushrooms, drained
2 cups shredded Cheddar cheese	⅓ cup mayonnaise
⅓ cup finely chopped onion	1 cup freshly grated Parmesan cheese
½ teaspoon nutmeg	
1 tablespoon cornstarch	
½ teaspoon salt	

Preheat oven to 350 degrees. Melt butter in skillet over medium heat. Add pecans and cook for 3 minutes. Cool completely and set aside. Cook noodles according to package directions. Drain and set aside. Squeeze spinach in between layers of paper towels to remove moisture.

Combine spinach, chicken, cheese, onion, nutmeg, cornstarch, salt, pepper, soy sauce, soup, sour cream, mushrooms, and mayonnaise in large bowl. Stir well to blend. Arrange 2 noodles in a lightly greased 11 x 7 x 1½-inch baking dish. Spread half of chicken mixture over noodles. Repeat with 2 more noodles and remaining chicken mixture. Top with remaining noodles and sprinkle with Parmesan cheese and butter pecan topping. Bake, covered, for 55 to 60 minutes, until hot and bubbly. Let stand 15 minutes before cutting.

Yield: 8 servings

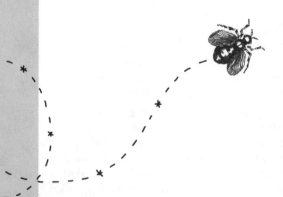

Chicken with Pasta, Portobello Mushrooms, and Sun-Dried Tomatoes

¼ cup dried packed sun-dried tomatoes
½ cup boiling water
6 ounces boneless, skinless chicken breasts
¼ cup dry white wine
1 tablespoon Italian seasoning
3 tablespoons chopped shallots
1¼ cups chopped fresh portobello mushrooms

8 ounces pasta, such as penne
5 cloves garlic, minced
1 tablespoon all-purpose flour
12 ounces evaporated skim milk
⅛ teaspoon ground nutmeg
⅛ teaspoon crushed red pepper flakes
½ cup chopped fresh basil

Preheat oven to 350 degrees. Place sun-dried tomatoes in a bowl, add boiling water, and set aside for tomatoes to reconstitute, approximately 10 to 15 minutes.

Place chicken in a shallow baking dish. Pour wine over chicken and sprinkle with Italian seasoning. Bake 15 to 20 minutes, until the meat is no longer pink and juices run clear. Remove chicken from baking dish, reserving cooking juices; cool and shred chicken.

Drain and thinly slice sun-dried tomatoes. Pour reserved cooking juices into a sauté pan. Add shallots, mushrooms, and tomatoes. Sauté over low heat for 5 minutes, until liquid is absorbed and vegetables are wilted. Remove from heat, cover, and keep warm.

Cook pasta according to package directions. While pasta is cooking, prepare sauce. Preheat a small, heavy saucepan for about 1 minute over medium heat. Spray with Pam or vegetable oil. Sauté garlic and flour, then whisk in evaporated milk. Add nutmeg and pepper flakes, whisking constantly. Bring mixture to boil and continue to cook for 5 to 10 minutes, until thickened. Reduce heat to lowest setting and add basil. Transfer drained pasta to a warm serving bowl; add chicken, vegetables, and sauce. Toss to coat.

Yield: 6 to 8 servings

Rouxminations

Cash Poor

William Russell, Alexander Majors, and William Waddell were the founders of the Pony Express. The company was Central Overland California and Pike's Peak Express Company, or C.O.C. & P.P., as it was known. The Pony Express was a subsidiary for the freight and stage company. Some creative types have claimed the initials C.O.C. & P.P. really stood for "Clean out of cash and poor pay."

Rouxminations

Mouths Were Watering

The Junior League of St. Joseph partnered with the talented cooks of the Albrecht-Kemper museum in distributing Palette to Palate in 1988. The book was featured in several national cooking columns, and though currently out-of-print, the book remains in great demand.

Pasta Puttanesca

1	pound angel hair or linguine pasta	½	cup black olives
2	(2 pound, 3 ounce) cans peeled Italian plum tomatoes	¼	cup drained capers
		4	cloves garlic, chopped
¼	cup olive oil	⅓	tube anchovy paste
1	teaspoon oregano	½	cup chopped Italian parsley
⅛	teaspoon red pepper flakes	2	teaspoons salt

Bring 4 quarts of water to a boil in a large pot. Add salt and pasta. Cook until tender but still firm. Drain and transfer to 4 plates.

While pasta is cooking, drain tomatoes, cut into halves and squeeze out as much liquid as possible. Combine tomatoes and olive oil in a skillet, and bring to a boil. Keep at a full boil and add remaining ingredients at a time, stirring frequently. Reduce heat slightly and continue to cook for a few minutes, until sauce has thickened to your liking. Serve over hot pasta and garnish with additional chopped parsley and grated cheese, if desired.

Yield: 6 servings

Pasta with Gorgonzola Tomatoes

3	tablespoons extra virgin olive oil	6	ounces Gorgonzola cheese, at room temperature, crumbled
1	medium onion, chopped	½	cup butter, softened
4	cloves garlic, chopped	1	pound penne pasta
1	(14½ ounce) can Italian plum tomatoes, drained and chopped		Salt and pepper
		1	cup grated Parmesan cheese, Reggiano, if possible
½	cup chopped fresh basil		

Heat oil in large skillet over medium heat. Add onion and garlic. Sauté until tender, 6 to 8 minutes, but do not brown. Stir in tomatoes. Cook until mixture thickens, stirring occasionally, about 15 minutes. Add basil and simmer 5 minutes. In a small bowl, combine Gorgonzola and butter. Cook pasta in boiling salted water until just tender, or al dente. Drain and return pasta to pot. Using a whisk, add Gorgonzola mixture to tomato sauce. Add sauce to pasta and toss to coat. Season with salt and pepper, sprinkle with Parmesan, and serve immediately.

Yield: 4 servings

Pasta with Chicken and Pepper-Cheese Sauce

3 tablespoons all-purpose flour, divided
½ teaspoon salt
¼-½ teaspoon ground red pepper
⅛-¼ teaspoon ground white pepper
⅛-¼ teaspoon ground black pepper
4 medium chicken breasts, skinned, boned and cut into 1-inch pieces
2 tablespoons cooking oil
1 medium onion, chopped
1 sweet red bell pepper, chopped
1 tablespoon seeded and chopped jalapeño pepper
2 cloves garlic, minced
¾ cup chicken broth
½ cup milk
1 teaspoon Worcestershire sauce
1 cup shredded Monterey Jack cheese
¼ cup sour cream
8 ounces linguine, cooked and drained

Combine 1 tablespoon flour, salt, and ground peppers. Toss with chicken to coat. Cook chicken in hot oil in a 10-inch skillet, until tender, about 4 to 5 minutes. Remove chicken. Add onion, red pepper, jalapeño, and garlic. If necessary, add more oil. Cook until tender. Stir in remaining flour. Add broth, milk, and Worcestershire sauce. Cook and stir until bubbly. Stir in cheese and melt. Stir 1 cup of hot mixture into sour cream, and then return to skillet. Add chicken and heat through, but do not boil. Serve over linguine.

Hint: Wear gloves when seeding and chopping the jalapeño pepper. Spinach linguine is great with this recipe.

Yield: 4 servings.

Rouxminations

Be Home By Dark

Among the youngest Pony Express riders was 15 year-old "Buffalo Bill" Cody. Other legends claim the youngest rider was 11 year-old Bronco Charlie Miller.

We're Number One

While several diary and newspaper reports name William Richardson as the first Pony Express rider, Johnny Fry is the one embraced by most St. Joseph residents as being the first rider.

Smoked Cheddar Mac and Cheese with Apples

½ cup chopped onion
1 cup chicken broth
¾ cup half-and-half
1 tablespoon all-purpose flour
½ teaspoon dry mustard
¼ teaspoon pepper
3 ounces smoked Cheddar or Gouda cheese, shredded

8 ounces large elbow pasta, cooked according to package directions
1 medium tart apple, diced (about ⅔ cup)
3 tablespoons shredded Parmesan cheese

Preheat oven to 350 degrees. Place onion and chicken broth in a saucepan. Bring to a boil, cover, reduce heat and cook until onion is tender, about 5 minutes. Combine half-and-half, flour, mustard, and pepper in a screw-top jar, cover, and shake well. Add to chicken broth, and cook until bubbly. Remove from heat, add cheese, and stir until melted. Pour sauce over pasta and toss to coat. Transfer to a greased 1½ to 2-quart casserole dish. Bake covered for 10 minutes. Uncover and bake 10 more minutes, until bubbly. Let stand 5 minutes. Top with apples and Parmesan.

Yield: 6 servings

Zucchini Linguine

6 ounces linguine
3 cloves garlic, minced
1 onion, chopped
2 teaspoons olive oil
3 medium zucchini, quartered lengthwise and sliced

½ teaspoon salt
1 tablespoon balsamic vinegar
2 tomatoes, seeded and diced
4 teaspoons grated Parmesan cheese

Prepare linguine according to package directions. Drain and set aside. Heat oil in a Dutch oven, add garlic and onion, and sauté until softened. Add zucchini and sauté 2 to 3 minutes longer. Add salt, vinegar, and tomatoes. Stir until sauce is slightly thickened. Add linguine and mix to heat through. Sprinkle with Parmesan and serve.

Yield: 4 servings

Rouxminations

Monopolizing The Mail

The Pony Express was organized by Russell, Majors, and Waddell whose headquarters were in St. Joseph's Patee House. Between 80-100 riders, mostly orphans, were hired and nearly 500 horses were used.

Like A Flash

Pony Express riders were allowed two minutes for the mount and the mochila exchange but many riders were able to cut the time to 15 seconds.

French Rice

1½ cups wild rice	1 cup sliced fresh mushrooms, sprinkled with freshly squeezed lemon juice
1 cup long grain white rice	2 cups whipping cream
4¼ cups chicken broth, preferably homemade	½ teaspoon salt
1 large onion, chopped	1 teaspoon freshly ground black pepper
1 green bell pepper, chopped	½-¾ cup freshly grated Parmesan cheese, divided
8 tablespoons butter	

Preheat oven to 350 degrees. Place wild and white rice in a 3-quart saucepan and add broth. Bring to a boil, cover, and cook over medium heat until done, about 45 to 60 minutes.

Sauté onion and green pepper in butter in a skillet until tender. Add to cooked rice. Add mushrooms, cream, salt, pepper, and half of Parmesan cheese, mixing well. Spoon rice mixture into a buttered 9 x 13-inch casserole dish. Sprinkle with remaining cheese. Cover and bake until bubbly, about 20 minutes. Uncover and continue baking until slightly browned, about 10 minutes longer.

Hint: 1 cup sliced carrots or sugar pea pods may be substituted for the mush-rooms.

Yield: 12 servings

Classic Creamed Rice

2 tablespoons butter	3 cups cooked white basmati rice
2 ounces prosciutto or country ham, minced	½ cup chicken broth
½ cup minced shiitake mushroom caps	½ cup whipping cream
½ cup grated zucchini	⅓ cup grated Parmesan cheese
¼ cup grated carrots	3 slices bacon, cooked crisp and crumbled

Melt butter in a large skillet. Add prosciutto, mushrooms, zucchini, carrots, and rice in layers. Top with broth and cream. Cover and simmer over medium heat for 8 to 10 minutes, until most of the liquid is absorbed. Do not stir. Just before serving, stir cheese into rice and sprinkle with bacon.

Yield: 6 to 8 servings

Rouxminations

Neither Rain, Nor Snow, Nor Sleet, Nor Hail

From a Pony Express map: "Communication between St. Joseph, on the fringe of Western settlement, and gold mining communities of California challenged the bold and made the skeptical timid. Into this picture rode the Pony Express. In rain and in snow, in sleet and in hail, over moonlit prairie, down tortuous mount path harried by lurking savage, pounding pony feet knitted together the ragged edges of a rising Nation…"

Morel Mushroom Risotto

1	cup dried morel mushrooms	1½	cups Arborio rice
4	tablespoons unsalted butter, divided	½	cup dry sherry
4	tablespoons olive oil, divided	2	cloves garlic, minced
	Salt and pepper	5-6	cups heated stock
⅔	cup minced shallots	1	cup spinach
1	medium onion, minced	½	cup grated Asiago cheese

Rehydrate mushrooms by soaking in ¾ cup warm water for 10 to 15 minutes. Remove from liquid, reserving it. Coarsely chop mushrooms. Heat 2 tablespoons butter and 2 tablespoons olive oil in a small skillet, add mushrooms, and cook about 3 minutes. Season with salt and pepper to taste and set aside.

In a large saucepan, heat remaining butter and oil. Add shallots and onion. Sauté over medium heat until translucent, about 5 minutes. Stir in rice and cook over medium heat until translucent. Stir in sherry and garlic, and cook until all the liquid is absorbed. Add reserved mushroom liquid. Add stock, 1 cup at a time, stirring continuously. Each cup must be absorbed before adding the next. With the final cup of stock, stir in spinach. Finished risotto should be firm to the bite, yet creamy. Remove from heat, stir in mushrooms and cheese. Season with salt and pepper to taste.

Yield: 4 to 6 servings

Wild Thing

3	cups cooked wild rice	1	clove garlic, minced
1	can French onion soup	¼	cup butter, melted
8	ounces fresh mushrooms, sliced	½	cup slivered almonds
⅓	cup chopped celery	½	cup shredded Monterey Jack cheese
¼	cup chopped red bell pepper		Salt and pepper to taste

Preheat oven to 325 degrees. Prepare rice according to package directions, substituting soup for part of the water. Add mushrooms, onion, celery, red pepper, and garlic to butter in a medium skillet, and sauté until tender. Combine cooked rice, vegetable mixture, almonds, cheese, salt, and pepper in a 2-quart casserole. Cover and bake for 35 to 40 minutes.

Yield: 6 servings

Rouxminations

Who Said A Stamp Costs Too Much?

The cost to carry a piece of mail was $5 per half ounce; later, the price was dropped to $1 per half ounce. The mail was carried in a pouch called a mochila.

Wild Thing

While not an actual Pony Express rider, Wild Bill Hickock is nevertheless associated with the mail delivery service due to a gun fight at Rock Creek station. (Hickock was probably a stock tender there.) Hickock was charged with murder but acquitted. He later became a scout and, ironically, a frontier peace officer.

Blue String Potatoes

1	(36 ounce) package frozen shredded hash brown potatoes	1½-2	teaspoons salt
¼	cup butter, melted	¼-½	teaspoon pepper
½	cup warm milk	½	cup chopped green onions
6	ounces Roquefort or blue cheese, crumbled	6	slices crisp cooked bacon, crumbled or ½ cup Bacos
2	tablespoons chopped fresh parsley	16	ounces nonfat sour cream
		16	ounces regular sour cream

Preheat oven to 350 degrees. Defrost potatoes and pour into large mixing bowl. Mix together remaining ingredients in a large bowl and pour over potatoes, mixing thoroughly. Spoon into 9 x 13-inch pan which has been coated with nonstick spray. Bake until hot and bubbly, about 1 hour.

Yield: 8 servings

Garlic Cheese Twice-Baked Potatoes

4	large russet potatoes	1	teaspoon seasoned salt
½	cup melted butter	½	teaspoon pepper
3	cloves garlic, minced	1	teaspoon dried parsley
¾	cup chopped green onion	2	cups shredded Cheddar cheese, divided
¾	cup sour cream		
1	teaspoon dill weed		

Preheat oven to 350 degrees. Microwave potatoes on high for about 20 minutes, until tender. Cut each potato in half lengthwise and scoop pulp into a bowl, leaving a ¼-inch layer of potato inside the skin. Add butter, garlic, green onion, sour cream, dill weed, seasoned salt, pepper, parsley, and 1¾ cups cheese to the potato pulp, mixing well.

Fill potato shells with mixture and place into a 9 x 13-inch pan. Sprinkle with remaining cheese and bake for 30 minutes, until hot and bubbly.

Hint: These freeze well.

Yield: 8 servings

Rouxminations

Not Quite As Fast As Network News

The shortest Pony Express ride was seven days. The rider carried President Abraham Lincoln's Inaugural Address.

Change Horses In Our Town

The entire Pony Express trek was 2000 miles. Pony Express riders averaged 10 miles per hour. Riders changed every 75-100 miles and horses were changed every 10-15 miles. It is estimated there were approximately 150-190 changing stations along the way.

Gold Rush Potatoes

2½ cups whipping cream
1½ cups milk
3½ pounds Yukon gold potatoes, peeled and thinly sliced into rounds
1½ teaspoons salt
1 teaspoon freshly ground pepper
8 ounces arugula, trimmed, coarsely chopped
2 cups grated Gruyère cheese
12 bacon slices, chopped, cooked crisp, drained

Preheat oven to 375 degrees. Butter a 9 x 13-inch baking dish. Mix cream and milk. Layer a third of potatoes in prepared dish, overlapping slightly. Sprinkle with ½ teaspoon salt and ¼ teaspoon pepper. Layer with a third of arugula, a third of cheese, and a third of bacon. Pour 1⅓ cups cream mixture over all. Repeat layering until all ingredients are used.

Bake, uncovered, until potatoes are tender and cream mixture thickens, about 1 hour and 15 minutes. Let stand 10 to 15 minutes before serving. (Can be made 1 day ahead. Cool slightly, chill uncovered until cold, then cover and keep refrigerated. Rewarm, covered with foil, in 375 degree oven for about 30 minutes.)

Hint: This is also good without the arugula.

Yield: 8 servings

Prime Tuber Chips with Lime Salt

1 teaspoon finely grated lime zest
1 teaspoon salt
1 large sweet potato (about ¾ pound)
1 large russet potato (about ¾ pound)
5 cups vegetable oil

In a small cup, stir zest together with salt. Peel potatoes and, using a vegetable peeler or mandolin, shave as many slices of potato as possible from each potato. Heat oil in a deep 10-inch heavy skillet, over moderately high heat, until it is 375 degrees. Fry potato slices in batches, stirring frequently, until lightly browned and bubbling stops, about 1 minute. Transfer chips with a slotted spoon to paper towels to drain. Sprinkle with lime salt.

Hint: Use other root vegetables (beets, rutabagas, etc.) to make it even more colorful! You can prepare these the day ahead, store in an airtight container, and reheat in a 350 degree oven the next day.

Yield: 10 servings

Potato Horseradish Gratin with Caramelized Onions

2½ pounds red potatoes	2 large onions, thinly sliced
1 teaspoon salt, divided	1 teaspoon sugar
1 teaspoon pepper, divided	1 tablespoon balsamic vinegar
2 cups half-and-half (do not substitute)	1 cup shredded Swiss cheese
½ cup cream-style horseradish	¼ cup chopped fresh parsley, divided
¼ cup butter	

Preheat oven to 400 degrees. Cook potatoes in boiling water for 20 minutes, until almost tender. Drain and cool slightly. Peel potatoes and cut into ¼-inch rounds. Arrange slices in a lightly greased 9 x 13-inch baking dish. Sprinkle with ½ teaspoon salt and ½ teaspoon pepper. Stir together half-and-half and horseradish and pour over potatoes. Bake, covered, for 40 minutes and remove from oven.

Meanwhile, melt butter in a large skillet over medium heat. Add onion and remaining salt and pepper. Cook, stirring occasionally, for 20 minutes. Add sugar and continue cooking, until onions are a nice caramel color, about 5 to 8 more minutes. Stir in vinegar and cook until liquid evaporates, about 2 minutes. Remove from heat and cool 5 minutes. Fold cheese and half of parsley into onions. Reduce oven temperature to 350 degrees and uncover potatoes. Top with onion mixture. Bake for 30 minutes. Remove from oven and let stand 5 minutes. Top with remaining parsley.

Yield: 8 servings

Sweet Potato Puree

2½ pounds red-skinned sweet potatoes, peeled and cubed	2 tablespoons butter
4 ounces soft fresh goat cheese, crumbled	1 teaspoon truffle oil
	Salt and pepper

Cook potatoes in large pot of boiling salted water until tender, about 15 minutes. Drain. Transfer sweet potatoes to processor or blender. Add cheese and process until smooth Add butter and truffle oil. Process until blended. Season with salt and pepper to taste. (Can be prepared 1 day ahead. Cover and refrigerate.) Stir puree in large saucepan over medium heat until heated throughout. Transfer puree to bowl and serve.

Yield: 6 servings

Rouxminations

The Alpha and The Omega

April 3 is a significant date in St. Joseph history because two important historical events occurred on this day, though not in the same year. The Pony Express left the stables in St. Joseph on April 3, 1860; also on this date, in 1882, Jesse James was shot and killed. "Where the Pony Express began and Jesse James ended" was once a popular advertising slogan for the city of St. Joseph.

Potato Quiches

3 cups frozen shredded potatoes	¼ cup finely chopped onion or chives
½ teaspoon onion salt	2 large eggs, beaten
½ teaspoon garlic salt	½ cup milk
⅓ cup butter or margarine, melted	½ teaspoon salt
1 cup finely chopped chicken	¼ teaspoon pepper
1 cup (4 ounces) shredded Cheddar cheese	¼ cup grated Parmesan cheese

Preheat oven to 425 degrees. Thaw potatoes between layers of paper towels to remove excess moisture. Add onion salt and garlic salt. Press potatoes into bottom and up sides of an ungreased 9-inch pie plate. Drizzle with butter. Bake for 25 minutes, until lightly browned. Cool on wire rack for 10 minutes. Reduce oven temperature to 350 degrees.

Combine chicken, cheese, and onion or chives; spoon into potato shell. Combine eggs, milk, salt, and pepper, stirring well. Pour over chicken. Bake until set, 25 to 30 minutes. Sprinkle with Parmesan cheese the last 5 minutes. Let stand 10 minutes before serving.

Yield: 6 servings

Sweet Potato Orchard Bake

3 medium sweet potatoes	¼ teaspoon cinnamon
3 medium tart apples	¼ teaspoon margarine
⅓ cup chopped pecans	2 cups miniature marshmallows
¾ cup packed brown sugar	

Peel sweet potatoes and cut into 1 to 1½-inch thick rounds. Cook in slightly salted water until just tender.

Preheat oven to 350 degrees. Quarter and slice each unpeeled apple into eighths. Combine brown sugar and cinnamon. Place alternating slices of apples and sweet potatoes in greased shallow 9 x 13-inch casserole. Sprinkle sugar mixture and nuts over top. Dot with butter and bake for 35 to 40 minutes.

Remove from oven, sprinkle with marshmallows and return to oven until marshmallows are slightly browned.

Hint: This is a unique twist on the old classic.

Yield: 8 servings

Roasted Garlic Potato Salad

1½ pounds small red new potatoes, cut into 1-inch cubes
4 tablespoons olive oil, divided
¼ teaspoon kosher salt, divided (may substitute table salt)
¼ teaspoon pepper
4 sprigs fresh rosemary

Salt and freshly cracked pepper to taste
1 tablespoon white wine vinegar
2-3 teaspoons Dijon mustard
½ head roasted garlic
4-8 green onions, thinly sliced (white and lightest green parts only)

This can be done either in the oven or on the grill. Preheat oven to 450 degrees or preheat grill temperature to very hot. Make an aluminum foil tray by folding foil over for double strength. Coat with nonstick spray. If using the oven method, may use cookie sheet.

In a medium-sized bowl, combine 1 tablespoon olive oil, ¼ teaspoon salt, and ¼ teaspoon pepper; mix well with a fork. Add potatoes and toss until well coated. Spoon mixture onto foil tray or cookie sheet, being sure to keep potatoes in a single layer. Top with rosemary sprigs.

To grill: Place foil tray about 5 inches over hot coals and tent with foil. Grill 25 to 30 minutes, turning occasionally, until tender and crisply browned. Remove from heat and discard rosemary.

To roast in oven: Bake potatoes, uncovered, 30 to 40 minutes, stirring occasionally. Remove from oven when tender and nicely browned. Discard rosemary.

While potatoes are cooking, whisk together vinegar, mustard, and salt and pepper to taste. Gradually add remaining 3 tablespoons oil and whisk. Squeeze roasted garlic to taste into mixture and combine well, mashing with a fork, if necessary. Add green onions and potatoes to the dressing. Toss gently to coat; serve warm.

Yield: 4 to 6 servings

Rouxminations

Breaker 1-9. We've Got A Convoy Here!

Many of the original St. Joseph families arrived in the new town by steamboats, and the freight that they brought with them for the use of Western-bound travelers provided the economic foundation of the town. In many ways, the steamboats on the Missouri River were like modern-day 18-wheel trucks on today's interstate highways, loaded with wholesale good for retail sale.

St. Joseph's Emerald Jewel

It could be said that the Krug brothers were jacks of all trades. After all, they were grocers, meat cutters, bakers and eventually, bankers. The Krugs started the German-American bank, invested in the city's stockyards, and owned an electric street car company in St. Joseph.

Perhaps the best-loved legacy of the Krugs is the land, some 160 acres, donated to the city to be used as a park. In the late 1800's, a grand entry to the park was constructed. Possibly reminiscent of homeland Germany, the castle entrance had three turreted towers of white limestone on each side of the entrance.

Rudolph Rau, superintendent of parks from 1887 to 1917, is credited with the vision which made the park a showplace. Being both a florist and a landscape architect, he developed lavish flowerbeds for visitors to admire. A conservatory exhibited all types of plants with a special mum show in the fall.

There were pony rides for children as well as a zoo. Band concerts, a lily pond, a Japanese bridge, a grotto and a lovers' walk were also part of the park. Although the magnificent entrance was torn down in 1936, Krug Park is still a favorite picnic and recreational spot for citizens. The lagoon with its paddle boats, fish, turtles, and ducks offer children and adults hours of recreation. And the rose garden bursts with color each summer season.

In recent years the park is home to the Sacred Hills encampment, and during December it becomes Holiday Park and delights thousands with Christmas lights and displays. Krug Park continues to be the crown jewel of the park system after over 100 years.

Vegetables and Side Dishes

Krug Park

Vegetables and Side Dishes

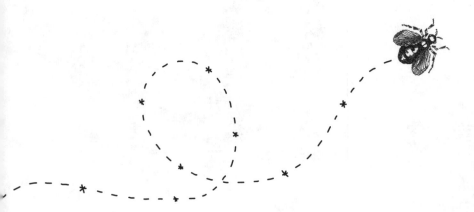

Stuffed Artichoke Bottoms

3 ounces cream cheese, softened
3 ounces blue cheese, crumbled
4 tablespoons unsalted butter
2 tablespoons minced chives
¼ teaspoon salt
⅛ teaspoon white pepper
2 (14 ounce) cans artichoke bottoms, drained
Sliced black olives, optional

Preheat oven to 350 degrees. Combine cream cheese, blue cheese, butter, chives, salt, and white pepper in a small bowl, blending well. Fill each artichoke bottom with some of mixture. Arrange on a baking sheet and bake for 10 minutes. Remove from oven and garnish with an olive slice, if desired.

Hint: Can be prepared up to 2 days ahead. Store covered in the refrigerator. These could also be used as appetizers; but, if so, cut into ¼-inch slices before garnishing.

Yield: 8 servings

Asparagus Gratin with Parmigiano-Reggiano Cheese

24 medium asparagus spears (about 1½ pounds)
½ cup freshly grated Parmigiano-Reggiano cheese
2 tablespoons fine plain dry bread crumbs
½ teaspoon grated lemon zest
3 tablespoons unsalted butter, melted

Bring 3 quarts salted water to a boil in a large saucepan. Trim woody ends from asparagus. With a vegetable peeler, peel bottom half of stalks and add to boiling water. Cook until tender but still crisp, about 6 minutes. Drain well.

Meanwhile, toss cheese, bread crumbs, and lemon zest together in a small bowl until blended.

Preheat broiler. Arrange asparagus in a single layer in an 8-inch square flameproof baking dish. Drizzle with melted butter and sprinkle with an even layer of cheese mixture. Broil about 4 inches from the heat until the bread crumb mixture is golden brown, about 3 minutes. Serve hot.

Yield: 4 to 6 servings

Rouxminations

A Crown Jewel

Krug Park was constructed because Mr. Krug did not want children going to the beer gardens along St. Joseph Avenue, near his home. The park's construction started in 1890 with 10 acres and is now 160 acres.

Animal Farm

The Frieburg Passion Play with a cast of over 1200 performed in 1928 at the Krug Bowl. The animals left over from the play became part of Rau's Zoo in Krug Park. Other animals in the zoo included bears, monkeys, alligators, buffalo, deer, and the only two camels in captivity in Missouri at the time.

Smoky Beans

5   slices bacon, cut into ½-inch dice
1   cup diced yellow onion
1-2 tablespoons minced garlic
½   cup ketchup
¼   cup dark molasses
¼   cup honey mustard
¼   cup bourbon
2   tablespoons brown sugar
2   tablespoons Worcestershire sauce
3-4 dashes Tabasco sauce
2   (28 ounce) cans baked beans, rinsed and drained
    Kosher salt and freshly ground pepper

Preheat oven to 325 degrees. In a large sauté pan over medium heat, cook bacon, stirring occasionally, until crispy, about 10 minutes. Add onions and garlic, cooking until soft, about 5 minutes. Add ketchup, molasses, mustard, bourbon, brown sugar, Worcestershire sauce, and Tabasco. Bring to a boil, reduce heat, and simmer for about 5 minutes.

Place beans in a 2-quart casserole or Dutch oven. Add sauce and stir to combine thoroughly. Bake, uncovered, for 1 hour. Season with salt and pepper to taste. Serve warm.

Yield: 6 to 8 servings

Grand Marnier-Glazed Carrots

3   tablespoons butter
1   pound baby carrots
3   tablespoons orange marmalade
⅓   cup Grand Marnier liqueur
2   tablespoons chopped fresh parsley

Melt butter in a large skillet over medium-high heat. Add carrots and toss to coat. Stir in marmalade and heat until melted. Add Grand Marnier and bring to a boil. Lower heat and simmer, covered, for 5 minutes. Uncover carrots and continue to cook until tender and the liquid has been reduced to a glaze, about 5 minutes. Sprinkle with parsley and serve at once.

Hint: If you do not have a bottle of Grand Marnier on hand, you can always purchase small trial sizes at your local wine shop.

Yield: 4 servings

Company Celery

2   stalks celery, sliced in bite-size
    pieces
1   teaspoon salt

1   cup canned button mushrooms,
    drained, or 8 ounces fresh
    button mushrooms
½   cup butter (1 stick)
1   cup slivered almonds

Place celery in a saucepan. Add salt and enough water to cover. Bring to a boil and cook until celery is crisp but tender, about 3 to 5 minutes. Drain water. Return to stove and add remaining ingredients. Cook on medium heat until heated through.

Hint: If using fresh mushrooms, sauté in the butter until tender.

Yield: 8 servings

Creamy Tex-Mex Corn with Lime

3   cups corn kernels
1   large shallot, chopped
1   clove garlic, chopped
1   teaspoon ground cumin
1   teaspoon chili powder
1   cup nonfat milk

4   ounces reduced fat cream
    cheese, cubed
2   tablespoons minced lime zest
¼   cup minced fresh chives
    Salt and pepper

Heat a large nonstick frying pan over medium heat. Coat with nonstick spray. Add corn, shallot, garlic, cumin, and chili powder. Sauté until corn starts to soften, about 4 minutes. Stir in milk and cheese and simmer, uncovered, until liquid thickens, about 4 minutes. Mix in lime zest and chives. Season with salt and pepper to taste and serve immediately.

Yield: 4 servings

Rouxminations

Honk, Daddy

Today the Krug Park bowl attracts several outdoor concerts each year and is the site for many summer reunions and weddings in the rose garden. The lagoon literally bubbles with fish as visitors throw bread crumbs. Perhaps the thing children and adults will most remember is instructing the driver to honk loud and long as the car passes through the tunnels in Krug Park.

Mummy Dearest

The chrysanthemums at an annual exhibit were described as being as small as a "brass button" and as large as a "head of cabbage." Visitors could see over 50 varieties of chrysanthemums at the exhibit. The conservatory and hothouses were removed from Krug Park in 1924-25.

Our Winter Wonderland

Krug Park is transformed annually into the Holiday Park. It includes hundreds of thousands of Christmas lights throughout the park, a Santa's workshop for children, a Nativity, "Christmas in Many Lands," and company sponsored light displays. A lighting ceremony is held annually to open the holiday season. The project was started by the East Side Optimists in 1981 and is visited by thousands during the holiday season.

Frederick Avenue Corn

3 tablespoons butter	2 pounds frozen corn, thawed
½ cup chopped onion	2 stalks celery, chopped
2 tablespoons flour	8 slices bacon, cooked and
½ teaspoon salt	crumbled
1 cup sour cream	

Preheat oven to 350 degrees and butter a 2-quart casserole dish. Melt butter in a large skillet, add onion, and sauté for 7 to 8 minutes over medium heat. Blend in flour and salt, stirring constantly. Gradually stir in sour cream until smooth. Add corn and celery, heating thoroughly. Stir in crumbled bacon, saving some for topping. Pour into prepared dish and sprinkle with reserved bacon. Bake until bubbly, 30 to 45 minutes.

Hint: Perfect dish to take when you have to go some place.

Yield: 8 servings

Green Bean and Carrot Sauté

32 unpeeled cloves garlic	1½ pounds baby carrots
2 tablespoons olive oil	1 teaspoon salt
1½ pounds green beans	2 tablespoons sugar

Boil garlic in 2 cups of water for 3 minutes. Drain and peel. Heat oil in an ovenproof dish. Add garlic, cover, and bake at 275 degrees for 30 minutes. Remove cover and bake an additional 15 minutes, until golden brown.

Cook green beans in boiling water for 4 minutes. Drain and rinse with cold water. Cook baby carrots in boiling water with salt and sugar for 10 minutes. Drain and rinse with cold water. Combine garlic, green beans, and carrots in a large bowl. Cover and refrigerate overnight.

Before serving, sauté in butter until heated through. Season with salt and pepper to taste.

Yield: 12 servings

Green Beans with Shallots, Rosemary, and Hazelnuts

2 pounds trimmed fresh green beans	1 tablespoon chopped fresh rosemary or 1 teaspoon dried
¼ cup butter	Salt and pepper
⅔ cup chopped shallots	½ cup hazelnuts, toasted, husked, and chopped

Cook green beans in boiling salted water until crisp tender, about 5 minutes. Drain and rinse in cold water. Drain well and set aside.

Melt butter in skillet over medium-high heat. Add shallots and rosemary. Sauté until shallots are tender, about 5 minutes. Add green beans and toss until heated through, about 5 minutes. Season to taste with salt and pepper. Add chopped hazelnuts and toss. Serve immediately.

Yield: 8 servings

Cranberry Chutney

6 cups cranberries	12 dried dates
1½ cups sugar	¼ cup crystallized ginger, chopped
1 unpeeled orange, chopped and seeded	½ cup cider vinegar
1 cup orange juice	1 teaspoon salt
1 small onion, finely chopped	1 teaspoon dry mustard
¼ cup raisins	3 tablespoons chopped fresh sage or 1 teaspoon dry
¼ cup slivered almonds	

Place all ingredients, except ⅔ of sage, in a non-aluminum pan and cook over medium-low heat, stirring until sugar dissolves. Increase heat and boil until berries pop and mixture thickens, 5 to 10 minutes. Add remaining sage. Ladle into sterilized jars and seal.

Rouxminations

One's Pain Is Another's Gain

Hyde Park was a homestead of blacksmith Anliff C. Hyde. Hyde reportedly had gold fever and made a trek to California. His homestead was plundered by post Civil War bushwhackers. One of his grandsons, Calvin, donated the farmland to the city and it is now a favorite recreational area called Hyde Park.

Sweet and Sour Green Beans

4	slices bacon	2	cans cut green beans, drained
1	cup sugar	1	onion, chopped
½	cup vinegar		

Cook bacon until crisp. Remove bacon with slotted spoon and drain on paper towels. Add sugar and vinegar to bacon drippings and cook until sugar is dissolved. Crumble bacon, and add to sugar mixture. Add green beans, and onion. Simmer for 45 minutes on low.

Yield: 6 servings

Rouxminations

Early Synchronized Swimming

Hyde Park, in the city's south end, was known for water ballets and band concerts in the early 1900's. Ice skating was also popular at the Park. Families gathered at Hyde Park to participate in events that represent a bygone era.

Spinach Pie

3	cups chopped yellow onion	½	cup freshly grated Parmesan cheese
2	tablespoons good olive oil	3	tablespoons plain dry bread crumbs
2	teaspoons kosher salt		
1½	teaspoons freshly ground black pepper	½	pound good feta, cut into ½-inch cubes
3	(10 ounce) packages frozen chopped spinach, defrosted	½	cup pine nuts
6	extra-large eggs, beaten	¼	pound salted butter, melted
2	teaspoons grated nutmeg	6	sheets phyllo dough, defrosted

Preheat oven to 375 degrees. In a medium sauté pan over medium heat, sauté onions in olive oil until translucent and slightly browned, 10 to 15 minutes. Add salt and pepper and allow to cool slightly.

Squeeze out and discard as much liquid from spinach as possible. Put spinach in a bowl. Gently mix in onions, eggs, nutmeg, Parmesan cheese, bread crumbs, feta, and pine nuts.

Butter an ovenproof, nonstick, 6-inch sauté pan and line it with 6 stacked sheets of phyllo dough, brushing each with melted butter and letting the edges hang over the pan. Pour the spinach mixture into middle of phyllo and neatly fold edges up and over top to seal in filling. Brush top well with melted butter. Bake for 1 hour, until crust is golden brown and the filling is set. Remove from oven and allow to cool completely. Serve at room temperature.

Yield: 6 to 8 servings

Oven Roasted Vegetables with Fresh Herbs

30 cloves garlic, peeled
1 red onion, peeled and cut into 6 wedges
3 leeks, white parts only, rinsed, and cut in half crosswise, and then in half lengthwise
1 fennel bulb, trimmed and cut into 8 wedges
1 pound red potatoes, cut into 1½-inch pieces
1 pound sweet potatoes, peeled and cut into 1½-inch pieces
¾ pound carrots, peeled and cut into 1½-inch lengths
1½ pounds banana squash, butternut squash, or pumpkin, peeled, seeded, and cut into 1½-inch cubes
1 cup extra virgin olive oil
1 tablespoon salt
1 teaspoon pepper
30 sprigs fresh thyme
4 sprigs fresh rosemary
40 leaves fresh sage

Preheat oven to 425 degrees. Immerse garlic cloves in boiling water for 3 minutes. Drain and pat dry with paper towels. In a small, heavy saucepan or skillet, heat enough olive oil to cover at least half of the cloves. Add garlic. Cook over medium high heat for about 7 minutes, turning continuously, until brown. Remove and drain on paper towels. Cool garlic oil and reserve for other uses such as salad dressings, or sautéing vegetables or chicken. May be prepared in large batches and stored in refrigerator for up to 2 weeks.

Combine all vegetables and roasted garlic in a large bowl. Add salt and pepper to the 1 cup olive oil, stir well, and pour over vegetables. Toss well to combine. Strip leaves off thyme and rosemary sprigs and add to vegetables, along with sage leaves. Toss again and then spread vegetables evenly in a large, shallow roasting pan. Roast for 35 to 45 minutes, until all the vegetables are tender when pierced with a fork.

Hint: Stove top roasted garlic provides an alternative to the traditional method.

Yield: 8 to 10 servings

Old St. Jo-Style Sautéed Mushrooms

2 tablespoons butter
¼ cup olive oil
1 onion, sliced
12 ounces fresh mushrooms, sliced
¼ cup red wine
2 cloves garlic
¼ cup Worcestershire sauce

Melt butter in saucepan over medium heat. Add olive oil. Add remaining ingredients and sauté until onions and mushrooms are tender.

Yield: 4 servings

Rouxminations

Quality Is Job #1

Throughout 80 years of the Junior League of St. Joseph's existence, the organization and individual members have been recognized for outstanding achievements in project development and volunteer service.

Rouxminations

End Of The Road

As the Gold Rush reached fever pitch in 1849, St. Joseph was the optimum north and west point on the Missouri River which could safely be reached by steamboat. Thousands of passengers made the steamboat trip to St. Joseph where they bought wagons and supplies for the hazardous trip to Marysville, Kansas, where the California Trail met the Oregon Trail.

Caramelized Onion and Pecan Brussels Sprouts

1	large onion	1	cup pecans pieces
1	pound Brussels sprouts	1	teaspoon salt
¼	cup butter	½	teaspoon pepper

Cut onion in half, and thinly slice. Microwave or boil Brussels sprouts until just tender and slice in half.

Melt butter in a large heavy skillet over medium-high heat. Add pecans and sauté until toasted, about 5 minutes. Remove pecans from skillet. Add onions and cook 15 minutes, until caramel in color. Add pecans and Brussels sprouts and cook until heated through, about 3 more minutes. Sprinkle with salt and pepper and serve immediately.

Yield: 6 to 8 servings

Vegetable Provençal

⅓	cup olive oil		Salt and freshly ground black pepper
3	medium onions, sliced		
5	cloves garlic, thinly sliced	12	fresh tomatoes, sliced, or
3	medium zucchini, sliced		1 (14½ ounce) can stewed
8	sprigs fresh thyme		tomatoes

Heat olive oil in a large skillet. Add onions and cook over medium-low heat until browned and caramelized, about 30 minutes. Add garlic and cook 1 minute. Increase heat to medium-high and add zucchini. Add additional oil if needed. Cook until tender, about 8 minutes.

Strip leaves from thyme sprigs and sprinkle over skillet. Add salt, pepper, and tomatoes. Stir until combined. Continue cooking until tomatoes are heated through, about 5 minutes.

Yield: 8 servings

Stir-Fried Sesame Snow Peas

2 tablespoons soy sauce
2 teaspoons sugar
2 tablespoons oriental sesame oil

2 large cloves garlic, chopped
2 pounds snow peas, trimmed
4 teaspoons sesame seeds

Stir soy sauce and sugar in small bowl until sugar dissolves. Heat oil in heavy large skillet. Add garlic and stir 15 seconds. Add snow peas and stir-fry until crisp-tender, about 4 minutes. Add soy mixture and toss until peas are coated, about 1 minute longer. Season with salt and pepper. Transfer to bowl, sprinkle with sesame seeds, and serve.

Yield: 6 to 8 servings

Vegetable Bundles

5 large carrots, peeled and cut into 5 x ½ x ¼-inch strips
2 pounds fresh green beans, trimmed
12 green onions

8 tablespoons butter, divided and melted
1 tablespoon fresh thyme or 1 teaspoon dried
Salt and pepper to taste

Bring large pot of salted water to a boil. Add carrots and cook about 1½ minutes. Add green beans and cook until vegetables are crisp and tender, approximately 2 to 3 minutes. Remove from heat and drain in colander. Drizzle 4 tablespoons of melted butter evenly over vegetables and gently toss to coat.

Cut green tops off onions and cut into strips 8 to 9 inches long and approximately ½ inch wide. Spray strips with Pam or rub butter on them to make them pliable. Using equal amounts of carrots and green beans, create a bundle and tie it with 1 green onion strip. Place on rimmed baking sheet lined with foil and coated with olive oil spray. Repeat procedure until all vegetables are used (approximately 12 bundles). Cover and refrigerate.

Preheat oven to 350 degrees. Add thyme to remaining melted butter. Brush bundles with mixture and sprinkle with salt and pepper. Bake until just heated through, about 8 minutes. Serve immediately.

Hint: These may be assembled a day ahead. Reheat just before serving.

Yield: 12 servings

Rouxminations

Golden Opportunity

The Gold Rush meant prosperity for St. Joseph's merchants. In 1848, the city had a population of 1800 and 19 stores. In 1849, three new stores opened and inventories increased to $400,000. St. Joseph boasted two flour mills, two steam saw mills, nine blacksmith shops, four wagon shops, two sheet ironware manufacturers, and two saddle and harness makers. Anything an emigrant could want, from hardware to frying pans, was available in St. Joseph.

Refried White Beans

2 teaspoons vegetable oil	1½ teaspoons cumin
½ cup finely chopped carrot	2 (15 ounce) cans cannellini or
1 cup chopped green onion	other white beans, undrained
3 large cloves garlic, minced	¼ cup chopped fresh cilantro

Heat oil in a large nonstick skillet over medium-high heat. Add carrots and sauté 5 minutes. Add onions and garlic and sauté until tender, about 2 minutes. Stir in cumin and beans; partially mash mixture with a potato masher. Cook 10 minutes or until thick, stirring frequently to keep beans from sticking. Stir in cilantro.

Hint: A great side dish and a must in the Portobello Mushroom Nachos (page 25).

Yield: 4 to 5 cups

Zucchini Feta Gratin

2½ cups hot cooked long grain rice	½ teaspoon salt
	⅛ teaspoon pepper
1 cup (4 ounces) crumbled feta cheese, divided	1 tablespoon chopped fresh mint or 1 teaspoon dried
4 cups ¼-inch-thick sliced zucchini (about 1½ pounds)	Dash of ground nutmeg
	3 large eggs, lightly beaten

Preheat oven to 375 degrees. Combine rice and ½ cup feta cheese in a bowl. Blend well. Press mixture into a 10-inch quiche dish or pie plate coated with nonstick spray.

Steam zucchini slices, covered, for 5 minutes. Press gently between 2 paper towels to remove excess moisture. Combine zucchini, remaining feta cheese, salt, and pepper in a medium bowl. Arrange mixture evenly over rice. Combine mint, nutmeg and eggs, stirring well with a whisk. Pour over zucchini mixture. Bake until set, about 40 minutes.

Yield: 6 servings

Stuffed Yellow Banana Pepper

6 large fresh banana peppers	½ teaspoon dried oregano
1 cup crumbled feta cheese	2 tablespoons olive oil
1 (3 ounce) package cream cheese, softened	

Preheat oven to 400 degrees. Scoop seeds and membrane from peppers. Stir together feta cheese, cream cheese, and oregano. Carefully spoon cheese mixture into peppers. Place peppers on an aluminum-foil-lined jelly-roll pan. Drizzle with olive oil. Bake for about 20 minutes, until peppers are tender. Serve warm or at room temperature.

Hint: Garnish with small strips of cooked bacon, if desired. Banana peppers can range from mild and sweet to very hot.

Yield: 6 servings as a side dish; 12 servings as an appetizer

Rouxminations

No April's Fools

The Pony Express and Jesse James all come back to life during first weekend in April. Since both events share the same day in history, April 3, Pony Express stables and Patee House jointly celebrate the beginning of the Pony Express and the ending of outlaw Jesse James.

Pineapple Soufflé

½ cup margarine	4 cups fresh packed bread pieces, crust removed (about 11 slices)
2 cups sugar	
4 eggs	
¼ cup milk	2½ pounds canned crushed pineapple, undrained

Preheat oven to 325 degrees. Grease a 9 x 13-inch casserole dish. Cream margarine and sugar until light and fluffy. Beat eggs for about 4 to 5 minutes. Add to creamed mixture. Add milk and beat until well blended. Fold bread pieces, crushed pineapple, and juice into mixture. Turn into prepared dish and bake for 1½ hours.

Hint: This unique side dish is especially good with pork.

Yield: 8 servings

Crock Pot Apple Butter

4 pounds Golden Delicious apples, peeled and sliced	1 cup packed brown sugar
½ cup apple cider vinegar	1 teaspoon cinnamon
3 cups sugar	1 teaspoon nutmeg

Place apples and vinegar in a crock pot. Cook on high for 6 hours. Reduce setting to low, stir in sugars and spices and cook for 4 hours. Cool. Store in refrigerator for 1 week or freeze in plastic containers.

Hint: This is perfect in roasted baby pumpkins. To do this, preheat oven to 350 degrees. Cut around the stem of each pumpkin. Scoop out seeds and sprinkle insides with salt. Place pumpkins on a greased baking sheet and fill with apple butter. Replace tops and roast until tender, 45 minutes to 1 hour. This makes a festive presentation and can also be done with applesauce.

Yield: 2 quarts

Christmas Grits

¾ pound breakfast sausage	4 tablespoons unsalted butter, divided
½ cup finely diced red bell pepper	1½ teaspoons minced garlic
4 large jalapeño chiles, seeded, finely diced or ½ cup finely diced green bell peppers	1½ teaspoons salt
	⅛ teaspoon cayenne pepper
3 cups milk	1½ cups quick cooking grits
3 cups water	1 cup shredded sharp Cheddar cheese

Coat a 9 x 13-inch baking dish with nonstick spray. Crumble sausage into a skillet and sauté for 2 minutes, breaking up chunks. Add bell pepper and jalapeños and sauté until tender, about 5 minutes. Remove from heat.

In a large saucepan, over high heat, bring milk, water, 2 tablespoons butter, garlic, salt, and cayenne pepper to a boil. Slowly whisk in grits. Reduce heat to medium. Whisk until thick, about 8 minutes. Add sausage mixture and cheese. Stir until cheese is melted. Pour into prepared pan and spread evenly. Drizzle with remaining butter. Let cool, cover, and refrigerate up to 2 days.

When ready to serve, bake in preheated 350 degree oven until warm, 15 to 30 minutes. You may also heat in microwave.

Yield: 8 servings

Broccoli with Balsamic Butter

1 large head broccoli, trimmed
and broken into large florets
2 tablespoons balsamic vinegar
2 tablespoons dry red wine

6 tablespoons unsalted butter,
cold and cut into small pieces
Salt and pepper to taste

Steam the broccoli in a vegetable steamer over boiling water just until crisp-tender and set aside. Combine the vinegar and wine in a small saucepan and cook over medium-high heat until reduced by half. Remove from the heat and whisk in the butter, bit by bit until all is incorporated and the sauce is creamy. Season with salt and pepper. Pour the balsamic butter over the broccoli and toss to coat well. Serve at once.

Yield: 4 to 6 servings

Acorn Squash in Honey Bourbon Sauce

2 acorn squash halved
lengthwise, seeded, peeled,
and cut into 1-inch slices
1 stick butter, cut into pieces

4 tablespoons bourbon
6 tablespoons honey
2 teaspoons grated orange zest
6 tablespoons water

Preheat oven to 400 degrees. In a 9 x 13-inch dish arrange the squash in a single layer. In a saucepan, combine the butter, bourbon, honey, orange zest, and the water. Bring the mixture to a boil over high heat, stirring occasionally then ladle the sauce over the squash. Bake the squash, covered with foil for 20 to 25 minutes, or until it is tender and the sauce is thickened. Divide the squash between serving dishes and spoon the sauce over it.

Yield: 4 servings

Rouxminations

Something For Everyone

The complete St. Joseph boulevard system, including all attached parks along its course, is the only one in the National Register of Historic Places. The boulevard runs from one end of the city to the other. It is popular for the bike and walking trail; other recreational facilities include baseball diamonds, an ice skating rink, tennis courts, basketball, roller blading, fishing, swimming, as well as a public golf course along the way.

Love at First Sight

Heavy on the romance is the story of Eugene Field and Julia Comstock. They met in St. Joseph, and if there is love at first sight, this was probably proof positive of that.

Eugene Field was a newspaperman and a poet when he met young Julia. The two fell in love almost immediately. During their courtship the couple often took long drives along Rochester Road, a popular site for young couples because of the beautiful trees which hung over the road from both sides and provided shade, privacy, and atmosphere for young lovers. Since Julia was 14 at the time, her father implored that the couple wait until she was 18 to marry. However, he soon relented and allowed his daughter to marry at age 16.

Field worked at the St. Joseph News-Press as a reporter while the couple lived in St. Joseph. In later years when the Fields were living in London, he wrote a poem "Lovers Lane, Saint Jo" which recalled moments of their courtship riding down Rochester Road.

To honor Eugene Field and his poem, Rochester Road was renamed Lovers Lane by the city.

Today, Lovers Lane still has stately trees along the road, but the lane is lined with a variety of homes with well-kept lawns and gardens.

A monument erected by The Lovers Lane Association stands along Lovers Lane honoring Eugene Field. We think you'll fall in love here too.

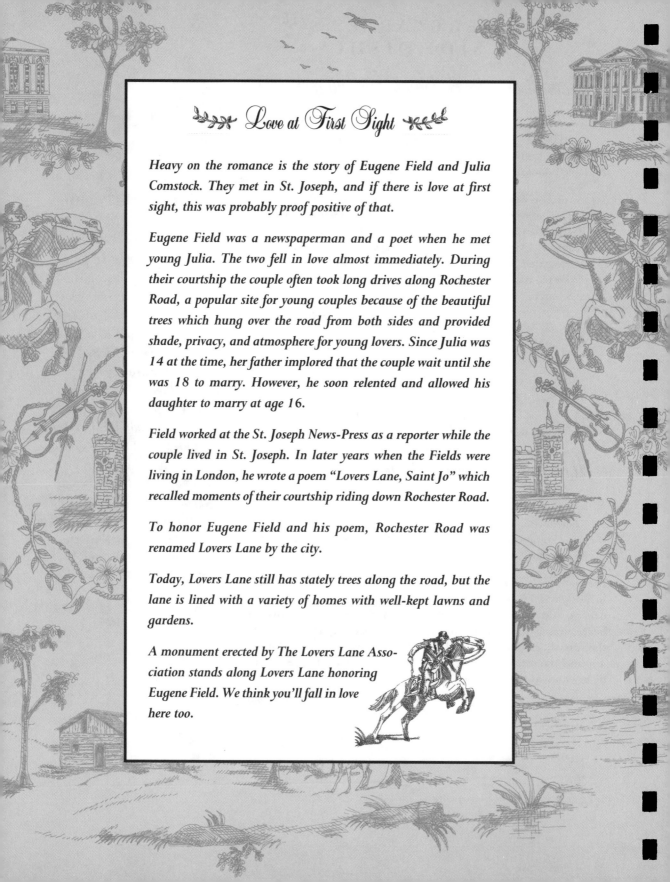

Desserts

Lovers Lane

Desserts

Double Crusted Apple Tart with Sweet Cornmeal Crust

Crust

1½ cups all-purpose flour
⅓ cup yellow cornmeal
¼ cup sugar

¾ cup butter, chilled and cut in small pieces
1 large egg

Filling

⅓ cup Craisins (dried cranberries)
⅛ cup Calvados (apple brandy) or brandy
6-7 medium Granny Smith apples, peeled, cored, and cut into ⅓-inch slices
½ cup plus 1 teaspoon sugar, divided
1½ teaspoons cinnamon

2 tablespoons all-purpose flour
2 tablespoons fresh orange juice
2 tablespoons unsalted butter, melted
Caramel sauce (purchased, or our favorite "Awesome and Easy Caramel Sauce" on page 245)

Put Craisins in a small bowl and cover with Calvados. Allow to soak for several hours, or at least while proceeding with recipe.

For Crust: Preheat oven to 375 degrees. Coat a 9-inch springform pan with nonstick spray. In a large bowl, combine flour, cornmeal, and sugar. Stir and mix well. With fork or pastry blender, cut in butter until the mixture resembles coarse crumbs. Add egg and mix lightly with fork until dough is moist enough to hold together. Press three-quarters of dough into prepared pan, covering the bottom and 2 inches up the sides. Roll out remaining dough into a circle on a piece of wax paper to just fit inside the top of the springform pan. (You may need to sprinkle a little flour when rolling to prevent dough from sticking to the rolling pin.) Refrigerate both crusts.

For Filling: In a bowl, mix apples, Calvados-soaked Craisins, ½ cup sugar, cinnamon, and flour. Remove springform pan from refrigerator and transfer apple mixture into prepared crust. Combine melted butter and orange juice. Slowly pour over filling, being sure to get some over the whole surface, but do not pour so much that it in any way pools up on the bottom of the crust. Invert the wax paper over the pan to cover the filling with the top crust. Seal crusts, crimping them together. Sprinkle remaining teaspoon of sugar over crust. Cut slits to vent. Bake until crust is golden, about 1 hour. To serve, splash each plate with caramel sauce, top with a slice of tart, and serve with vanilla ice cream.

Hint: The recipe works without the Craisins but is so much better when they are included. Brandy can be omitted.

Yield: 10 servings

Rouxminations

Waxing Poetic

Eugene Field, the famous poet, served at the city editor of the St. Joseph Gazette in during 1875-76. Field met Julia Comstock, who was 14 years old. They married two years later. The newlyweds lived a part of their lives at 425 N. Eleventh. That residence is still standing.

Pumpkin Crunch Torte

Crunch Topping

1½ cups finely chopped walnuts
1½ cups vanilla wafer crumbs, about 36 cookies

1½ cups packed light brown sugar
¾ cup butter, melted

Torte

1¼ cups sugar
¾ cup butter (1½ sticks), softened
1 cup solid pack canned pumpkin
2½ cups all-purpose flour
½ cup plain yogurt

1 tablespoon pumpkin pie spice
2¼ teaspoons baking powder
¾ teaspoon baking soda
½ teaspoon salt
3 large eggs
Vanilla wafer crumbs, optional

Filling

3 cups whipping cream

3 tablespoons powdered sugar

For Crunch Topping: Preheat oven to 350 degrees. Mix walnuts, vanilla wafer crumbs, brown sugar, and butter in large bowl until well blended. Divide evenly among 4 9-inch cake pans. With fingers, evenly pat topping to cover bottom of each pan; set aside.

For Torte: In large bowl, with mixer at low speed, beat sugar and butter just until blended. Increase speed to high and beat 10 minutes or until light and fluffy, scraping bowl often with rubber spatula. Reduce speed to low; add pumpkin, flour, yogurt, pumpkin pie spice, baking powder, baking soda, salt, and eggs. Beat until well mixed, scraping bowl frequently. Increase speed to high and beat 2 minutes. (Batter will be thick) Spoon batter into prepared pans, dividing evenly. Spread evenly with spatula. Stagger the 4 cake pans on 2 oven racks, so layers are not directly on top of 1 another. Bake until toothpick inserted in center comes out clean, about 20 minutes, rotating pans between upper and lower racks after 10 minutes.

Cool cake layers in pan on wire rack 10 minutes. With spatula, loosen each cake layer from edge of pan and invert onto wire racks to cool completely.

In small bowl, with mixer at medium speed, beat cream for 30 seconds. Add powdered sugar and then beat until stiff peaks form. Place 1 cake layer, crunch topping side up on a cake plate. Top with a quarter of whipped cream. Repeat layering, ending with a cake layer, topping side up. Spoon remaining cream with a teaspoon in 8 rounded

(Pineapple Crunch Torte continued)

dollops around the outer edge of the cake, or ice the entire top, if you prefer. Sprinkle lightly with vanilla wafer crumbs, if desired. Refrigerate if not serving right away.

Yield: 10 servings

Mocha Brownie Torte

4 ounces unsweetened baking chocolate	1 teaspoon salt
⅔ cup shortening	1½ cups chilled whipping cream
2 cups sugar	⅓ cup packed brown sugar
4 eggs	1 tablespoon instant coffee crystals
1 teaspoon vanilla	Shaved chocolate or chocolate covered coffee beans
1¼ cups all-purpose flour	
1 teaspoon baking powder	

Preheat oven to 350 degrees. Line 2 (9-inch) layer cake pans with wax paper; set aside. Melt chocolate and shortening in large saucepan over low heat. Remove from heat. Mix in sugar, eggs, and vanilla. Stir in dry ingredients. Spread batter in prepared pans. Bake until a tester inserted in center comes out clean, 20 to 30 minutes, testing after 20 minutes. Cool 5 minutes, then remove from pan. Remove waxed paper and cool thoroughly.

Meanwhile, beat chilled whipping cream until it begins to thicken. Gradually add sugar and instant coffee; continue beating until stiff. Spread 1 cake layer with 1 cup cream mixture. Top with second layer and frost with remaining cream. Garnish with chocolate shavings or chocolate covered coffee beans. Chill at least 1 hour before serving.

Hint: The brownie part of this recipe can baked in a 9 x 13-inch pan for 30 minutes to make ordinary brownies. Add 1 cup coarsely chopped walnuts, if desired.

Yield: 10 servings

Three Layer Strawberry Meringue Torte

Torte

1½ cups sifted cake flour	¾ cup sugar
1½ teaspoons baking powder	6 egg yolks
⅜ teaspoon salt	4½ tablespoons milk
¾ cup butter-flavored vegetable shortening	1½ teaspoons vanilla

Meringue

6 egg whites	1½ cups sugar
¾ teaspoon salt	¾ teaspoon vanilla
¾ teaspoon cream of tartar	

Filling and Frosting

3 cups whipping cream	2 cups sliced strawberries
12 tablespoons powdered sugar	8 large whole strawberries

For Torte: Preheat oven to 350 degrees and coat 3 9-inch layer cake pans with nonstick spray. Sift flour, baking powder, and salt together 3 times. Set aside. Cream shortening in large bowl of an electric mixer; add sugar and beat until fluffy. Beat egg yolks until thick and add to creamed mixture. Stir in milk and vanilla. Add dry ingredients and beat until batter is smooth. Spread an even amount into each of the prepared pans. Set aside.

For Meringue: Beat egg whites, salt, and cream of tartar in clean bowl with clean beaters until soft peaks form. Add sugar, 2 table-spoons at a time (very important to follow this direction; the sugar will not dissolve completely if more than this is added at a time), beating well after each addition. Add vanilla. Carefully spoon a third of meringue over the batter in each pan. Bake until peaks are only slightly browned, about 12 minutes. DO NOT overbake. Remove from oven, loosen sides of tortes from pans and transfer to wire racks, meringue side up. Cool completely.

For Filling: Whip cream until it begins to stiffen, add powdered sugar, and whip until stiff.

Assembly: Place 1 torte on a plate and spread with a ½-inch layer of cream filling. Arrange half of sliced strawberries on top of filling and spread another ½-inch layer of cream over strawberries. Top with

(Three Layer Strawberry Meringue Torte continued)

another torte and repeat process. Top with final torte. Spread remaining cream over top and sides using an offset spatula to smooth sides. Cut whole strawberries in half lengthwise and encircle the base of the torte. Keep refrigerated until ready to serve. Splash strawberry sauce (either homemade or purchased) on plate and top with a slice of torte.

Yield: 10 servings

Apple Bundt Cake

4	medium Golden Delicious apples (about 1½ pounds) peeled and diced	¼	cup orange juice
2½	cups plus 5 tablespoons sugar, divided	1	tablespoon grated orange zest
2	teaspoons cinnamon	1	teaspoon vanilla
4	large eggs	3	cups all-purpose flour
1	cup vegetable oil	3½	teaspoons baking powder
		½	teaspoon salt
			Powdered sugar

Preheat oven to 350 degrees. Oil and flour a 12-cup Bundt pan. Mix apples, 5 tablespoons sugar, and cinnamon in medium bowl. Combine remaining sugar, eggs, vegetable oil, orange juice, orange zest, and vanilla in large bowl; whisk to blend. Stir flour, baking powder, and salt into egg mixture. Spoon 1½ cups batter into prepared pan. Top with half of apple mixture. Cover apples with 1½ cups batter. Top with remaining apples, then remaining batter.

Bake cake until top is brown and tester inserted in center comes out with moist crumbs attached, about 1 hour and 30 minutes. Cool cake in pan on racks 15 minutes. Run knife around sides of pan to loosen and turn cake onto rack. Cool at least 45 minutes. Dust with powered sugar. Serve slightly warm or room temperature.

Hint: This cake has a crispy outside and a moist inside.

Yield: 10 servings

Rouxminations

Cry Me A River

Eugene Field and Julia held their wedding breakfast at the Pacific House located at Third and Francis Street. According to history, "rivers of champagne" were served. Every style of oyster, steaks, turkeys, quail, and prairie chicken were also served to the guests. The Fields then invited the wedding party to St. Louis to continue the celebration.

Rouxminations

A Tug of
The Heart Strings

Eugene Field and Julia Comstock lived at 425 North 11th street, and it was here their first children were born. The subsequent death of his first born son inspired one of Field's famous poems, "Little Boy Blue." A statue commemorating the poem was given to the St. Joseph Public Library in 1943 by the St. Joseph Women's Press Club.

Tiramisu Toffee Torte

Cake

1	(1 pound, 2½ ounce) package pudding-included white cake mix	4	egg whites
1	cup strong coffee, room temperature	4	(1.4 ounce) toffee candy bars, very finely chopped

Coffee Drizzle

½	cup strong coffee, room temperature	½	cup Baileys or Kahlúa liqueur

Frosting

⅔	cup sugar	2	cups whipping cream, whipped
⅓	cup chocolate syrup	2	teaspoons vanilla
4	ounces cream cheese, softened		

Garnish

Chopped toffee candy bars or chocolate curls

For Cake: Preheat oven to 350 degrees. Grease and flour 2 (8 or 9-inch) round cake pans. In a large bowl, combine cake mix, 1 cup coffee, and egg whites on low speed until moistened. Beat 2 minutes at high speed. Fold in toffee bars. Spread batter evenly into prepared pans. Bake until toothpick inserted in center comes out clean, about 30 minutes. Cool 10 minutes. Remove from pans and cool completely.

For Drizzle: Combine coffee and liqueur in small bowl. Stir well and set aside.

For Frosting: Combine sugar, chocolate syrup, and cream cheese in medium bowl. Beat until smooth. Add whipped cream and vanilla. Beat until light and fluffy. Refrigerate until ready to use.

To assemble cake, slice each layer in half horizontally to make a total of 4 layers. Drizzle each cut side with ¼ cup of coffee drizzle. Place 1 layer on serving plate coffee-side-up and spread with ¾ cup frosting. Repeat with second and third layers. Top with remaining layer and frost sides and top of cake.

Hint: Make cake portion 1 day ahead. After layers are completely cooled, wrap loosely and store in freezer overnight. It is much easier to slice a frozen layer of cake in half than it is to slice a room temperature layer. The frozen state also cuts down on crumbs getting in the way. For nonalcoholic version, use an additional ½ cup strong coffee instead of liqueur.

Yield: 10 servings

Chocolate Birthday Cake

Cake

½ cup (1 stick) butter, softened
1 cup sugar
4 eggs

1 teaspoon vanilla
1 (12 ounce) can chocolate syrup
1 cup self-rising flour

Icing

½ cup (1 stick) butter
½ cup whipping cream

1 (6 ounce) package semisweet
    chocolate morsels
1½ cups powdered sugar, sifted

For Cake: Preheat oven to 350 degrees. Grease and flour 2 (8-inch) cake pans. Line with wax paper and grease and flour paper. Cream butter and sugar together in bowl of an electric mixer. Add eggs 1 at a time, beating well after each addition. Add vanilla. Add chocolate syrup and flour alternately. Beat only until ingredients are just blended.

Pour batter into prepared pans. Bake until a tester inserted in center comes out clean, about 25 minutes. Cool slightly and unmold layers on a rack. Cool completely before icing.

For Icing: Melt butter, cream, and chocolate together in a double boiler or heavy bottomed saucepan. Cool. Whisk in sifted powdered sugar until desired spreading consistency.

Hint: Make sure icing is cool before adding powdered sugar.

Yield: 10 servings

Rouxminations

Little Boy Blue

Aye, faithful to Little Boy Blue they stand,

Each in the same old place -

Awaiting the touch of a little hand,

The smile of a little face;

And they wonder, as waiting the long years through

In the dust of that little chair,

What has become of our Little Boy Blue,

Since he kissed them and put them there.

(Excerpt from Eugene Field's "Little Boy Blue.")

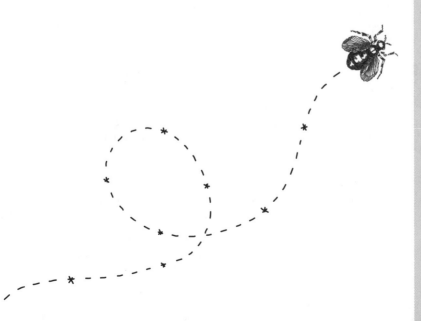

Be All and End All Chocolate Cake with Hershey Bar Frosting

Cake

3½ cups sifted cake flour
½ teaspoon baking soda
½ teaspoon baking powder
½ teaspoon salt
6 ounces unsweetened chocolate
1 cup water
16 tablespoons (2 sticks) unsalted butter, softened to consistency of mayonnaise

2 cups sugar
½ cup firmly packed light brown sugar
1½ tablespoons vanilla
6 extra large eggs, room temperature
1 cup buttermilk

Frosting

5 cups powdered sugar
¾ cup unsweetened cocoa (not Dutch)
7 tablespoons whole milk
14 tablespoons (1¾ sticks) unsalted butter, softened

14 ounces Hershey's milk chocolate, melted (2 giant bars)
2 tablespoons vanilla

For Cake: Preheat oven to 350 degrees. Butter 3 (9 x 1½-inch) round cake pans. Line with wax paper and butter paper. Sift flour, baking soda, baking powder, and salt together. Combine chocolate and 1 cup water in a medium heat proof bowl. Melt over barely simmering water, stirring occasionally, until perfectly smooth. Remove from heat. In a large bowl, beat butter on medium speed until creamy. Continue beating while sprinkling in both sugars a tablespoon at a time. Add vanilla and beat until very light. Add eggs, 1 at a time, beating until thoroughly blended after each addition. Beat batter until very light and creamy. Blend in chocolate. Add flour in 3 parts (sprinkling over the bowl), alternating with buttermilk in 2 parts, beating on lowest speed manageable and just until each addition disappears. Fold batter with a large flexible rubber spatula to finish blending. Divide batter among prepared pans, smoothing tops, then pushing batter slightly up against the sides. Bake 2 layers on middle rack and 1 on lower rack, staggering them to allow circulation. Bake until a toothpick emerges clean from center of cakes, 30 to 35 minutes. Cool in pan on racks for 15 minutes, then turn out onto racks, top sides up, to cool completely. Make the day of serving.

For Frosting: In food processor or mixing bowl, blend sugar and cocoa. Melt butter with milk over low heat. Add while hot to sugar

(Be All and End All Chocolate Cake with Hershey Bar Frosting continued)

mixture and vanilla. Beat or process until smooth. Control thickness with hot milk or sugar. Spread at once.

To Assemble Cake: Place 1 layer bottom up on cake plate and spread with ⅔ cup frosting. Top with second layer, bottom up, and spread with ⅔ cup frosting. Place top layer on, top side up. Frost top and sides with remaining frosting. Some frosting can be piped to decorate.

Hint: Get measurements right! A standing mixer is easier. Cake is tall and is great for birthdays!

Yield: 10 servings

Chocolate Lava Cake

Cake

6 (10 ounce) semisweet chocolate bars	½ cup all-purpose flour
10 tablespoons (1¼ sticks) butter	3 tablespoons cocoa
½ cup sugar	¾ teaspoon baking powder
	3 eggs

Garnish

½ cup whipping cream	1 (10 ounce) package frozen raspberries, thawed and pureed in blender
1 teaspoon vanilla	

Coat 6 (6-ounce) custard cups with nonstick spray. In 1-quart saucepan, melt chocolate, butter, and sugar over low heat, stirring until melted and blended. Remove from heat and pour into large mixing bowl. Add flour, cocoa, and baking powder and mix with a mixer on medium speed until blended. Add eggs, 1 at a time, beating until blended. Beat 6 minutes. Pour into custard cups, filling two-thirds full. Cover with plastic wrap and freeze for at least 2 hours or overnight. Preheat oven to 375 degrees. Place frozen custard cups on cookie sheet and bake 15 to 18 minutes.

While cake is cooking, mix cream and vanilla together and spoon on small dessert plates. Place dots of raspberry puree in circle around the outer edge of cream mixture. Using a toothpick, draw through the circles to make heart shapes. Remove cakes from oven, cool slightly, and invert on prepared plates.

Hint: Make sure to invert these individual cakes while they are still warm–chocolate fudge "lava" will ooze out of the volcano shaped cake.

Yield: 6 servings

Rouxminations

Lovers' Lane, Saint Jo

Saint Jo, Buchanan County,

Is leagues and leagues away;

And I sit in the gloom of this rented room,

And pine to be there today.

Yes, with the London fog around me

And the bustling to and fro,

I am fretting to be across the sea

In Lover's Lane, Saint Jo.

(Excerpt from Eugene Field's "Lovers' Lane, Saint Jo.")

Rouxminations

Forget The Lettuce, Give Me The Chocolate

In the late 1800's, G.W. Chase could be found selling produce and candies from his vendor's wagon. This was the forerunner of the Chase Candy Company which started in 1876 in downtown St. Joseph.

Lazy Day Cake

1 cup flaked coconut
1 cup chopped pecans
1 box German chocolate cake mix and the ingredients it calls for
½ cup butter or margarine, softened
8 ounces cream cheese, softened
1 pound powdered sugar

Preheat oven to 350 degrees. Grease bottom of 9 x 13-inch baking pan. Spread coconut evenly on bottom of pan. Sprinkle pecans over coconut. Mix cake mix and ingredients according to package directions. Pour over pecans. Mix butter, cream cheese, and powdered sugar together. Randomly drop by large spoonfuls onto the cake batter. DO NOT STIR. Bake for 40 to 45 minutes.

Hint: Delicious hot or cold.

Yield: 10 servings

Goddess Cake

1 box German chocolate cake mix and the ingredients it calls for
1 can sweetened condensed milk
1 jar caramel ice cream topping
1 container frozen dairy topping, thawed
6 Heath bars, crushed

Prepare and bake cake according to package directions in a 9 x 13-inch pan or 2 (8-inch) cake pans, if you are inclined to split the recipe (i.e. 1 for you, 1 for the neighbors). When cool, poke holes all over cake with wooden spoon handle. Whisk together condensed milk and ice cream topping. Pour over cooled cake. Refrigerate cake for at least 30 minutes before spreading with dairy topping. Sprinkle crushed Heath bars over top of cake. Refrigerate.

Hint: This is so easy and EVERYONE who eats it LOVES IT! We love it because it is the perfect thing to whip up to take places - meals for new parents, meetings, etc. - when you simply don't feel like working.

Yield: 10 to 12 servings

Heath Brickle Coffee Cake

2	cups all-purpose flour	1	teaspoon baking soda
½	cup (1 stick) butter, softened	1	egg
1	cup packed brown sugar	1	teaspoon vanilla
½	cup sugar	1	cup Heath brickle, divided
1	cup buttermilk	¼	cup chopped pecans

Preheat oven to 350 degrees. Coat a 9 x 13-inch pan with nonstick spray. Blend flour, butter, and sugar. Take out ½ cup of mixture and reserve. Add buttermilk, baking soda, egg, vanilla, and ½ cup Heath brickle to the remaining mixture. Blend well. Pour into prepared pan.

Mix remaining Heath brickle with pecans and add to reserved flour mixture. Sprinkle over top of batter. Bake until a tester inserted in center comes out clean, about 30 minutes.

Yield: 10 to 12 servings

Incredible Cream Cheese Chocolate Chip Cake

1	cup unsalted butter	3	teaspoons baking powder
8	ounces cream cheese, softened	1	teaspoon salt
1½	cups sugar	2	teaspoons vanilla
4	eggs	½	cup milk
3	cups all-purpose flour	12	ounces mini chocolate chips

Preheat oven to 325 degrees. Butter and flour a tube pan. Cream together butter and cream cheese. Gradually add sugar, eggs, and the remaining ingredients in order. Pour batter into prepared pan and bake 60 to 65 minutes, until a knife inserted in the center comes out clean. Cool for 10 minutes on a cake rack.

Hint: For an added indulgence, drizzle slices of cake with Chocolate Fudge Sauce on page 246.

Yield: 10 servings

Rouxminations

St. Joseph's Sweet Tooth

The Chase Candy Company's most famous product is the Cherry Mash, a palm-sized mixture of cherries surrounded by milk chocolate and roasted peanuts, first introduced in 1918. Today, Chase Candy makes 16 different types of candy, but the Cherry Mash is its only 12-month product. About 30 million Cherry Mash candies are sold through the Midwest and as far away as Texas and Colorado. Chase Candy also makes 50 tons of peanut brittle a year, still cooked in a copper kettle.

Pear Spice Cake with Pecan Praline Topping

1 cup unsalted butter, divided	½ cup minced crystallized ginger
1 (1 pound, 2¼ ounce) box spice cake mix	2 pears, peeled, cored, and cut into ½-inch pieces
¾ cup canned pear nectar (juice)	¾ cup packed golden brown sugar
3 large eggs	¼ cup whipping cream
2 tablespoons mild molasses	1½ cups pecan halves, toasted

Position rack in center of oven and preheat to 350 degrees. Butter 9-inch springform pan with 2¼-inch high sides. Stir ½ cup butter in small saucepan over medium heat until melted and brown, about 3 minutes. Pour into a large bowl. Add cake mix, pear nectar, eggs, molasses, and ginger. Using electric mixer, beat batter 2 minutes. Fold in pears. Pour batter into prepared pan. Bake until cake is golden brown and tester inserted into center comes out with some moist crumbs attached, about 1 hour and 10 minutes.

Cool cake in pan on rack 15 minutes. Run knife between pan sides and cake to loosen. Release pan sides and place cake on platter.

Stir sugar, cream, and remaining ½ cup butter in heavy medium saucepan over medium high heat until smooth. Boil 3 minutes, stirring often. Stir in pecan halves. Spoon warm topping over warm cake. Serve warm or at room temperature.

Yield: 10 servings

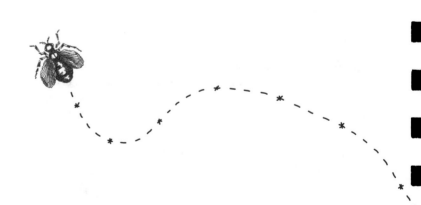

Pumpkin Sheet Cake

1	cup vegetable oil	1	teaspoon baking soda
4	extra large eggs	½	teaspoon salt
2	cups sugar	2	teaspoons cinnamon
1	(1 pound) can solid pack pumpkin	½	teaspoon ginger
2	cups unsifted all-purpose flour	½	teaspoon cloves
2	teaspoons baking powder	½	teaspoon nutmeg

Cream Cheese Frosting

1	(3 ounce) package cream cheese, softened	1	tablespoon milk
6	tablespoons margarine, softened	1	teaspoon vanilla
		1¾	cups powdered sugar

Preheat oven to 375 degrees. Grease and flour a 10 x 15-inch jelly-roll pan. Place oil, eggs, and sugar in large bowl of mixer. Beat on medium speed until blended. Add pumpkin and mix thoroughly. Sift together flour, baking powder, baking soda, salt, and spices. Gradually add flour mixture to pumpkin mix. Mix on medium speed until smooth, scraping down sides of bowl frequently. Pour batter into prepared pan. Bake until wooden pick inserted in center comes out clean, 20 minutes or longer. Cool and frost.

For Cream Cheese Frosting: Beat cream cheese with mixer until very soft. Add margarine and beat thoroughly, getting out all lumps. Add milk and vanilla. Gradually add powdered sugar and beat until smooth.

Yield: 12 servings

Rouxminations

Peek-A-Boo

Before the construction of the Christ Episcopal Church at Seventh and Francis streets, services were held in the garden orchard of Kate Howard. According to legend, curious Indians often peered through the bushes and listened to the music. Christ Episcopal Church was built at Seventh and Francis Streets and is the oldest Protestant church in continuous use in St. Joseph.

Red Cake... Sure to be a Valentine's Day Tradition

Cake

2½ cups self-rising flour
1   cup buttermilk
1½ cups vegetable oil
1   teaspoon baking soda
1   teaspoon vanilla
¼   cup red food coloring

1½ cups sugar
1   teaspoon unsweetened cocoa
    powder
1   teaspoon white vinegar
2   large eggs

Frosting

⅓   pound butter, softened
    (1⅓ sticks)

10 ounces cream cheese, softened
1   pound powdered sugar

For Cake: Preheat oven to 350 degrees. Coat 3 (9-inch) cake pans with nonstick spray. Mix all cake ingredients together until lumps are gone. Pour batter equally in the 3 pans. Bake until a tester inserted in center comes out clean, about 20 minutes. Cool layers in pans on wire racks for 10 minutes. Carefully remove from pans.

For Frosting: Combine butter, cream cheese, and powdered sugar, and beat until fluffy. Spread between layers and over outside of cake. Refrigerate at least 1 hour before serving.

Hint: You can add chocolate shavings on the top for garnish. If you are out of buttermilk you can always add 1 teaspoon vinegar to 1 cup of milk as a substitute. This cake is very moist, easy to make, and basically foolproof.

Yield: 10 servings

Rouxminations

You Gotta Have Heart

Heartland Regional Medical Center developed from a merger of Missouri Methodist Hospital and St. Joseph's Hospital, also known as Sisters Hospital. Heartland in the region's largest employer, with more than 2,600 employees. In 1999, Heartland was named a Top 100 Hospital in the nation for heart specialties - the only hospital in Missouri to receive the award. In 1999 and in 2000, Heartland was named a Top 100 Hospital for orthopedic specialties.

Rum Cake

Cake

1 cup chopped pecans or walnuts	4 eggs
1 (18½ ounce) package yellow cake mix	½ cup cold water
	½ cup vegetable oil
1 (3¾ ounce) package instant vanilla pudding mix	½ cup Bacardi dark rum (80 proof)

Glaze

¼ pound butter (do not substitute)	1 cup sugar
¼ cup water	½ cup Bacardi dark rum (80 proof)

For Cake: Preheat oven to 325 degrees. Grease and flour a 12-cup Bundt pan or 10-inch tube cake pan. Sprinkle nuts over bottom of pan. Mix remaining cake ingredients together. Pour batter over nuts. Bake until a tester inserted in center comes out clean, about 1 hour. Cool on rack. Invert onto serving plate. Using a cooking fork, prick top and sides. Drizzle and smooth glaze evenly over top and sides. Allow cake to absorb glaze and repeat until all glaze is used. This cake is best made the day before serving.

For Glaze: Melt butter in saucepan. Stir in water and sugar. Boil 5 minutes, stirring constantly. Remove from heat and stir in rum.

Hint: This freezes well. For holidays or special occasions or just because you feel creative, decorate with whole drained maraschino cherries and a border of sugar frosting or whipped cream at base and top of cake. Decorate also with seedless white grapes which have been washed and dusted with powdered sugar while still a bit damp. Looks like a million. We also love it with the Awesome and Easy Caramel Sauce, page 245.

Yield: 10 servings

Rouxminations

The Art 4-1-1

The Albrecht-Kemper Museum of Art houses one of the finest collections of 18th, 19th, and 20th century American art in the Midwest. The Museum began in 1913 with the foundation of the St. Joseph Art League. Artists on permanent display at the museum include Mary Cassatt and Thomas Hart Benton.

Rouxminations

Parlez-Vous Francais

Joseph Robidoux's predecessors were French and were the earliest and most successful fur traders in the young American plains. Because of his strong French heritage, Robidoux spoke French fluently and also learned several Indian dialects.

Zucchini Cakebread

1 cup extra virgin olive oil, plus more for pan
2 cups unbleached all-purpose flour, plus more for pan
2 teaspoons cinnamon
1 teaspoon salt
1 teaspoon baking soda
3 large eggs
1⅔ cups granulated sugar
2 teaspoons vanilla extract
2 cups shredded trimmed, firm zucchini
1 cup chopped walnuts, divided
¾ cup golden raisins
Grated zest of 1 lemon (yellow part only, without the underlying pith)

Place a rack in center position in oven and preheat oven to 325 degrees. Lightly brush a 9 x 5 x 3-inch pan with olive oil and sprinkle with flour, tapping pan to coat evenly and remove any excess.

Sift flour, cinnamon, salt, and baking soda together into a small bowl. In a large bowl, with an electric mixer at medium speed, beat eggs and olive oil together until well blended. Gradually add sugar while continuing to beat, and beat until mixture is foamy and pale yellow, and the sugar dissolved. Beat in vanilla. Add dry ingredients and beat at low speed just until blended. Don't overmix. Add zucchini, ¾ cup walnuts, raisins, and lemon zest and fold in with a rubber spatula until evenly distributed. Transfer batter to prepared pan. Spread batter evenly in pan and sprinkle with remaining walnuts.

Bake until cake has risen above sides of pan and a tester inserted in center comes out clean, about 1 hour and 10 minutes. Cool cake on a wire rack for 20 to 30 minutes. Remove cake from pan by inverting it onto a kitchen towel. Continue cooling cake, right-side-up, on wire rack until completely cool before slicing. The cake can be wrapped tightly in plastic wrap and stored in refrigerator for up to 5 days.

Hint: Keeps fresh for several days.

Yield: 8 to 12 servings

Banana Split Cheesecake

Crust

1 cup Oreo cookie crumbs	1 tablespoon butter or margarine, melted
2 tablespoons sugar	

Filling

1 (8 ounce) package fat-free cream cheese, softened	1½ cups sugar
3 (8 ounce) package ⅓ less fat cream cheese, softened	1½ cups mashed ripe banana
	3 tablespoons all-purpose flour
1 (8 ounce) carton low-fat sour cream	2 teaspoons vanilla
	4 large eggs

Toppings

⅓ cup canned crushed pineapple in juice, drained	⅓ cup chocolate syrup
⅓ cup chopped fresh strawberries with juice	¼ cup chopped pecans, toasted
	16 maraschino cherries, drained

For Crust: Preheat oven 325 degrees. Combine all ingredients in a bowl and toss with a fork until crumbs are moist. Press into bottom of a 9-inch springform pan which has been coated with nonstick spray.

For Filling: Beat cheeses and sour cream at high speed of a mixer until smooth. Add sugar, banana, flour, and vanilla. Beat well. Add eggs, 1 at a time, beating well after each addition. Pour into prepared pan and bake until set in the middle, about 1 hour and 15 minutes. Remove from oven and run a knife around outside edge. Cool to room temperature, cover and chill for at least 8 hours.

When ready to serve, top each slice with 1 teaspoon each of pineapple, strawberries, and chocolate syrup, ¾ teaspoon pecans, and 1 cherry.

Yield: 10 to 12 servings

Rouxminations

Something For Everyone

The Hotel Robidoux had several different personalities on display. The lobby was decorated in Italian Renaissance style while the Pompeiian had beautiful frieze with figures representing the sports of the early Roman period. The Grill room was decorated in an old English style, with a series of ten hand-painted panels representing all phases of the hunt. The ballroom and banquet hall had a uniquely beautiful art glass ceiling, and the Rathskeller had landscapes of Dutch scenery and clusters of artificial grapes and foliage on the ceiling. The hotel was imploded in the 1970s.

DESSERTS

Coconut Chocolate Almond Cheesecake

1½ cups chocolate wafer or sandwich cookie crumbs
1 cup plus 3 tablespoons sugar, divided
¼ cup butter or margarine, melted
4 (8 ounce) packages cream cheese, softened
3 large eggs
1 (14 ounce) package flaked coconut

1 (12 ounce) package semisweet mini chocolate morsels
½ cup slivered almonds, toasted
1 teaspoon vanilla
½ cup semisweet chocolate morsels
½ cup chopped almonds or pecans, toasted

Preheat oven to 350 degrees. Coat a 10-inch springform pan with nonstick spray. Stir together cookie crumbs, 3 tablespoons sugar, and butter. Press mixture evenly into bottom only of prepared pan. Bake for 8 minutes. Remove from oven and allow to cool

Beat cream cheese, eggs, and remaining sugar at medium speed of an electric mixer until fluffy. Stir in coconut, chocolate mini morsels, almond slivers, and vanilla. Pour into crust. Bake for 1 hour, remove from oven, and cool on a wire rack.

Place semisweet morsels in a zip-top plastic bag. Submerge in very warm water until morsels melt. Snip a tiny hole in 1 corner of bag; drizzle chocolate over cheesecake. For garnish, shake chopped nuts along outer rim of top of cheesecake. Cover and chill at least 8 hours and up to 5 days.

Yield: 10 to 12 servings

Rouxminations

The Eyes Have It

Joseph Robidoux's father was engaged in the fur business for several years; and while his wealth was accumulating, his eyesight was deteriorating. Young Robidoux learned the trade as a young teenager and quickly earned a reputation for dealing fairly and successfully with the Indians. He brought his success to the Missouri River Valley and eventually called that area home.

216

Easy No Bake Chocolate Crust Cheesecake

7 ounces chocolate wafer cookies	2 (8 ounce) packages cream cheese, softened
⅔ cup plus 3 tablespoons sugar, divided	4 tablespoons freshly squeezed lemon juice
6-8 tablespoons butter, melted	½ cup whipping cream

Coat an 8-inch springform pan with nonstick spray. Place cookies in a food processor and process until finely ground. Combine cookies and 3 tablespoons sugar in a bowl. Add 6 tablespoons melted butter and mix until mixture holds together. If needed, add remaining 2 tablespoons butter. Transfer to prepared pan and pat out evenly over bottom and about 1 inch up the sides. Place in freezer while proceeding.

Combine cream cheese, lemon juice, and remaining sugar in a mixer and beat until combined. Whip cream until soft peaks form. Fold into cream cheese filling. Remove crust from freezer, and pour filling evenly into pan. Cover with plastic wrap and place in freezer for 30 minutes (or up to 1 week). Transfer to refrigerator to allow to soften a bit before serving.

Hint: Drizzle Raspberry Coulis on plate, top with slice of cheesecake, and drizzle Chocolate Fudge Sauce on top. (Both the "Raspberry Coulis" and "Chocolate Fudge Sauce" recipes are on page 246.)

Yield: 8 to 10 servings

Rouxminations

I'll Drink To That

In 1899, St. Joseph had 116 saloons.

World Class

The Hotel Robidoux, named for St. Joseph's founding father, Joseph Robidoux, had a Rathskeller, bowling alley, Billiard Room, and Barber shop which could all be utilized by the public. The Hotel also had a Japanese room, Cotillion room, Lounging and smoking room, and several banquet rooms. A popular place in the hotel was the Pony Bar'n.

Pumpkin Cheesecake with Bourbon Sour Cream Topping

Crust

¾ cup graham cracker crumbs
½ cup finely chopped pecans
¼ cup firmly packed light brown sugar
¼ cup granulated sugar
¼ cup (½ stick) unsalted butter, melted and cooled

Filling

1½ cups solid pack pumpkin
3 large eggs
1½ teaspoons cinnamon
½ teaspoon freshly grated nutmeg
½ teaspoon ground ginger
½ teaspoon salt
½ cup firmly packed light brown sugar
3 (8 ounce) packages cream cheese, cut into bits and softened
½ cup granulated sugar
2 tablespoons whipping cream
1 tablespoon cornstarch
1 teaspoon vanilla
1 tablespoon bourbon liqueur or bourbon, if desired

Topping

2 cups sour cream
2 tablespoons sugar
1 tablespoon bourbon liqueur or bourbon or to taste
16 pecan halves for garnish

For Crust: In bowl, combine cracker crumbs, pecans, and sugars. Stir in butter. Press mixture into bottom and ½ inch up sides of a buttered 9-inch springform pan. Chill crust 1 hour.

For Filling: Preheat oven to 350 degrees. In bowl, whisk together pumpkin, eggs, cinnamon, nutmeg, ginger, salt, and brown sugar. In a large bowl with an electric mixer, cream together cream cheese and granulated sugar. Beat in cream, cornstarch, vanilla, bourbon liqueur and pumpkin mixture and beat the filling until smooth. Pour into crust. Bake in middle of oven for 50 to 55 minutes, until center is just soft. Let cool in pan on racks for 5 minutes.

For Topping: In bowl, whisk together sour cream, sugar, and bourbon liqueur. Spread over top of cheesecake and bake for 5 more minutes. Let cheesecake cool in pan on rack and chill it, covered, overnight. Remove sides of pan and garnish with pecans around the outside edge.

Hint: We've tried many pumpkin cheesecake recipes and think this one is the best. It is perfect for the holidays!

Yield: 10 servings

Chocolate Estate Torte

8 ounces Baker's semisweet chocolate	4 eggs, beaten
½ pound unsalted butter, melted	1 pint whipping cream
1 cup sugar	¼ cup powdered sugar
½ cup coffee, room temperature	Shaved chocolate curls

Preheat oven to 350 degrees. Line bottom and sides of a 9-inch spring-form pan with foil. In a medium mixing bowl, melt chocolate in micro-wave using short intervals so the chocolate does not burn. Add melted butter, sugar, eggs, and coffee. Beat with a mixer until smooth. Pour into prepared pan. Bake for 30 minutes, until torte starts to crack in the middle and pull away from the sides of the pan. Remove from oven and let cool. Cover with foil and freeze for at least 8 hours.

Before serving, remove from pan and allow to partially thaw. While torte is thawing, whip cream and sugar until stiff peaks form. Cut torte into slices and top with whipped cream and chocolate curls. Refrigerate unused portions.

Hint: You can "mass produce" these. After first 24 hours in freezer remove torte from springform pan and wrap tightly in foil. Store in freezer for up to 2 months. Just be sure to get it out far enough in advance to give it time to sit on the counter and soften up a bit. This is perfect for last minute company or to lighten the holiday load!

Yield: 10 servings

Mocha Cocoa Torte

1½ cups crushed almond macaroons	½ gallon coffee ice cream, softened
½ gallon chocolate ice cream, softened	¼ cup Irish Mist, Kahlúa, or Bailey's liqueur
1½ cups chocolate syrup or fudge sauce, divided	½ cup crushed toffee candy bars

In a 10-inch springform pan, layer macaroons, chocolate ice cream and ½ cup chocolate syrup or fudge sauce. Freeze. Add a layer of coffee ice cream and pour on liqueur. Caution: Do not use more or it will not freeze. Top with candy. Freeze until firm, preferably overnight. Unmold on serving dish. Warm remaining syrup and serve with torte.

Hint: Amaretto cookies may be substituted for macaroons. This is a very versatile recipe. It can be made using any combination of ice cream flavors, cookies, and candy bars.

Yield: 10 servings

Rouxminations

Fare Enough

The steamboats along the Missouri River could accommodate several hundred passengers, including immigrants on the lower deck. The cabin fare from St. Louis to St. Joseph ranged from $10 to $15, including meals. The cooks on board the steamboats were generally described as excellent.

Caramel Nut Tart

Crust

1¼ cups all-purpose flour	1 large egg yolk
½ cup chilled butter, cut into pieces	2 tablespoons ice water, approximately
1 teaspoon vanilla extract	

Filling

⅔ cup firmly packed brown sugar	2½ cups mixed unsalted nuts (such as cashews, pine nuts, almonds, walnuts, hazelnuts, or pecans)
½ cup butter	
⅓ cup plus 1 tablespoon honey	
2 tablespoons sugar	
⅓ cup whipping cream	

For Crust: Preheat oven to 325 degrees. Blend flour and salt in processor. Add butter and cut in using off/on turns until mixtures resembles coarse meal. Blend in vanilla and yolks using off/on turns. Blend in enough water until dough begins to clump together. Gather into ball and chill for 30 minutes. Roll out dough on a lightly floured surface to an 11-inch round. Transfer to a 9-inch tart pan with removable bottom. Trim edges and line with foil. Fill with pie weights or dried beans and bake 15 minutes. Remove foil and beans and return to oven until golden brown, about 15 minutes more.

For Filling: Combine brown sugar, butter, honey, and sugar in a heavy medium saucepan. Stir over high heat until butter melts and mixture comes to a boil. Continue to boil until candy thermometer reaches 240 degrees, the softball stage, stirring frequently. Boil about 2 minutes more, stirring frequently. Remove pan from heat and add cream, whisking until smooth. Mix in nuts and cool 5 minutes. Spoon filling into crust. Bake until filling darkens in color, about 30 minutes. Remove from oven and cool 20 minutes. Serve warm or at room temperature.

Hint: Incredible dessert which is easy to cut.

Yield: 10 servings

Chocolate Tart with Glazed Fruit

Crust

1 cup all-purpose flour	1 rounded teaspoon instant coffee (not freeze-dried)
1/3 cup powdered sugar	1/2 cup plus 2 tablespoons cold unsalted butter, cut into small pieces
2 rounded tablespoons cocoa powder	

Filling

12 ounces cream cheese, room temperature	1 rounded teaspoon instant coffee (not freeze-dried)
1 rounded tablespoon cocoa powder	1/2 cup powdered sugar
	1 large egg
	1/2 teaspoon vanilla

Topping

1 (6 ounce) basket raspberries	4 strawberries or more, cut in half
3 peaches or nectarines, pitted and thinly sliced	12 blackberries
	2/3 cup apricot jam

For Crust: Preheat oven to 350 degrees. Combine flour, sugar, cocoa powder, coffee, and butter in a food processor and process until dough forms a large ball, or mix dough using your usual pie crust method. Press dough to about 1/8-inch thickness on the bottom and up the sides of a 9 or 10-inch fluted tart or quiche pan. Bake for 10 minutes. Remove from the oven and set aside.

For Filling: Reduce oven temperature to 325 degrees. In a food processor or mixer, mix all filling ingredients until smooth. Spoon into baked crust and bake for 30 minutes. Remove from oven and allow to cool at least 15 minutes before adding the fruit topping. (May be made a day ahead up to this point. Let cool, cover loosely with aluminum foil, and refrigerate.)

For Topping: Arrange fruit over cooled filling. Heat jam over very low heat in a small saucepan until hot and liquid, stirring continuously, as it burns easily. Brush onto fruit with a pastry brush, coating it well.

Hint: Drizzle plate with chocolate sauce first and garnish with whipped cream. Can use just strawberries and no other fruit. It is easier, if a less impressive presentation. Increase strawberries to 2 small baskets and omit remaining fruit.

Yield: 10 servings

Rouxminations

War Games

In 1908, St. Joseph hosted the largest military tournament ever held in the United States in the city's south end. There were 5000 soldiers that participated in exhibitions, contests, and parades. Despite the city's 29 hotels, it could not accommodate the more than 50,000 spectators.

Danish Apple Bar

2½	cups all-purpose flour	1	cup plus 2 tablespoons sugar, divided
1	teaspoon salt	1	tablespoon plus 1 teaspoon cinnamon, divided
1	cup Crisco shortening		
1	egg yolk	1	beaten egg white
	Milk	1	tablespoon margarine
1	cup crushed cornflake crumbs		
8-10	peeled, cored, and sliced apples		

Frosting

2	cups powdered sugar	1	teaspoon vanilla
2	tablespoons milk		

Sift flour and salt together in a large bowl. Cut in shortening until crumbly. Place egg yolk in a cup measure and beat lightly. Add enough milk to make ⅔ cup. Add to flour mixture and work just to blend. Roll out half of dough on a lightly floured work surface. Arrange in bottom of a jelly-roll pan and sprinkle with cornflake crumbs. Arrange apple slices over crumbs. Combine 1 cup sugar and 1 teaspoon cinnamon. Sprinkle over apples. Roll out remaining dough and place over apples. Seal edges with water. Do not cut vents. Beat egg whites until stiff and brush over crust. Melt margarine and brush over crust. Sprinkle with remaining sugar and cinnamon. Bake in a preheated 375 degree oven for 1 hour. Dribble with frosting while still warm.

For Frosting: Combine all ingredients until smooth.

Hint: These ship well in the mail - just ask our children. Once you taste them, you will want to fix them often!

Yield: 10 to 12 servings

St. Charles Little Lemon Tarts

Lemon Curd

¾	cup sugar
1	tablespoon plus 2 teaspoons cornstarch
½	teaspoon grated lemon zest

⅓	cup water
⅓	cup fresh lemon juice
1	egg, lightly beaten
2	drops yellow food coloring

Tart Shell

2	cups flaked coconut
½	cup sugar
¼	cup plus 2 tablespoons flour

1	teaspoon vanilla
2	egg whites

Topping

½	cup frozen reduced fat Cool Whip, thawed

2	tablespoons or more flaked coconut, toasted

For Lemon Curd: Combine sugar, cornstarch, and lemon zest in saucepan and stir well. Gradually add water and lemon juice and stir with wire whisk until blended. Put on stove, bring to a boil and boil for 1 minute, stirring constantly. Spoon a little of hot lemon mixture into egg, whisking. Stir egg mixture into pan and cook, stirring constantly, until thickened. Add food coloring and stir. Cover with plastic wrap and refrigerate until ready to use.

For Tart Shells: Coat tiny muffin tins with nonstick spray. Combine all tart shell ingredients and press into bottom and sides of 14 to 16 muffin tins. Bake at 400 degrees 13 minutes, until lightly browned. Cool and remove from pan.

To assemble, fill tart shells about ⅔ full with lemon curd, top with Cool Whip, and sprinkle with coconut.

Yield: 14 to 16 tarts

Rouxminations

And the award for the Best Supporting role goes to...

The St. Charles Hotel was one of St. Joseph's most popular hotels. It was established in 1879 and became a popular spot for travelers stopping over in St. Joseph. The hotel was used for one of the sets of the Ryan and Tatum O'Neal film, Paper Moon. *The hotel today is merely a shell of its once grand majesty. It is in disrepair from water damage and vandals and has been red-tagged for demolition.*

Rouxminations

Red Lights Galore!

Between 1920-1930, St. Joseph had more than 80 bordellos. The red light district was located in the 7th and Messanie area of town. St. Joseph's most famous madam was Lizzie King, and other well known ladies were "Diamond Tooth" Nell Williams and Minnie Himmelberg. The red lights were used to warn the police it was an inopportune time to make their usual raid.

A "Pear" of Hearts

1	package puff pastry sheets, thawed	½	cup milk
1	egg beaten with 1 tablespoon water	10	ounces mixed berry jam
16	ounces sour cream	2	(1 pound, 13 ounce) cans pears, drained
¾	cup plus 2 tablespoons sugar, divided		Powdered sugar

Preheat oven to 400 degrees. Using a heart-shaped cookie cutter, cut hearts out of pastry sheets and brush with egg wash. Bake until golden brown, 8 to 10 minutes. Cool and split in half.

Mix sour cream, ¾ cup sugar, and ½ cup milk in a bowl and set aside. Strain berry jam and thin with ¼ to ½ cup water. Add 2 tablespoons sugar to strained mixture.

Spread ¼ cup sour cream mixture on a plate and top with bottom half of pastry heart. Arrange a pear half on pastry, cut-side-down, and place pastry top over pear, slightly off to the side. Drizzle berry mixture over top, spilling over to plate. Dust with powdered sugar.

Hint: Can use any shape cookie cutter depending on the holiday. Be sure to use good pears; inexpensive ones tend to loose their shape and fall apart. You will have extra berry mixture.

Yield: 12 servings

Wild Woman Pie

1	cup sugar	½	cup chopped pecans or walnuts
1	cup packed brown sugar	½	cup chocolate chips
1	cup all-purpose flour	1	unbaked (10 inch) pie shell
2	large eggs, lightly beaten		
1	cup unsalted butter, melted		

Preheat oven to 325 degrees. Mix sugar, brown sugar, and flour together. Stir in eggs, then butter, combining well. Fold in nuts and chocolate chips. Spread in crust and bake until knife inserted in center comes out clean, 60 to 70 minutes.

Yield: 8 servings

Black Bottom Banana Cream Pie

1 (9 inch) pie crust	¼ teaspoon salt
3 tablespoons cornstarch, divided	2 large eggs
½ cup plus 2 tablespoons sugar, divided	1 tablespoon butter
2 tablespoons unsweetened cocoa	2 teaspoons vanilla
Dash of salt	2 ounces cream cheese, softened (may use low fat)
1⅓ cups milk, divided (may use 1% or skim)	2 cups sliced ripe banana (about 2 large)
1 ounce semisweet chocolate, chopped	1½ cups thawed whipped topping
	Chocolate curls, optional

Bake pie crust and cool completely on wire rack.

Combine 1 tablespoon cornstarch, 2 tablespoons sugar, cocoa, and dash of salt in a small, heavy saucepan. Gradually add ⅓ cup milk, stirring with a whisk. Cook 2 minutes over medium-low heat. Stir in chocolate. Bring to a boil over medium heat. Reduce heat to low and cook 1 minute, stirring constantly. Spread chocolate mixture into bottom of prepared crust.

Combine remaining cornstarch, sugar, ¼ teaspoon salt, eggs, remaining milk, and butter over medium heat in heavy saucepan. Stir constantly with a whisk. Bring to boil, reduce heat to low, and cook until thick, about 30 seconds. Remove from heat and add vanilla. Beat cream cheese until light and fluffy. Add ¼ cup hot custard to cream cheese, and beat until just blended. Stir in remaining custard.

Arrange banana slices on top of chocolate layer and spoon custard over bananas. Press plastic wrap over custard and chill 4 hours. Remove wrap and spread whipped topping evenly over custard. Garnish with shaved chocolate, if desired. Chill until ready to serve.

Yield: 10 servings

Rouxminations

Sanity Now Rules

The Buchanan County Courthouse was the second largest in size in Missouri when it was built in 1876. It was described as one of the outstanding buildings in the United States. In 1882, Bob and Charlie Ford were tried here for shooting Jesse James and were sentenced to hang. Over the years, the courthouse has served as offices for attorneys, a temporary asylum, sleeping rooms and a concert hall for the Mendelssohn Society.

Coffee Toffee Ice Cream Pie

Pie Crust

1½ cups crumbled Oreo cookies
½ cup dry roasted peanuts

¼ cup butter or margarine, melted

Filling

3 pints coffee ice cream, softened

10 (1.2 ounce) Heath bars, crushed

Topping

1 (12 ounce) jar fudge topping
2-3 tablespoons brewed coffee

1-2 tablespoons Kahlúa liqueur

For Crust: Process cookies in a food processor until ground. Remove and set aside. Place peanuts in processor and process until ground. Combine with cookies and stir in melted butter. Press crumbs into bottom and up sides of a 9-inch pie plate that has been coated with nonstick spray. Bake at 325 degrees for 7 minutes. Cool completely before filling.

For Filling: In a chilled, large mixer bowl, combine ice cream and toffee pieces with a wooden spoon until well mixed. Freeze 1 hour and spoon into crust. Freeze 1 more hour, cover with plastic wrap, and freeze until firm, several hours or overnight. Soften pie 5 to 10 minutes before serving.

For Topping: In saucepan, combine fudge topping, coffee, and liqueur. Heat through and serve over slices of pie.

Hint: Place the pie on a hot, wet towel to loosen crust from the plate so that it will release easily after it is cut.

Yield: 8 servings

Rouxminations

Early Website

William Webb came to St. Joseph in the 1870s and eventually acquired four drug stores. In addition to being one of the first druggists to put in a soda fountain, he was also among the first to serve lunches. The Webb Drug Store was best known for its homemade ice cream.

Blackberry Delight

Crust

1 cup butter, softened
1½ cups all-purpose flour

½ cup chopped pecans

Filling

2 cups sugar
½ cup water

2 (12 ounce) packages frozen
blackberries
5½ tablespoons cornstarch

Topping

2 cups powdered sugar
3 (8 ounce) packages cream
cheese, softened

Whipped cream and fresh
blackberries, optional

For Crust: Preheat oven to 350 degrees. Combine ingredients and lightly pat into bottom of a 9 x 13-inch baking pan. Bake until golden brown, 10 to 20 minutes. Cool completely!

For Filling: Combine sugar and water in saucepan and cook over low heat, stirring, until sugar is melted. Add blackberries and cornstarch, stirring frequently. Bring to boil, reduce heat, and simmer for 3 minutes. Cool completely. Spread in cooled crust.

For Topping: Cream together sugar and cream cheese until light and fluffy. Spread over blackberry layer. Cover and refrigerate until chilled. Serve with dollop of whipped cream and a fresh blackberry, if desired.

Yield: 10 to 12 servings

Rouxminations

Goods For You

The Brittain-Richardson and Company building at 4th and Jules was constructed in 1882 by John S. Brittain and John D. Richardson. Brittain's business became one of the largest wholesale dry goods firms in the country.

Butter Croissant Pudding with Cinnamon Sauce

1	cup whipping cream	3	medium croissants, cut into ½-inch slices
1	cup milk		
1	tablespoon vanilla	2	tablespoons butter, melted
¼	teaspoon salt	2	tablespoons powdered sugar
3	eggs	3	tablespoons raisins, optional
9	tablespoons sugar		

Cinnamon Sauce

1½	cups packed brown sugar	½	cup whipping cream
½	cup light corn syrup	1	tablespoon vanilla
¼	cup water	1½	teaspoons cinnamon
3	tablespoons butter		

Preheat oven to 375 degrees. Bring cream, milk, vanilla, and salt to a simmer in heavy medium saucepan. Beat eggs and sugar to blend in medium bowl. Gradually whisk in cream mixture and stir well.

Lightly brush croissant slices with melted butter. Arrange in a 6-cup soufflé dish or an 8-inch round cake pan. Sprinkle with raisins, if desired. Pour cream mixture over croissants. Gently press slices down to absorb liquid. Sprinkle with the powdered sugar. Set dish in a large baking pan and add hot water to large pan to come 1 inch up sides of soufflé dish. Bake until a tester inserted in middle comes out clean, 40 to 45 minutes.

For Cinnamon Sauce: Cook brown sugar, syrup, water, and butter until it forms a soft ball (235 degrees on a candy thermometer). Remove from heat and stir in cream and vanilla. Serve with pudding.

Hint: This sauce is wonderful on ice cream, waffles, or pancakes. Keeps well in the refrigerator.

Yield: 6 servings

Chocolate Bread Pudding with Vanilla Sauce

5 cups stale French bread, torn into chunks	⅔ cup cocoa
1 cup whipping cream	3 eggs, lightly beaten
2 cups milk	1 teaspoon cinnamon
¼ cup butter, melted	1 tablespoon vanilla
¾ cup sugar	¼ teaspoon salt
	Strawberries, optional

Vanilla Sauce

½ cup butter	2 tablespoons cornstarch
1 cup sugar	¼ cup cold water
2 cups milk	

Break bread into small chunks in a large bowl. In separate bowl mix cream, milk, butter, sugar, cocoa, eggs, cinnamon, vanilla, and salt. Combine well. Pour over bread and let soak 10 minutes. Stir well. Spoon mixture into a lightly greased 12 x 8-inch baking dish. Bake at 350 degrees until a knife inserted in center comes out clean, 40 to 45 minutes. Serve with vanilla sauce and garnish with strawberries.

For Sauce: Combine butter, milk, and sugar in a saucepan and cook over low heat until butter melts and sugar dissolves. Combine cornstarch and water. Add to saucepan Add vanilla, bring mixture to a boil and cook 1 minute.

Yield: 8 servings

Rouxminations

Honoring Our Past

The Coleman Hawkins Jazz Festival is a relatively new festival for St. Joseph having been started in 1999. It spotlights St. Joseph's native son and father of the jazz saxophone, Coleman Hawkins. The Festival is the second Saturday in June.

Home Is Where The Artifacts Are

The St. Joseph Museum was built as a residence in 1879 by William M. Wyeth and has 21,000 square feet of floor space, with 43 rooms. The building was later purchased by the widow of another early pioneer, Milton Tootle. In 1948, Goetz and Goetz Brewing Company donated $35,000 for the purchase of the building; not as a residence but as a museum.

Cherry Berries on a Cloud

Meringue

6 egg whites, room temperature	¼ teaspoon salt
½ teaspoon cream of tartar	1¾ cups sugar

Filling

6 ounces cream cheese, softened	2 cups whipping cream, whipped
1 cup sugar	2 cups miniature marshmallows
1 teaspoon vanilla	

Topping

2 cups fresh strawberries, sliced	1 (1 pound, 5 ounce) can cherry pie filling
3 tablespoons sugar	1 teaspoon lemon juice

For Meringue: Preheat oven to 250 degrees. Grease a 9 x 13 x 2-inch pan. Beat egg whites, cream of tartar, and salt until frothy. Gradually beat in sugar. Beat until very stiff and glossy, about 15 minutes. Spread into prepared pan and bake 1 hour. Turn off oven and leave meringue in oven for 12 hours or overnight. DON'T PEEK.

For Filling: Mix cream cheese, sugar, and vanilla. Gently fold in whipped cream and marshmallows. Spread over cooled meringue. Refrigerate 12 hours or overnight. Cut into serving pieces and top with spoonful of topping.

For Topping: Sprinkle strawberries with sugar. Add pie filling and lemon juice and blend well. Cover and chill several hours.

Hint: Great dessert for luncheons - women love it!

Yield: 10 to 12 servings

Cream Cheese Coffee Cake Pastry

2 packages yeast
¼ cup warm water (110 degrees)
2½ cups all-purpose flour
1 cup plus 1 tablespoon sugar, divided
1 teaspoon salt
1 cup margarine
4 egg yolks

8 ounces cream cheese, softened
1 egg yolk
Egg white
½ cup chopped pecans
Powdered sugar icing (powdered sugar, milk, and vanilla to the desired consistency)

Dissolve yeast in water and let stand 3 to 5 minutes. Measure flour, 1 tablespoon sugar, salt, margarine, and 4 egg yolks into a bowl. Mix with a pastry blender. Stir yeast and add to bowl. Mix well until a dough forms. Cover and refrigerate 2 hours.

Mix cream cheese, remaining sugar, and 1 egg yolk. Beat until smooth. Divide chilled dough in 2 parts. Roll out 1 part on a floured surface and press into a 10 x 15-inch pan. Spread with cream cheese mixture. Roll remaining dough into a 10 x 15-inch rectangle and place over filling. Pinch edges together. Beat egg white slightly and brush over top. Sprinkle with nuts. Let rise in warm place 1 hour. Bake at 350 degrees until pastry is golden, 30 to 35 minutes. Cool slightly then drizzle powdered sugar icing over top.

Hint: This is wonderful - very rich and people always love it. Can make ahead. Assemble night before except for egg whites, cover with plastic wrap and refrigerate. Take out and let sit for 30 minutes to 1 hour, brush with egg white, and bake.

Yield: 12 servings

Rouxminations

The Voodoo That You Do

It was reported Mary Alicia Owen made "important discoveries" in voodoo magic. She was the president of the American Folklore Society and studied rites and customs of the Sac Indians who formerly occupied the land north of St. Joseph. According to legend, she was permitted to join secret Indian Societies.

Almond Biscotti

⅓ cup margarine or butter, room temperature	1½ cups slivered almonds, finely chopped
2 cups all-purpose flour, divided	1 egg yolk
⅔ cup sugar	1 tablespoon milk or water
2 eggs	2 tablespoons shortening
2 teaspoons baking powder	1 cup milk chocolate or semisweet chocolate pieces
2 teaspoons vanilla	

Preheat oven to 325 degrees. In a mixing bowl, beat margarine until creamy. Add 1 cup flour, sugar, 2 eggs, baking powder, and vanilla. Beat until combined. Stir in remaining flour and nuts. Divide dough in half. Shape each portion into a 9-inch log (approximately 2 inches wide). Place 4 inches apart on a lightly greased cookie sheet. Stir together egg yolk and milk or water. Brush onto logs.

Bake for 25 minutes. Cool on cookie sheet for 1 hour. Cut each cooled log diagonally into ½-inch slices. Lay slices cut-side-down on an ungreased cookie sheet. Bake for 15 minutes. Turn slices over and bake until dry and crisp, about 15 minutes more. Cool.

Combine shortening and chocolate pieces in a small saucepan. Melt over low heat, stirring, until smooth. Drizzle over cooled biscotti or dip 1 end of biscotti into mixture.

Yield: 4 dozen

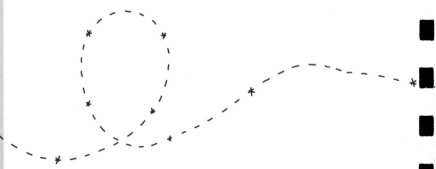

Cranberry Hazelnut Biscotti

1½ cups hazelnuts	4 large eggs
3¾ cups all-purpose flour	1 egg yolk
2 cups sugar	2 teaspoons vanilla
1 teaspoon baking powder	1½ cups Craisins (dried cranberries)
1 teaspoon salt	1 tablespoon water

Toast hazelnuts in a 350 degree oven for 20 minutes. Cool and rub hazelnuts in a dish towel to remove skins. Finely chop nuts or place in baggy and roll with rolling pin until finely crushed.

Mix flour, sugar, baking powder, and salt in a medium bowl. Beat eggs and egg yolk with vanilla in a large mixing bowl. Add dry ingredients and blend well. Mix in Craisins, water, and hazelnuts. Gather into a ball.

Preheat oven to 350 degrees. Grease 2 cookie sheets. Divide dough in half and shape each into a 3 x 14-inch log on prepared cookie sheets. Bake until lightly golden, 35 to 40 minutes. Cool 10 minutes and cut diagonally into ½-inch pieces. Lay slices cut-side-down and continue baking 10 minutes on each side. Cool and keep in an airtight container up to 3 weeks.

Yield: 4 dozen

Rouxminations

Tennis, Anyone?

Dr. Renee Richards and Andre Agassi played in the annual Pony Express Tennis Tournament, a tournament famous for drawing up and coming tennis players.

Hair Today, Gone Tomorrow

W. H. Rhodes sold men's wigs and toupees at 607 Edmond Street, establishing his business in 1890, and advertising "women do not like to trade with a bald clerk."

Rouxminations

The Plaza Hotel, St. Joe Style

Hotel Patee House was the center of the nation's Westward expansion. It was opened by John Patee as a luxurious hotel in 1858 to serve travelers as the railroad pushed west to St. Joseph.

The Multi-Purpose Building

The Patee House cost $180,000 and had 140 guest rooms. The Patee House served as a hotel three times, a college twice, and a shirt factory for 80 years. During the Civil War, the Patee House housed the U. S. Provost Marshal's office; and the Union army recruiting office was in the Patee House.

Patee Hall Praline Cookies

1⅔ cups all-purpose flour, sifted
1½ teaspoons baking powder
½ teaspoon salt
½ cup unsalted butter, room temperature
2½ cups firmly packed light brown sugar, divided
1 large egg
1 teaspoon vanilla
½ cup whipping cream, or more if necessary
1 cup sifted powdered sugar
1 cup pecan halves, toasted and broken into large pieces

Preheat oven to 350 degrees. Sift together flour, baking powder, and salt in medium bowl. Set aside. In bowl of an electric mixer fitted with a paddle attachment, cream butter and 1½ cups brown sugar on medium speed until light and fluffy, about 2 minutes. Add egg and vanilla. Beat until fully combined. Add flour mixture, and beat on low speed until combined. Drop batter by rounded teaspoons onto greased baking sheets, 2 inches apart. Bake 10 to 12 minutes, until firm and barely golden. Cool on baking sheet 5 minutes. Transfer cookies to wire racks placed over parchment-lined baking sheets.

In a small saucepan, combine remaining 1 cup brown sugar and cream. Bring to a boil over medium heat. Cook, stirring constantly, for 2 minutes. Remove from heat. Add powdered sugar and whisk until smooth. If frosting thickens too much, thin with more cream. Add pecan pieces. Spoon about ½ teaspoon praline mixture on each cookie.

Yield: 4 dozen

Chocolate Chip, Cherry, and Walnut Rugalach

Dough

2 cups all-purpose flour	1 cup (2 sticks) unsalted butter, chilled and cut into ½-inch pieces
2 tablespoons sugar	
¼ teaspoon salt	6 ounces chilled cream cheese, cut into ½-inch pieces

Filling

½ cup sugar	8 tablespoons miniature semisweet chocolate chips
1 teaspoon ground cinnamon	
12 tablespoons cherry preserves	8 tablespoons finely chopped walnuts
8 tablespoons dried tart cherries	
	⅓ cup (about) whipping cream

Combine flour, sugar, and salt in a food processor and process until blended. Add butter and cream cheese and cut in using on/off switch, until dough begins to clump together. Gather dough into ball. Divide into 4 equal pieces and flatten into disks. Wrap each in plastic and refrigerate at least 2 hours. (Can be prepared 2 days ahead. Keep refrigerated. Let soften slightly at room temperature, about 5 minutes, before rolling out.)

Grease a large baking sheet. Mix sugar and cinnamon in small bowl. Roll out 1 dough disk on a well-floured surface to 9-inch round. Spread 3 tablespoons preserves over dough, leaving a 1 inch border. Sprinkle with 2 tablespoons cherries, 2 tablespoons chocolate, 2 tablespoons cinnamon-sugar mixture, and 2 tablespoons walnuts. Cut dough into 8 equal wedges. Starting at wide end of each wedge, roll up tightly. Arrange cookies tip side down on prepared baking sheet, spacing 1½ inches apart and bending slightly to form a crescent. Repeat 3 more times with remaining dough discs. Place baking sheets in freezer for 30 minutes.

Position rack in center of oven and preheat oven to 375 degrees. Brush cookies lightly with cream. Bake until golden brown, about 40 minutes. Transfer cookies to racks to cool completely. (Can be made ahead and stored in airtight container for up to 1 week or frozen for up to 1 month.)

Hint: These burn easily, so watch them carefully!

Yield: 3 dozen

Rouxminations

Corporate Headquarters

The Patee House served as the headquarters for the Pony Express. Also, the Hannibal and St. Joseph Railroad's office was in the Patee House. Today a restored railroad office and the last Hannibal steam locomotive are displayed there.

Not Exactly As He Had Planned It

In 1865, Confederate leanings left Mr. Patee short of cash and he held a lottery to dispose of Patee House. He had to buy the last 100 tickets to get them sold, and on April 28 when the hotel was raffled, he held the winning ticket.

Chunky Peanut Butter Cookie Fingers

1 cup extra-crunchy peanut butter	1½ cups all-purpose flour
¾ cup firmly packed brown sugar	½ teaspoon baking soda
½ cup butter, softened	½ teaspoon salt
¼ cup honey	½ cup wheat germ
½ teaspoon vanilla	1½ cups semisweet chocolate
1 large egg	morsels

Preheat oven to 325 degrees. Combine peanut butter, brown sugar, butter, honey, vanilla, and egg in a mixing bowl. Beat at medium speed of an electric mixer until creamy. Combine flour, baking soda, salt, and wheat germ. Gradually add to butter mixture, beating well.

Shape dough into 1-inch balls (about 1 teaspoon). Roll balls into 2½-inch logs. Place 2 inches apart on an ungreased cookie sheet. Bake until lightly browned, about 12 minutes. Cool 1 minute on cookie sheets; remove to wire racks and cool completely.

Melt chocolate morsels in microwave, stirring until smooth. Dip 1 end of each cookie into chocolate, return to wire racks, and let stand until chocolate is firm.

Hint: More nutritious than average peanut butter cookie.

Yield: 4 dozen

Decadent Double Chocolate Cookies

4 tablespoons butter	1 cup all-purpose flour
12 ounces semisweet chocolate chips	1 teaspoon vanilla
14 ounces sweetened condensed milk	12 ounces almond bark or white chocolate

Preheat oven to 350 degrees. Melt butter and chocolate chips in condensed milk in a double boiler over simmering water. Remove from heat and add flour and vanilla. Let mixture cool 10 minutes. Drop by teaspoonfuls onto a greased cookie sheet and bake for 7 minutes. Cool slightly and remove from pan.

Melt white chocolate in double boiler and drizzle over cookies. Set pan in refrigerator to set chocolate.

Hint: Very easy to make. Freezes well!

Yield: 2 to 2½ dozen

Coconut Pecan Crisps

1 cup sugar, plus more for pressing cookies
1 cup firmly packed brown sugar
1 cup butter, softened
1 cup vegetable oil
1 egg
1 teaspoon vanilla
3½ cups sifted all-purpose flour

1 teaspoon cream of tartar
1 teaspoon baking soda
1 teaspoon salt
1 cup Rice Krispies
1 cup flaked coconut
1 cup oatmeal
1 cup chopped pecans

Blend butter and sugar together. Add oil, egg, and vanilla. Sift flour, cream of tartar, soda, and salt together. Add to butter mixture. Fold in cereals, coconut, and pecans.

Chill dough for an hour. Preheat oven to 350 degrees. Pinch off teaspoonfuls of dough and shape into balls. Arrange on a baking sheet and flatten with bottom of a greased and sugared glass. Bake for 10 to 12 minutes.

Hint: These cookies freeze well.

Yield: About 7 dozen

Hazelnut Butter Cookies

2 cups all-purpose flour
¼ teaspoon baking soda
Pinch of salt
1 cup butter
1 cup finely chopped toasted hazelnuts

½ cup sugar
1 egg yolk
2½ teaspoons vanilla extract
2 cups powdered sugar

Preheat oven to 350 degrees. Combine flour, baking soda, and salt in a large bowl. Add butter and cut in until mixture resembles coarse meal. Add chopped nuts, sugar, egg yolk, and vanilla, and mix until smooth dough forms. Shape dough into 1-inch balls. Place on a cookie sheet and press with back of fork in a crisscross pattern to form ¼-inch thick cookies. (A cookie stamp can be used.) Bake cookies until a pale golden brown, about 20 minutes. Cool and roll cookies in powdered sugar.

Hint: A delicate and delicious tea cookie which freezes well.

Yield: 4 dozen

Rouxminations

Informative, Yet Profoundly Disturbing

Tourists to St. Joseph can visit the Glore Psychiatric Museum which is arguably the largest and best single exhibition explaining the evolution of mental health in the United States. Tourists can see 19th century restraints, and treatments including the "Bath of Surprise," a "Fever Cabinet," and the amazing contents of one patient's stomach.

Rouxminations

Cows, Kettles, and Cholera

Passengers on the Missouri River steamboats brought with them their livestock, household goods, supplies for stores on the Western end of the trip, and cholera. In 1849, hundreds of people died of the disease in St. Joseph and along the trail to the California gold.

We Is Learning Good

When the St. Joseph schools were reopened following the Civil War in 1864 , there were 67 public schools and teachers earned an average annual salary of $564. Today, St. Joseph has about 30 public and private schools.

Country Club Crunchy Cookies

3½ cups all-purpose flour	1 tablespoon milk
3 teaspoons baking soda	2 teaspoons vanilla
1 teaspoon salt	1 cup vegetable oil
½ cup butter	1 cup cornflakes, preferably
½ cup margarine	Honeynut
1 cup firmly packed light brown sugar	1 cup quick oats
1 egg	6 ounces chocolate chips
1 cup sugar	6 ounces butterscotch chips

Preheat oven to 350 degrees. Stir together flour, baking soda, and salt. Soften butter and margarine to the point of almost being melted through. Combine with brown sugar, white sugar, egg, milk, and vanilla in a large bowl. Stir in flour mixture, alternating with oil, until well blended. Do this by hand for best results. Stir in flakes, oats, and chips until well blended. Drop by tablespoonfuls, about 2 inches apart, onto ungreased cookie sheets. (Do not use Teflon coated sheets.) Bake for 10 to 12 minutes.

Hint: For a cakier cookie, do not melt butter and margarine, simply soften slightly. You may use 12 ounces of any chip you like. In fact, these cookies are amazingly flexible. You may substitute different cereals for the cornflakes; potato chips even work in a pinch.

Yield: 4 dozen

Lavender Cookies

1 cup butter, softened	2 cups all-purpose flour
¾ cup sugar, divided	¼ cup lavender flowers
¼ teaspoon salt	

Preheat oven to 350 degrees. Cream butter and ½ cup sugar. Mix in salt and flour and gather into a ball. Cover and chill dough 1 hour.

Place flowers and remaining sugar in a food processor. Process until a fine powder. Remove dough from refrigerator and form into 1-inch balls. Roll each ball in lavender sugar. Arrange on an ungreased cookie sheet and bake until golden, 10 to 12 minutes.

Yield: 2½ dozen

German Chocolate Sandwich Cookies

Filling

²⁄₃ cup sugar
¼ cup butter, softened
1 (5 ounce) can evaporated milk

1 egg, lightly beaten
1⅓ cups flaked coconut
¾ cup finely chopped pecans

Cookies

1½ cups sugar
¾ cup butter, softened
¼ cup milk
2 eggs

1½ teaspoons vanilla
1¾ cups all-purpose flour
¾ cup unsweetened cocoa
1 teaspoon baking soda

For Filling: Combine sugar, butter, milk, and egg in a 2-quart saucepan. Cook over medium heat, stirring constantly, until mixture comes to a boil and thickens, 8 to 10 minutes. Stir in coconut and pecans. Cover and refrigerate at least 1 hour.

For Cookies: Preheat oven to 350 degrees. Combine sugar and butter in a large mixer bowl. Beat at medium speed, scraping bowl often, until creamy, 1 to 2 minutes. Add milk, eggs, and vanilla; continue beating until well mixed, 1 to 2 minutes. Reduce speed to low; add flour, cocoa, and baking soda. Beat until well mixed. Drop dough by rounded teaspoonfuls 2 inches apart onto greased cookie sheets. Bake until top springs back lightly when touched, 9 to 11 minutes. Cool completely. Spread 1 level tablespoonful filling on flat side of 1 cookie; top with a second, flat-side-down. Squeeze together gently.

Hint: Make sure size of cookie is a teaspoon. They make really large cookies.

Yield: 3 dozen

Rouxminations

On Eagle's Wings

The German-American Bank was designed by E. J. Eckel and Mann and features a German Imperial Eagle and the American Eagle in mosaic panels. The owners of the bank were members of the Krug family who came to St. Joseph from Germany. Due to anti-German sentiment during World War I, the name of the bank was changed to the American National Bank and the German shield was covered.

And, They're Off

The mass emigration to California started in the spring of 1848.

Lemon Butter Cookies

1 cup (2 sticks) margarine, softened	Pinch of salt (not too much)
1 cup sugar	1½ teaspoons lemon extract
2 egg yolks	2½ cups all-purpose flour
	1½ teaspoons baking soda

Preheat oven to 350 degrees. Cream together margarine and sugar. Add egg yolks, salt, and lemon extract. Sift together flour and soda and stir into creamed mixture until blended. Form balls the size of walnuts. Dip tops into sugar or roll in sugar.

Place on ungreased cookie sheets and bake for 8 to 10 minutes. Do not overbake.

Hint: Use pure lemon extract, as opposed to imitation. The added flavor is worth the extra cost!

Yield: 4 dozen

Pony Express Cowboy Cookies

1½ cups margarine, softened	1½ teaspoons vanilla
1½ cups sugar	2 cups quick oats
1½ cups firmly packed brown sugar	2 cups Rice Krispies with marshmallows
3 eggs, beaten	1 (12 ounce) package chocolate chips
3 cups all-purpose flour	
1½ teaspoons baking soda	1 cup flaked coconut
¾ teaspoon baking powder	1 cup peanuts
¾ teaspoon salt	¼ cup peanut butter

Preheat oven to 350 degrees. Cream margarine and sugar together in a large mixing bowl until light and fluffy. Add eggs and vanilla. In a separate bowl, combine remaining ingredients. Add to creamed mixture and mix well. Drop by teaspoonfuls on an ungreased cookie sheet. Bake for 8 to 10 minutes.

Yield: 6 dozen

Rouxminations

A Real Ladies Man

Certainly one of the most colorful of the Pony Express riders was Johnny Fry. It is said that young Kansas girls waited along the trail for Johnny Fry and offered him cookies and sweets. But because Fry was traveling so fast at times, it became difficult to hand these goodies to him. According to legend, one young woman invented a cookie with a hole it, making it easier for Johnny to pick it up. Thus was the beginning of the doughnut.

Pumpkin Fest Cookies

1	cup Crisco shortening	2	cups all-purpose flour
1	cup sugar	1	teaspoon baking soda
1	cup solid pack canned pumpkin	1	teaspoon cinnamon
1	egg	½	teaspoon salt

Frosting

3	tablespoons butter	1	cup powdered sugar
4	teaspoons milk	¾	teaspoon vanilla
½	cup firmly packed brown sugar		

For Cookies: Preheat oven to 350 degrees. Cream shortening and sugar until light and fluffy. Add pumpkin. Add egg and mix well. Sift together flour, soda, cinnamon, and salt. Add to creamed mixture and blend well. Drop by teaspoonfuls onto cookie sheet. Bake for 10 to 12 minutes.

For Frosting: Combine butter, milk, and brown sugar in a saucepan and cook, stirring, until brown sugar melts. Cool and add powdered sugar and vanilla. Beat until smooth. Spread on warm cookies.

Yield: 3 dozen

Corby Pond Cookies

1	cup butter	1	teaspoon baking soda
1	cup sugar	1	teaspoon baking powder
1	cup firmly packed brown sugar	2½	cups powdered oats (blend in blender)
2	eggs	1	(12 ounce) bag chocolate chips
1	teaspoon vanilla	1	(4 ounce) Hershey bar, melted
2	cups all-purpose flour	1½	cups chopped nuts, optional
½	teaspoon salt		

Preheat oven to 375 degrees. Cream together butter, sugar, and brown sugar. Add eggs and vanilla and mix well. Combine flour, salt, baking soda, and baking powder. Add to creamed mixture and blend. Stir in powdered oats, chips, melted chocolate, and nuts. Form dough into balls slightly larger than golf balls and place on an ungreased baking sheet. Bake for 8 to 9 minutes. Do not overbake.

Yield: 7 dozen

Rouxminations

From Mill Shop
To Malt Shop

John Corby, an early day settler, built Corby's Mill on the 102 River in 1852. The 102 River was so named because it is 102 miles long. The river shrank, and the mill was hit by a tornado and eventually razed, but not before it served as Kleinbrodt's 101 Tavern. The Tavern was known for its barbecued beef sandwiches and ice cold beer.

Lucky 13

The Corby Place, a twelve floor building, was St. Joseph's first skyscraper. Because of prevailing superstitions, the building does not have a thirteenth floor.

Shortbread Cookies

¾ pound unsalted butter, room temperature
1 cup sugar (plus extra for sprinkling)
1 teaspoon vanilla
3½ cups all-purpose flour
¼ teaspoon salt

Preheat oven to 350 degrees. In the bowl of an electric mixer, mix together butter and 1 cup sugar until just combined. Add vanilla. In a medium bowl, sift together flour and salt. Add to creamed mixture. Mix on low speed until dough starts to come together. Turn out onto a surface dusted with flour and shape into a flat disk. Wrap in plastic and chill for 30 minutes.

Roll dough to ½-inch thickness and cut with a 3-inch cookie cutter of your choice. Place cookies on an ungreased baking sheet and sprinkle with sugar. Bake until the edges begin to brown, 20 to 25 minutes. Remove from oven and allow to cool to room temperature.

Hint: We adore these. For a fun twist, dip half in chocolate. Simply combine 1 cup semisweet chocolate chips, or any type you prefer, with 1 teaspoon shortening. Microwave for 45 seconds. Stir and, if necessary, microwave a bit more, until chocolate is melted and smooth. Dip cookies and place on wax paper.

Yield: 2 dozen

Chocolate Walnut Crumb Bars

1 cup (2 sticks) butter, softened
2 cups all-purpose flour
½ cup sugar
¼ teaspoon salt
2 cups chocolate chips morsels, divided
1¼ cups sweetened condensed milk
1 teaspoon vanilla
1 cup chopped walnuts

Preheat oven to 350 degrees. Beat butter in a bowl until creamy. Beat in flour, sugar, and salt until well blended. With floured fingers, press 2 cups crumb mixture onto bottom of greased 9 x 13-inch pan. Bake until lightly browned, 10 to 12 minutes. Reserve remaining flour mixture.

Warm 1½ cups chocolate chips and condensed milk in heavy saucepan over low heat, stirring until chips melt. Stir in vanilla and spread over hot crust.

Stir walnuts and remaining chocolate chips into reserved crumb mixture. Sprinkle over chocolate filling. Bake for 25 to 30 minutes.

Yield: 12 servings

Winken, Blinken, and Nod Cookies

3 cups all-purpose flour	1½ cups sugar
1 teaspoon baking powder	2 eggs
¼ teaspoon salt	1 tablespoon vanilla
1 cup unsalted butter, room temperature	

Icing

½ cup butter, softened but not melted	1 tablespoon of vanilla
	Skim milk
1 (1 pound) box powdered sugar	

Sift flour, baking powder, and salt together, and set aside. Cream butter in a mixing bowl. Add sugar and beat until light and fluffy. Beat in eggs, 1 at a time. Add vanilla and beat. Mix in reserved dry ingredients, blend well, and shape into 2 balls. Wrap in plastic and refrigerate at least 3 hours or overnight.

When ready to bake, preheat oven to 350 degrees and coat a cookie sheet with nonstick spray. Remove dough from refrigerator and knead a bit while still in plastic wrap to loosen it up for rolling. You may even want to put it out on the counter for 15 minutes or so to soften it up a bit. Don't leave it out too long because then it becomes too soft.

Lightly flour a work space and rolling pin. Remove dough from wrap and roll out to the thickness of about ½ inch. Cut with your favorite cookie cutter and transfer to prepared cookie sheets. Bake for 8 to 10 minutes. The biggest key is to not OVERBAKE! Err on the side of underbaking and get them out earlier then you would suppose. Let cool.

While cooling, make the icing. Cream together butter, sugar, and vanilla. Add enough milk to allow icing to spread easily, but not be runny.

Hint: The dough can be made up to a month in advance. The cookies can also be stored in the freezer for up to a month. Sure to become a holiday tradition!

Yield: 4 dozen

Rouxminations

Wynken, Blynken, and Nod -

Wynken and Blynken are two little eyes,

And Nod is a little head,

And the wooden shoe that sailed the skies

Is a wee one's trundle-bed;

So shut your eyes while Mother sings

Of wonderful sights that be

And you shall see the beautiful things

As you rock in the misty sea

Where the old shoe rocked the fishermen three:-

Wynken,

Blynken,

And Nod.

(Excerpt from Eugene Field's "Wynken, Blynken, and Nod")

Shortbread Caramel Bars

½ cup butter, softened	1½ cups firmly packed brown
½ cup powdered sugar	sugar
1 cup plus 2 tablespoons	½ teaspoon baking powder
all-purpose flour, divided	1 cup chopped pecans
2 eggs	1 cup Heath bar chips

Preheat oven to 375 degrees. Mix butter, sugar, and 1 cup flour. Press evenly into bottom of a 9 x 13-inch baking pan. Bake until lightly browned, 12 to 14 minutes.

Combine 2 tablespoons flour and remaining ingredients in a medium bowl and mix well. Spread over top of baked base. Bake until golden, 12 to 20 minutes. Cool and slice into bars.

Yield: 12 servings

Sour Cream Apple Squares

2 cups all-purpose flour	1 teaspoon baking soda
2 cups firmly packed brown sugar	½ teaspoon salt
½ cup butter, softened	1 cup sour cream
1 cup chopped English walnuts	1 teaspoon vanilla
or pecans	1 egg
1-2 teaspoons cinnamon	2 cups peeled, chopped apples

Preheat oven to 350 degrees. Combine flour, brown sugar, and butter until crumbly. Add nuts. Press 2¾ cups of mixture into bottom of an ungreased 9 x 13-inch pan. Add cinnamon, baking soda, salt, sour cream, vanilla, and egg to remaining dry mixture. Add apples and blend well. Spoon over crumb mixture. Bake for 25 to 35 minutes.

Hint: Very yummy and moist. Good served warm with ice cream.

Yield: 10 to 12 servings

Rouxminations

We're Bigger Than You Are

Before the Civil War, St. Joseph was about twice the size of neighboring city, Kansas City; and after the war St. Joseph exploded to about four times the size of Kansas City.

The Knockout Punch

Kansas City beat St. Joseph to the punch in building a permanent railroad bridge across the Missouri river in 1869. With that, tons of products could easily be shipped through Kansas City, straight to big markets, making Kansas City a railroad hub.

Cream Cheese Mints

1 (8 ounce) package cream
   cheese (may use ⅓ less fat)
¼ cup butter
1 (2 pound) package powdered
   sugar

½ teaspoon peppermint extract
6 drops red liquid food coloring
   (more or less for color if
   desired)

Combine cream cheese and butter in a saucepan over low heat. Cook, stirring constantly, until smooth. Gradually stir in powdered sugar, mixing until blended. Stir in extract.

Shape mixture, while keeping on low heat, into ½-inch balls and transfer to wax paper. Dip a 2-inch cookie stamp or bottom of a glass into powdered sugar and press each ball to flatten. (I use small hard heart-shaped candy to make designs in the mints.) Let stand uncovered 4 hours or until firm. They freeze well between layers of waxed paper in an airtight container.

Hint: Can be made for any holiday or occasion - just change food coloring and stamp design. Kids love them!

Yield: 4 dozen

Awesome and Easy Caramel Sauce

½ cup butter
1 cup firmly packed brown sugar

½ cup whipping cream
1 tablespoon vanilla extract

Combine butter and brown sugar in a heavy saucepan. Cook over medium heat, stirring often, until sugar melts. Stir in cream; bring mixture to a full boil. Remove from heat and stir in vanilla.

Hint: This sauce is wonderful! It is great over ice cream, the rum cake, and the double crusted apple tart, just to name a few. It can be made a day, or even 2, ahead and stored in refrigerator. Warm before serving.

Yield: 1¼ cups

Rouxminations

Bill, The Tool Man

The Wyeth Hardware and Manufacturing Company was started in 1859 when William M. Wyeth opened a hardware store to help outfit the wagon trains. It grew into a multi-million dollar business.

Chocolate Fudge Sauce

1¼ cups powdered sugar
½ cup whipping cream
¼ cup butter

2 ounces unsweetened chocolate
Dash of salt
1 teaspoon vanilla

Combine sugar, cream, butter, and salt in a heavy saucepan. Cook over medium heat until chocolate and butter have melted, stirring occasionally. Reduce heat to low and simmer about 30 minutes. Remove from heat and stir in vanilla. Serve warm or cool. Transfer to plastic squirt bottle and store in the refrigerator up to 2 weeks. Reheat in microwave.

Yield: 1 cup

Raspberry Coulis

1 (12 ounce) bag frozen raspberries

3 tablespoons sugar
2 teaspoons fresh lemon juice

Puree raspberries, then pass through a strainer to remove seeds. Add sugar and lemon juice. Stir well to combine. Transfer to plastic squirt bottle and store in refrigerator up to 1 week.

Yield: 2 cups

Chocolate Cheese Spread

1 (8 ounce) package cream cheese, softened
1 tablespoon powdered sugar

1½ teaspoons cocoa
2 tablespoons Kahlúa liqueur
Semisweet chocolate shavings

Combine cream cheese, powdered sugar, cocoa, and Kahlúa in a mixing bowl. Beat at medium speed of electric mixer until blended. Shape mixture as desired, cover, and chill. Garnish with chocolate shavings. Serve with shortbread cookies or animal crackers.

Hint: Great for holiday events. You can purchase a small trial size of Kahlúa at various liquor or wine shops.

Yield: 1 cup

Contributors

Diane Acuff
Carrie Adams
Janelle Aldrich
Melinda Allaman
Pam Allen
Candace Allison
Mary Ames
Bea Anderson
Jacqueline Andrews
Lynda Andrews
Tony Angelo
Helen Anno
Lisa Antle
Marian Armstrong
Roxanne Armstrong
Pat Auxier
Laura Baade
Jill Bagby
Kathy Bahner
Mary Ann Bailey
Kim Baker
Christy Barber
Linda Barbosa
Sue Barnes
Verda Barnes
Becky Barnett
Carol Barrie
Gwendolyn Bartlett
Susan Bartlett
Bickley Bayer
Francee Beaulieu
Adrine Beheler
Sandie Beihl
Joni Bestgen
Melisa Bird
Teri Bistritz
Kim Blakley
Monica Bolin
Erik Borger
Dale Boulware
Shirley Bradley
Suzanne Bradley
Nancy Briggs
Elizabeth Bristow
Mary Brock

Jean Brown
Mary Lynn Brown
Margaret Bucher
Sue Burmont
Carol Burns
Linda Burns
Merry Burtner
Judy Butler
Emily Cannon
Pam Canterbury
Mary Cargill
Betty Carmichael
Susan Carolus
Susan Carolus
Jane Carpenter
Rosalie Carter
Gale Casey
Jane Cathcart
Marcia Chapman
Angela Chavez
Kathy Chladek
Kim Chulick
Tom Chulick
Jenni Clayton
Cindy Clinch
Dawn Coates
Sally Coffman
Rita Connett
Cindy Cornelius
Nanette Corso
Alecia Cotter
Debbie Cotter
Joan Counts
Charis Cox
Julia Cox
Bobbie Cronk
Elizabeth Crotty
Jennifer Culver
Shelly Culver
Janie Custer
Anne Davis
Gloria Davis
Marian Davis
Daire Dawkins
Mignon DeShon

Richard DeShon
Lynne Dickens
Peggy Dillon
Veronica Dominguez
Patricia Donaher
Angela Dorsey
Colleen Dorsey
Rosemary Dorsey
Dorothy Douglas
Anne Douglass
Darla Downer
Heidi Downer
Theresa Drummond
Nancy Duggins
Leigh Ann Dunn
Inez Duncan
Dlo DuVall
Eileen Dyer
Cathy Echterling
Linda Eckard
Cheryl Ehlert
Dorothy Elliott
Marlene Elliott
Amy Enlow
Robyn Enright
Doug Euler
Rachel Euler
Ann Evans
Stephanie Everly
Kim Faynik
Kathleen Fiquet
Matilda Fitzpatrick
Sonya Flanders
Anne Fletcher
Karen Foley
Diane Ford
Hannah Ford
Barbara Fox
Barbara Fricke
Liz Fuehrer
Sherie Gabbert
Becky Garrison
John Gebhards
Helen Gettys
Connie Gibson

Angie Giddens
Judy Giddens
Shaun Gillam
Betty Glaze
Phyllis Gondring
Sheryl Gossett
Bill Grace
Karen Grace
Mary Grace
Brenda Graves
Karen Graves
Jacklynn Grimwood
Margi Grimwood
Teresa Gutman
Ashli Hanlan
Cosette Hardwick
Vickie Hargens
Christie Harr
Georgian Harris
Lanie Hauschel
Aimee Hausman
Cindy Hausman
Jane Hayward
Tracee Hegarty
Mary Herzog
Mary Pat Hewitt
Jane Hibler
Kim Hill
Kimberly Hill
Mary Hillix
Kathleen Hillyard
Mary Hinde
Vicki Hinde
Jen Hoecker
Becky Holden
Rachelle Holt
Wanda Hopkins
Heidi Hornaday
Mary Jo Hornaday
Noreen Houts
Jenni Howat
Phyllis Humbert
Mechele Humphreys
Jan Hurst
Barbara Ide

Gordon Ide
Thea Ide
Sara Jeffrey
Jalaina Johnson
Trisha Johnson
Janet Johnston
Cyndie Jones
Penny Jones
Sandra Jones
Jennifer Josendale
Jean Kincaid
Nancy Kirby
Donna Klein
Norma Laderoute
Marian Lam
Rosie Lammoglia
Greg Larson
Mary Larson
Brad Lau
Beth Lawrence
Dianne Lawson
Joanna Lehman
Joan Lehr
Peggy Leone
Gina Lewis
Natalie Lewis
Susan Lierz
Mary Liles
Sherri Lilly
Michelle Limbic
Lora Lorenz
Julie Love
Diane Loveless
Gail Lowdown
Lida Lowe
Diane Lucas
Christina Lund
Barbara Lutz
Donna Sue Lyon
Deborah Mahoney
Carlene Makawski
Judy Mannschreck
Sherri Manville
Pat Marston
Terrie Martin
Janet McCoy
Mary Jane McDaniel
Eleanor McDonald
Peggy McDonald
Kevin McGlade
Mary McGlade
Cathy McKim
Robin McLean
Dana Meers

Rhonda Meierhoffer
Melanie Meijering
Carol Meyers
Cindy Michalski
Ruth Miller
Shirley Miller
Jennifer Miner
Marjorie Miner
Betty Moles-Specker
Alicia Morgan
Cheryl Morrow
Phyllis Muff
Shelly Murray
Jas Nellestein
Juli Nelson
Katherine Nelson
Laura Nelson
Nancy Nelson
Nora Nelson
Pam Nelson
Robert Nelson
Diane Nicholas
Lori Norcross
Laura Olson
Jennifer Olvey
Margaret O'Malley
Jean Ann O'Meara
Christi O'Riley
Jean Orr
Alice Osborn
Tiffany Owens
Brenda Oxley
Norma Parker
Lynn Parman
Kay Partamian
Rachel Patterson
Kevin Pearson
B.J. Penland
Pamela Pike
Sally Pike
Jan Pray
Janice Pray
Stacy Pretz
Tara Proffit
Karen Read
Nancy Reed
Nancy Reese-Dillon
Patsy Remington
Clarine Reser
Sarah Richmond
Sharon Ritchey
Kellie Ritchie
Carolyn Robertson
Lisa Robertson

Matt Robertson
Tracy Robertson
Andrea Robinson
Jodie Rocha
Reva Rocha
Alexis Rodney
Brian Rose
Susan Roth
Michele Rowe
Patricia Runde
Carol Sanders
Madeleine Sanders
Mary Sanders
Sally Sanders
Jeanne Schanze
Paige Scheetz
Bob Schewe
Janet Schiesl
Pauline Schirmer
Beatrice Schmidt
Jean Schmidt
Enid Schneider
Shelly Schoeneck
Rhonda Schram
Margaret Schreiber
Mary Schreiber
Sharon Schultz
Patti Schwab
Debby Scroggins
Suzanne Shearer
Sonja Shinneman
Nancy Siemens
Sarah Siemens
Donna Silvey
Kay Simpson
Vicki Sindelar
Deborah Sisk
Barbara Smith
Betty Smith
Debbie Smith
Elizabeth Smith
Judy Smith
Pat Smith
Nancy Sokol
Nancy Speltz
Rebecca Spencer
Brenda Spinner
Debbie Sprague
Barbara Squires
Loah Stallard
Karen Steeby
Ramona Steele
Teri Steinbecker

Trish Steinbecker
Janet Steury
Janet Strop
Alane Studley
Joan Summers
Linda Summers
Susan Symington
Andrea Taylor
Janet Taylor
Marilyn Taylor
Sheridan Taylor
Susanne Teel
Lana Tewell
Alma Thackery
Amy Thedinger
Gloria Thomas
Patrick Thomas
Susan Thomas
Sydney Thomas
Jane Thompson
Jo Thompson
Erin Tieman
Ann Tootle
Judith Trout
Sherry Trout
Michelle Turner
Shirley Twombly
Sharon Vaughn
Barbara Voight
Patricia Waitkoss
Lynn Watkins
Cathie Wayman
Mildred Weaver
Sue Weisensee
Lisa Whitacre
Louise Wilcox
Marcia Williams
Gayle Winder
Rebecca Wissehr
Sandra Wolanski
Gena Wolsky
Helen Wood
Alice Woodbury
Ingrid Woodbury
Karen Woodbury
Alice Wray
Jean Wright
Judy Wright
Pamela Wright
Barbara Wurtzler
Lou Wyeth
Barbara Yoakum
Patricia Ziesel

Friends of the Cookbook...

Bea Anderson
Norm and Laura Baade
Jill Bagby
Gwen Bartlett
Bickley Bayer
Dr. and Mrs. Edward Beheler
Bender's Prescription Shop
Dolores Blair
Wally Bloss
Vickie Bradley
Carol Burns
Shawn and Emily Cannon
Mignon DeShon
Linda DeShon
Bea Dobyan
Dr. and Mrs. Juan Dominguez
Tony and Theresa Drummond
Eileen Dyer
Jo Eyberg
Matilda Fitzpatrick
Anne M. Fletcher
J. Franklin Gallery
Jeannie Franklin
Barb Fricke

Dr. Don and Sheryl Gosett
James and Karen Graves
Reed and Brenda Graves
Staci Gray
James and Ruth Gray
Bill and Jackie Grimwood
Glenda Hamilton
Cort and Tracee Hegarty
Brian and Mary Pat Hewitt
Mary Jo Hornaday
Barbara Blake Ide
Gordon and Thea Ide
Jeremy and Trisha Johnson
Sandra Jones
Ray and Marian Lam
Peggy Leone
Mark and Susan Lierz
Patt and Sherri Lilly
Jackie Looney
Shirley Miller
Michael and Jas Nellestein
Tom and Laura Nelson
Nodaway Valley Bank
John and Laura Olson

Pat and Margaret O'Malley
Seann and Christi O'Riley
Bud and Renee Potts
Pat and Nancy Dillon
Mrs. George Richmond
James and Andrea Robinson
George W. Roth
Bob and Susan Roth
Jacklyn Runyan
Stet and Jeanne Schanze
William and Margaret Lee
    Schreiber
The Schoeneck Family
Mr. and Mrs. Robert Simpson
Dr. Donald and Loah Stallard
Janet Steury
Janet Taylor
Amy Thedinger
Elanor Thomas
Pat and Susan Thomas
Jim and Jo Thompson
Barbara Wurtzler

A Special Thanks To...

Tom and Cathy Pankiewicz

Barbara Blake Ide

Bob Simpson

Erin Blevins

Mildred Dillon

Stanley K. Harris, Jr.

MacAndrew Burns

Marshall White

Greg Sekula

Fred Slater

Christy Barber

Bill McKinney

Cindy Weaver

Connie Burri

Hillyard Companies

St. Joseph Area Chamber of Commerce

The St. Jospeh Museum

St. Jospeh Convention and Visitors Bureau

St. Joseph Parks and Recreation Department

Western Robidoux, Inc.

City of St. Joseph

Pony Express Museum

Resources

Around St. Joseph: St. Joseph News-Press, 2000 Millennium Edition.

Beautiful Lake Contrary and Saint Joseph, MO: Cookman Instant Printing, reprint from 1907.

Davis, Robin and J. Marshall White. *Images of America. St. Joseph, Missouri: A Postcard History.* Charleston, SC: Arcadia, 1999.

Grenier, Mildred. *St. Joseph A Pictorial History.* USA: The Donning Company, 1981.

Heerlein, Birdie. *Dancing at the Frog Hop.* St. Joseph, MO: Oxley Printing, 1984.

Historic Downtown Walking Tour: Junior League of St. Joseph, 1992.

Hotel Robidoux. St. Joseph, MO: The Book Place. 1990.

Jesse James Home: Pony Express Historical Association.

Lake Contrary Days of Glory 1880-1964. USA: Blacksnake Creek Press, 1992.

Logan, Sheridan A. *Old Saint Jo.* John Sublett Logan Foundation, 1979.

Missouri Courthouses Buchanan County: University of Missouri-Columbia Extension Division.

Our Hidden Jewel: Leadership St. Joseph, 1997.

St. Joseph Journal of Commerce, circa 1900. Friends of the Park. St. Joseph Parks, Recreation and Civic Facilities, reprinted in 2000.

St. Joseph Magazine.

Schellhorn, Christina. *This IS St. Joseph.* USA: Pansophic Publishing. 1995.

Settle, Raymond W. and Mary Lund Settle. *Saddles and Spurs.* Lincoln: University Nebraska Press, 1955.

The Restored Buchanan County Courthouse: Buchanan County, St. Joseph, 1982.

Visscher, William Lightfoot. *The Pony Express.* Golden, CO: Outbooks, 1980.

Weeks, Clyde. *Krug Park St. Joseph's Crown Jewel.* St. Joseph: Blacksnake Creek Press, 1993.

INDEX

INDEX

INDEX

INDEX

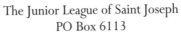

The Roux We Do

The Junior League of Saint Joseph
PO Box 6113
Saint Joseph, MO 64506
Telephone: (816) 279-3832 • E-mail: info@therouxwedo.com
Visit our web page at www.therouxwedo.com

Name _____

Address _____

City _____ State _____ Zip _____

Please send _____ copies   @ $19.95 each _____

Postage and Handling   @ $ 5.00 each _____

                                    Total Enclosed _____

Make checks payable to The Junior League of St. Joseph

Please charge to: ❑ Visa   ❑ MasterCard

Card Number: _____ Expiration Date: _____

Signature: _____

To open a wholesale account, call (816) 279-3832

- -

The Roux We Do

The Junior League of Saint Joseph
PO Box 6113
Saint Joseph, MO 64506
Telephone: (816) 279-3832 • E-mail: info@therouxwedo.com
Visit our web page at www.therouxwedo.com

Name _____

Address _____

City _____ State _____ Zip _____

Please send _____ copies   @ $19.95 each _____

Postage and Handling   @ $ 5.00 each _____

                                    Total Enclosed _____

Make checks payable to The Junior League of St. Joseph

Please charge to: ❑ Visa   ❑ MasterCard

Card Number: _____ Expiration Date: _____

Signature: _____

To open a wholesale account, call (816) 279-3832

Names and addresses of bookstores, gift shops, etc. in your area would be appreciated.

_____

_____

_____

_____

_____

_____

_____

_____

_____

_____

_____

_____

Names and addresses of bookstores, gift shops, etc. in your area would be appreciated.

_____

_____

_____

_____

_____

_____

_____

_____

_____

_____

_____

_____